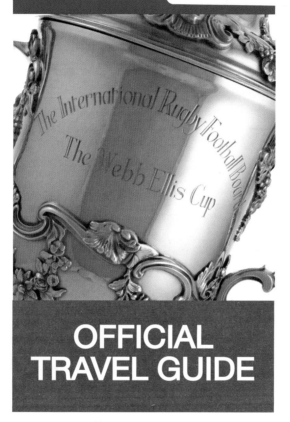

# OFFICIAL
# TRAVEL GUIDE

**Written by**
**Mike Gerrard, Donna Dailey**
**and Hope Caton**

## Publishing Information

Published in the United Kingdom in March 2007 by:
The Purple Guide Ltd
Teddington Studios
Broom Road
Teddington Middlesex
TW11 9NT

ISBN 978-0-9547234-8-4
ISBN-10  0-9547234-8-1

Printed in Slovenia.

## Sales and PR

For information, telephone our sales department on 020 8614 2277 or email: **sales@purpleguide.com**
Public Relations: Ptarmigan Sports Marketing 0113 242 1155
Distibuted in the UK and EU by NBN International: 01752 202327

## Write to us

We welcome the views and suggestions of our readers. Please post your comments on our website **www.purpleguide.com**

The publishers have done their best to ensure that the information in this book is current and accurate. Some information may be liable to change. The publishers cannot accept responsibility for any loss, injury or inconvenience that may result from the use of this book.

To find out more about Purple Guides visit
**www.purpleguide.com**

**Dr Syd Millar**
Chairman
International Rugby Board

In 1987 the Game of Rugby took a huge step forward in terms of global appeal and promotion with the kick-off of the first ever IRB Rugby World Cup in New Zealand and Australia. Little did we know that this historic tournament would change the face of the Game forever and the evolution Rugby has experienced since those pioneering days has been phenomenal.

With the kick-off of Rugby World Cup 2007 just around the corner the International Rugby Board is confident the Tournament will be the most successful yet in its colourful and exciting 20-year history.

There is little doubt that an exciting air of anticipation is starting to build in the world rugby community as France 2007 will offer an irresistible mix of world class rugby and the unique, colourful regional experiences that only France can offer. The teams and the substantial numbers of travelling supporters can look forward to world class venues and wonderful hospitality from the cities.

The Rugby World Cup plays an important part in the development of world Rugby as the revenue provides the financial platform for the global growth of the Game. In August last year the IRB announced a US$50 million strategic investment programme designed to increase the competitiveness of the Game around the world. The aim is to have more teams capable of winning RWC as the competitiveness of the international Game increases.

The growth in popularity and success of Rugby World Cup has continued steadily from 1987 and the expected cumulative TV audience for the Tournament is expected to be of over 4 billion. It is fair to say that Rugby World Cup is now one of the biggest sporting events in the world.

CONTENTS

According to legend, it was during a match in the autumn of 1823, that a young student, William Webb Ellis, *'with a fine disregard for the rules of football, first took the ball in his arms and ran with it, thus originating the distinctive feature of the rugby game.'*

The above is a quote from a plaque placed on the Doctor's wall of the school at Rugby, England, by the Old Rugbeian Society at the turn of the 20th century.

The game of football as played at Rugby between 1750 and 1823 included handling the ball, but no one was permitted to run towards the goal with the ball in his grasp. According to the rules, what William should have done, (having caught the ball in his arms) was to have *'retired back as far as he pleased without parting with the ball'*. Progress forward was by kicking, hacking (kicking an opponent in the shins) and an enormous rolling scrum involving up to sixty players. Running forward with the ball did not become accepted practice until the 1830s. That said, games played at Rugby were organised by students (not masters), and rules were a matter of custom and were frequently changed and modified: *'...the rules were discussed almost every time the boys went out to play and ...adjustments were frequently made [to the game]'*.

In those days, a match might see forty seniors take on two hundred younger pupils. One game played in 1839 was between School House, with 75 players, and the rest of the school – 225 players. It is difficult to imagine so many people on the pitch until one realises that the playing area was on the grass of the eight-acre Close with a row of trees along the perimeter with a cross-bar at each end. According to the rules, a point was scored when: *'a player having*

WILLIAM WEBB ELLIS BICENTENARY MATCH

*touched the ball straight for a tree, and touched the tree with it
...a player then may drop (kick) from either side if he can, but the
opposite side may oblige him to go to his own side of the tree'.*
This would seem to indicate that a player, after touching
the ball onto the tree, could take his kick towards the
cross-bar from either side of the trees unless one of the
opposition insist that he take the kick from his own side
of the trees. It was the job of the multitude of younger
players to prevent a senior player from touching a tree
with the ball. The distinctive game at Rugby was more
vigorous and entailed more contact with the ground (and
other players) than ball games at other Public Schools.
Perhaps this was due to the fact that at Rugby, the game
was played on eight acres of grass rather than cobbles or
paving stones.

The word 'try' originates from the period when a touch-
down (or tree-touch) allowed the player a try (or attempt)
at goal. If the kick failed no points were scored. As in
today's game, the kicked ball had to pass over the cross-
bar and the entire opposing team (often made up of
younger boys in top hats) would pack the goal mouth and
stand on the cross-bar to stop kicks at goal succeeding. It
wasn't until 1845 that players were banned from standing,
or sitting, on the cross-bar.

## Rugby School

Rugby School was founded in 1567, as a provision
in the will of Lawrence Sheriff, who had made his
fortune supplying spices to Queen Elizabeth I. It was
intended that the school be a free grammar school for
the education of Rugby's more promising boys. Though
today it is fee-paying, and co-educational, Rugby School
continues to offer scholarships to outstanding students
who come from state primary schools in the vicinity of
Rugby. The recently established Arnold Foundation for
Rugby School now offers complete fee and boarding
support for promising students outside the Rugby area.

Rugby is one of the nine 'great' English public schools
as defined by the Public School's Act 1868. The school's
most famous Head Master was Dr.Thomas Arnold,
immortalised in Thomas Hughes' book *Tom Brown's
School Days*. It was Arnold's reforms, with their emphasis
on sport, 'fair play' and the system of allocating
responsibility to boys, that led the British Public School
system towards the ethos which drove the British
Empire. The system has been copied around the world.

> 'with a fine disregard for the rules of football, (he) first took the ball in his arms and ran with it...'
>
> Mr Matthew Bloxham,
> a contemporay of Ellis

## William Webb Ellis (1807-1872)

William was born in Salford, near Manchester, the son of Ann Webb and James Ellis, an officer in the Dragoon Guards. After James was killed at the Battle of Albuera in 1812, Anne moved her sons, William and Thomas, to Rugby. As 'foundationers', pupils living within a radius of 10 miles of the Rugby clock tower, the boys were able to attend Rugby school for no cost. William attended from 1816 to 1825 and was noted as a good scholar and a good cricketer. Though it was noted that he was *'rather inclined to take unfair advantage at cricket'*. And, of course, there was the incident of breaking the rules by running forward with the ball during a football match.

After leaving Rugby, William attended Brasenose College, Oxford, where he established a reputation for playing cricket. He entered the Church and became chaplain of St Georges and then rector of St Clement Danes, in The Strand. In 1855 he became rector of Laver Magdalen, Essex, and a picture of him (the only known portrait) appeared in the Illustrated London News after he gave a particularly stirring sermon on the subject of the Crimean War.
He died in the south of France and is buried in Vieux Chateau, Menton, near the Italian border. He never knew the rugby legacy he left behind.

## Rugby in other nations

Games involving passing a ball and tackling other players have been played throughout the centuries. *Harpastum* was a game played by Romans during the Empire. *Caid*, played in Ireland, had two versions: a field game where the object was to put the ball (made out of animal skin with a natural bladder inside) through arch-like goals, formed from the boughs of two trees; and 'cross-country game' played during the daylight hours of a Sunday, in which the object was to carry the ball across a parish boundary. Both of these were rough contact sports where wrestling, pushing, and holding of opposing players was allowed. It was usually played by teams of unlimited numbers, representing communities, until a clear result was achieved or the players became too exhausted to continue. Caid was spread around the world through the Irish diaspora influencing other sports such as Australian Rules Football.

*Cnapan,* in Wales, involved teams of up to 1,000 players from adjacent parishes. The ball was passed, or smuggled, from one player to another, with the object of passing it to the opposing team's parish, church porch or another agreed destination. It was a running, handling and passing game with much physical contact and with elements that resembled scrums and lineouts. There was no kicking in the Welsh game, since the ball was made of wood and (to add interest) boiled in tallow to make it slippery.

In the 19th century rules for football were formulated and codified. The formalisation of rugby can be traced to three documented events: publishing of the first set of written rules in 1845; rejection by the Football Association in 1863 of the rules of running with the ball in hand and hacking; and the formation of the Rugby Football Union in 1871.

## IRB

In 1884, England had a disagreement with Scotland over an England try, disallowed by the referee, citing a foul by Scotland. England argued that since they invented the game, if they said it was a try, it was a try. Two years later, Scotland, Ireland and Wales formed the International Rugby Football Board (IRFB). England initially refused to to accept the IRFB as the governing body and wouldn't join until granted proportional representation on the board. The IRFB countered that member countries would not play England until the RFU agreed to accept its authority. England finally joined in 1890. In 1930 it was agreed that all international matches would be governed by the IRFB. In 1997, the IRFB moved from London to Dublin and in 1998 they dropped the F.

## Rugby Union

The Football Association was formed in 1863 with the intention to frame a code of laws that would gather all the various methods of play under the one heading of 'football'. Two contentious draft rules concerned 'running with the ball' and 'hacking'. A motion was proposed that these two rules be expunged from the FA rules. Francis Campbell of the Blackheath Club, argued that hacking is an essential element of 'football' and that to eliminate it would *do away with all the courage and pluck from the game, and I will be bound over to bring over a lot of Frenchmen who would beat you with a week's practice*. Campbell withdrew the Blackheath Club from the FA explaining that the rules that they intended to adopt would destroy the game and all interest in it. Twenty-one English clubs followed his lead and formed the Rugby Football Union. Three Rugby School alumni lawyers drew up the first rules of the game.

## La Soule

This French game was more like amicable warfare, in which the men from opposing villages would meet on a neutral field. The ball was made from wood or leather and a game could last several hours as the men tried to put the ball into their opponent's goal. So brutal were the clashes, with sometimes hundreds of men lying wounded, that the French authorities continually tried to outlaw the game and it began to decline in popularity in the late 19th century.

Rugby was introduced to French schools in the late 1880s by Baron Pierre de Coubertin, founder of the modern Olympics, who had seen the game being played in English public schools. It wasn't limited to schools for very long – two of the first cities to have organised rugby teams were Pau and Bordeaux.

**Bernard Lapasset**
President
French Rugby Federation
President
Organising Committee,
Rugby World Cup 2007

FRANCE

## An unforgettable experience

For the first time in history France has the honour
of organising the Rugby World Cup. This privilege
is all the greater because 2007 marks the twentieth
anniversary of this worldwide celebration of Rugby.

From the opening match of the tournament on
7 September 2007 to the Final at the Stade de France ®
on 20 October 2007, 2.4 million spectators will gather in
the twelve competition Host Cities. More than 700,000
of them will have come from all over the world, not
only to support their national team, but also to discover
France's regional charms and to make the most of its
internationally renowned heritage.

Rugby World Cup 2007 is the sporting event of the
decade in France and a fantastic opportunity for our
entire nation to provide accommodation and transport
for the benefit of Rugby fans. Social interaction,
friendliness and gastronomy are as much a part of
Rugby as they are features that draw people to France
– the world's number one tourist destination.

The French Rugby Federation and the Organising
Committee are working with the Host Cities, tourist
boards and the services of the French State to ensure
that each and every one of you has an experience of
Rugby World Cup 2007 that is as unforgettable as the
Tournament itself.

# PARIS

## & SAINT-DENIS

# From the first match to the action-packed final, Paris will be hosting the most important matches of Rugby World Cup 2007.

The tournament opens in Saint-Denis at Stade de France® with France v Argentina on Friday 7th September, followed by South Africa v Samoa at Parc des Princes on Sunday the 9th. Two of the tournament's most exciting contests will be held at Stade de France®: England v South Africa on Friday 14th September, and France v Ireland on the following Friday, the 21st. The Pool C and Pool D quarterfinal battle will be staged at Stade de France® as will the semi-finals and the thrilling final on the 20th October.

Directions and maps to the stadiums are on the next few pages together with details of the planned rugby festival and beer gardens in Saint-Denis. Fans and followers without tickets will be watching the tournament on large screens in the rugby bars of central Paris. At the time of printing large screens were planned for Hotel de Ville and a Rugby Village is proposed to be located under the Eiffel Tower.

# Getting around Paris

## Arrondissements

Paris is organised into districts called *arrondissements*. It is useful to acquaint yourself with the system because Parisians refer to them when giving directions and they feature in maps.

Arrondissements are numbered from 1-20 and are arranged in a spiral shape. Each arrondissement has its own character – the first arrondissement is the oldest and is at the centre of the spiral. Number 2 is the financial district, 4 takes in Notre Dame, Hotel de Ville and Le Marais, 5 & 6 include Saint Germain with its many bars and restaurants, 8 is the posh business and hotel district, and Montmartre is in the 18th arrondissement.

## Maps

The best Paris maps are the easy-to-read pocketbooks called *Paris Circulation,* with 70 plans, street finder, metro and RER maps, sold in most news kiosks for €5.

## Paris Visite

A pass that offers unlimited travel on all metro, RER trains and buses including excursions to Versailles and Disneyland.Valid for 1, 2, 3, or 5 days consecutive travel, the card is good value if only for the time saved standing in queues. On sale at RATP stations, Tourist Offices and some tobacconists.

## Tourist Offices

Paris Convention and Visitors Bureau

25 rue des Pyramides; carrousel du Louvre
0892 68 30 00 (€0.34/min)
09.00-19.00 daily; www.parisinfo.com
Pick up free brochures, Paris maps and purchase a Paris Visite card. If you're planning to visit many sights, purchase a Paris Museum Pass that allows repeat entry to more than 60 museums:
2 day pass €30; 4 days €45; 6 day €60.

## Trains

Paris has two train systems: a commuter fast train called RER and a city-wide underground service, the metro.

RER train lines are distinguished by letter while metro lines are numbered. Routes on both networks are identified by colour and the direction is indicated by the last stop. For example, to travel to Stade de France®, take metro line 13 (light blue) in the direction of St-Denis Université and alight at St-Denis porte de Paris.

## Metro

Trains are usually frequent but can be very crowded during rush hour which occurs about 6-7pm. Though the metro has 14 lines, chances are that few will travel direct to your destination and you will have to transfer. This may entail walking up and down stairs as Paris metro stations often are not equipped with escalators or elevators. Generally, choosing a smaller station will involve less walking.

Single tickets can be purchased for €1.40 at machines in the stations or in books of 10 *un carnet* for €10.50. Queues can be long and the instructions confusing for non-French speakers. A *Paris Visite* card is highly recommended.

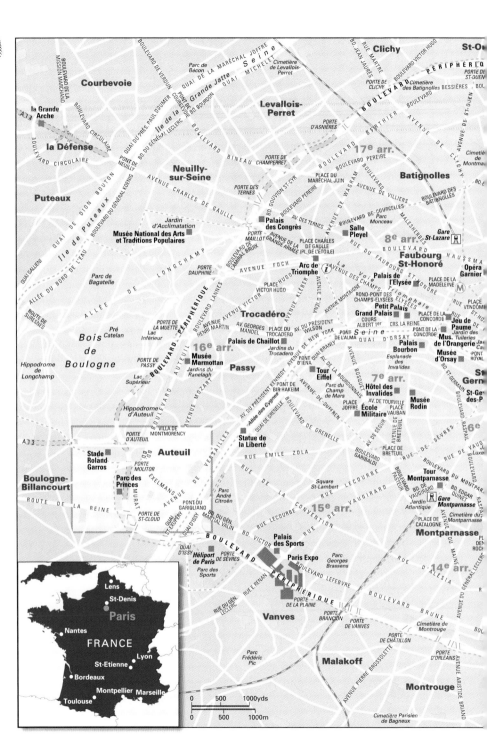

PARIS

## The Seine
• romantic river, where it all began

## Notre-Dame
• religious heart of France, dating back to 1163

## La Tour Eiffel
• symbol of the city, unmissable in more ways than one

## Musée du Louvre
• unrivalled collection set in a former royal palace

## Musée d'Orsay
• Impressionist collection in an old train station

## Musée National Picasso
• one of Paris's most popular museums, devoted to a genius

## Jardin du Luxembourg
• beautiful gardens in the heart of the city

## Arc de Triomphe
• one of three arches built in alignment

## Montmartre
• parts are tacky but elsewhere the atmosphere lingers

## Le Marais
• lovely area with plenty of bars, museums and the prettiest square in Paris: place des Vosges

## Pompidou Centre
• outstanding modern art collection in an unusual building

STADE DE FRANCE ®
FROM SAINT-DENIS.
ARCHITECTS: MICHEL
MACARY, AYMERIC ZUBLENA,
MICHEL REGEMBLA, CLAUDE
CONSTANTINI

## Stadium tours

ZAC du Cornillon
Nord
www.stadefrance.com
0892 700 900
10.00-18.00 daily,
hourly till 17.00 except
during events
meet at Gate H
€10 adults, €7 children
The behind-the-
scenes tour takes
in the VIP rooms,
players' locker rooms
and the edge of the
pitch. There is a
museum about the
construction of the
stadium with details
on the technology
used to build it.

| Stade de France ® capacity 80,000 | | |
| --- | --- | --- |
| **Matches** | **Date** | **Pool** |
| France v Argentina | 7 September, Fri | D |
| England v South Africa | 14 September, Fri | A |
| France v Ireland | 21 September, Fri | D |
| Quarter Final 4 W pool D v RU pool C | 7 October, Sun | |
| Semi Final 1 W QF1 v W QF2 | 13 October, Sat | |
| Semi Final 2 W QF3 v W QF4 | 14 October, Sun | |
| FINAL | 20 October, Sat | |

## The stadium and around

ZAC du Cornillon Nord
www.stadefrance.com
0892 700 900

This stadium holds a special place in French hearts for it was here that France won the coveted FIFA World Cup. It is passionately hoped by the country's rugby fans that the magic will be repeated for 'Les Bleus' in 2007.

Stade de France® was only commissioned once France

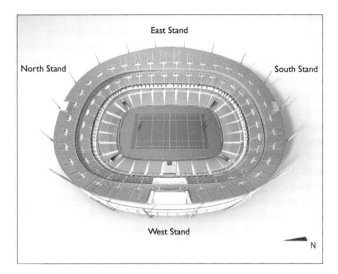

East Stand

North Stand

South Stand

West Stand

N

## Getting to the stadium

**Nearest stations**
• La Plaine-Stade de France, RER line B.
• St. Denis-Porte de Paris, metro line 13.

**Nearest airport**
Charles de Gaulle is located north-east of Paris on the RER B3 train line.

**Car**
Autoroute A1, A3, A86. Those travelling by car are advised to use public carparks in the city, available and well-indicated, then go to the stadium on foot or by public transport.

For those who have reserved parking, the carpark entrance is near Gate H.

**Trains**
• **Eurostar**
arrives at Gare du Nord take RER B one stop north to Stade de France.
• **TGV**
arrives at Charles de Gaulle, change to RER.
• **RER**
Line B to La Plaine-Stade de France.
Line D to Stade de France St Denis. Walk or take bus 139 to avenue du Stade de France.

**Metro**
The metro line 13 St. Denis-Porte de Paris stop is directly north of the stadium. Journey time 25 minutes from central Paris

was granted the rights to host FIFA World Cup 1998. The stadium was designed by four architects: Michel Macary, Aymeric Zubléna, Michel Regembla, Claude Constantini whose names must be credited on any photograph or description. It was completed in 31 months at a cost of €400 million, jointly financed by private interests and the French state.

The Stade is equipped with state-of-the-art technology and sound reinforcement that means every spectator can see and hear clearly.

Every summer the interior is transformed into a beach and in winter it becomes a ski resort.

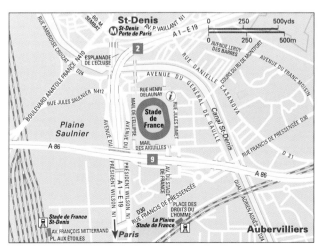

REMEMBER TO PURCHASE YOUR TRANSPORT TICKETS WELL IN ADVANCE OF THE MATCH TO SAVE TIME QUEUING.

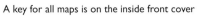

A key for all maps is on the inside front cover

## Saint-Denis 2007 Rugby Festival

metro: Saint-Denis – Porte de Paris

The city of Saint-Denis is pulling out all the stops to welcome international fans during Rugby World Cup 2007.

### Village Saint-Denis Rugbycolor

The main area, especially developed for the event, is an 8000 sq.metre village to be located near Stade de France®, adjacent to the metro station. It will be open each weekend of the tournament and promises to be a festive place with outdoor (under tents) restaurants, a giant screen broadcasting all the matches of Rugby World Cup 2007, and street entertainment.

### Opening weekend

The village will open on Thursday 6th September, matches will be broadcast on giant screens from Friday 7th. A street party with concerts and fireworks will be held on Saturday evening 8th September to inaugurate the village.

### Festival Planète Rugby

Free music concerts are scheduled to take place every weekend. On days that matches are held at Stade de France® concerts are planned before and after the match. On non-match days, concerts are planned for weekend evenings beginning at 7pm or 9pm.

| Large Screens Beer Gardens Restaurants Sports debates Free concerts Rugby Park Fireworks | **Saint-Denis tourism website** www.ville-saint-denis.fr <br> **Tourist Office** I rue de la République 01 55 87 08 70 09.30-18.00 Mon-Sat 10.00-16.00 Sun closed for lunch |
|---|---|

At press time, the programme was not confirmed but these artists are expected to perform: Kasabian, Gotan Project, Johnny Clegg and Soweto Gospel Choir, Carlos Nunez and Simple Minds.

### World Sports Forum

Join the lively debate on current issues in rugby politics. For topics covered and speakers check at the Tourist Office and/or the website listed above.

PREVIOUS CONCERT HELD AT SAINT-DENIS

# Five Legends, Five Opinions

## Have your say in Visa's Rugby World Cup Debate!

Five of the greatest rugby players – Zinzan Brooke, John Eales, Martin Johnson, Philippe Sella and Joel Stransky – will be discussing and debating the ins and outs of the game.

Don't miss this chance to go head-to-head with the Visa Rugby Legends and other fans around the world as they engage in Visa's Rugby World Cup Debate.

For more details log on to
**www.visarugby.com**

Visa is a proud worldwide partner of the Rugby World Cup 2007.

## Saint-Denis

One of the oldest villages around Paris was founded in the third century on the site of the burial of Saint-Denis. The relics of the saint are kept in the **Basilica Saint-Denis** and it is here that all the kings of France are interred, along with the remains of other notables such as Catherine de Medici and Marie Antoinette. The church dates from 1140 and is the oldest Gothic church in France. The crypt is even older and was first consecrated by Charlemagne in 775.

Saint-Denis was the first to bring the news of Jesus Christ to Roman Gaul. He was the first Bishop of Paris during the time of the Roman persecutions and like many early Christians was martyred for his faith. Saint-Denis was decapitated on Montmartre (mountain of the martyrs) but he did not die. The legend says he picked up his head and carried it as he walked, headless and barefoot, all the way to the village that then would take his name.

**Basilique Cathedral de Saint-Denis**
10.00-18.15 daily
12.00-18.15 Sunday
closed 1 hour earlier Oct-Mar
€6.10

---

### Marché aux Puces (Flea Market)

It all began with scavengers in the rag trade who would pick through other peoples rubbish for items they could sell at the market. After 1870 they set up their stalls near Porte de Clignancourt and the range of items on offer expanded to include antiques and objets d'art. In the early 1900s, journalists coined the phrase 'Flea Market' to describe the quantity and variety of small-sized items displayed by merchants, or perhaps the phrase described the buyers – flitting from one deal-of-the-century to the next.

north of the Périphérique between porte de Clignancourt and porte de St Ouen
10.00-18.00 Sat-Mon
metro: Garibaldi, porte de Clignancourt
Over 2,000 dealers in 16 distinct markets in small lanes

## Parc de La Villette

www.villette.com
inside the Périphérique between porte de Pantin and porte de la Villette
metro: porte de la Villette, porte de Pantin
10.00-18.00 daily, closed Monday

La Villette is the largest urban park in Paris. It was established in 1979 on 55 hectares of industrial wasteland on the borders of the 19th arrondissement and Seine-Saint-Denis. There is always something going on in the park and the website is kept regularly updated in French and English with listings of all activities.

**Cité des Sciences**. France is a world leader in technological innovation and this is celebrated in the excellent national museum of science and technology. With over 30,000 sq metres of exhibition space there is much room to explore and many exhibits are designed to be interactive.

First floor exhibits: Aeronautics, Automobiles, Space, Human body, Environment, Water and Oceans. Second floor: Biology, Stars and Galaxies, Light illusions, Medicine, Rocks and Volcanoes.

The museum's large windows offer views across the park, which includes a mirrored geodesic dome, **La Géode**. The dome houses a 400-seat cinema with a hemispherical screen.

At the south end of the park is the **Cité de la Musique**, a state-of-the-art music centre with concert halls, rehearsal studios, and Musée de la Musique with over 1,000 instruments.

### Cité des Sciences
www.cite-sciences.fr/english
10.00-18.00 Tues-Sat,
10.00-19.00 Sun
closed Monday
€7.50 adults, €7 under 25s, Planetarium €3

### La Géode
10.30-21.30 Tues,
Thurs-Sat
10.30-20.30 Wed, Sun
hourly show €9

### Cité de la Musique
12.00-18.00 Tues-Sat,
10.00-18.00 Sun

LA GÉODE

# PARC DES PRINCES

## Getting to the stadium

Parc des Princes is located just outside the Périphérique near Bois de Boulogne.

**Nearest airports**
**• Charles de Gaulle**
Located northeast of Paris on RER B line. Take RER B to St-Michel Notre-Dame and change to metro line 10.
**• Orly**
Located south of Paris with a connection to RER B, at Antony.

**Car**
The Périphérique exits of porte de St Cloud or porte d'Auteuil are closest to the stadium. Use public carparks in and around the city, available and well-indicated, and then go to the stadium on foot or by public transport.

**Trains**
**• Eurostar**
arrives at Gare du Nord, take metro line 4 to Strasbourg St-Denis, transfer to metro line 9.
**• TGV**
arrives at Charles de Gaulle, take RER B to St-Michel Notre-Dame change to metro line 10.
**• RER**
line C to Javel or Gare d'Austerlitz change to metro line 9

**Metro**
Line 9 (pont de Sèvres) exit porte de St. Cloud line 10 (Boulogne) exit porte d'Auteuil.

REMEMBER TO PURCHASE YOUR TRANSPORT TICKETS WELL IN ADVANCE OF THE MATCH TO SAVE TIME QUEUING.

| Parc des Princes capacity 47,870 | | |
|---|---|---|
| **Matches** | **Date** | **Pool** |
| South Africa v Samoa | 9 September, Fri | A |
| Italy v Portugal | 19 September, Wed | C |
| England v Tonga | 28 September, Fri | A |
| Ireland v Argentina | 30 September, Sun | D |
| 3rd place play-off | 19 October, Sat | |

## The stadium and around

24 avenue du commandant Guilbaud
www.psa.fr

The oval design of Parc des Princes makes for excellent views for the fans but creates an intimidating atmosphere for visiting players. Inaugarated in 1972, the stadium was designed for comfort and visibility by Roger Taillibert.

Paris's premier league rugby team, Stade Francais, play their international matches here to ever-increasing crowds. Their home stadium is actually Stade Jeanbouin, located nearby. Pre-game and half-time entertainment often features well choreographed chorus lines of beautiful can-can girls dressed in elaborate costumes inspired by famous Paris cabarets.

In addition to soccer and rugby, the stadium also hosts the Supercross, antique fairs, and a winter snow park.

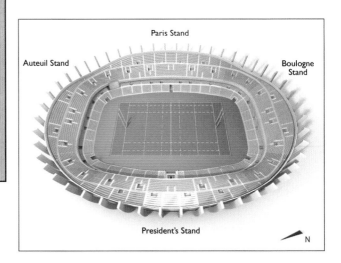

LE STADE

# Bars and restaurants near the stadium

### Les Princes
6 place du Docteur Paul Michaux (at the bottom end of avenue du Parc des Princes)
metro: porte de St Cloud
01 46 51 05 88
Having as its proprietors current France international and Stade Francais winger Christophe Dominici, and former international Christophe Juillet, you can guess that Les Princes is a very rugby-friendly bar indeed. It's in the perfect location right next to the stadium, with reasonably priced beer and food.

### Aux Trois Obus
120 rue Michel-Ange
metro: porte de St Cloud
01 46 51 22 58
Well located next to the metro and very close to the stadium entrance.

### Le Stade
2 rue du Commandant-Guilbaud
metro: porte de St Cloud
01 40 71 22 22
www.lestade-restaurant.com
This bar/restaurant owned and managed by rugby players Pieter de Villiers and Sylvain Marconnet, caters to hungry sports fans at lunch and in the evenings. They also own a wine company, Tresors du Cap.

### PSG
24 rue du Commandant-Guilbaud
metro: porte de St Cloud
01 47 43 72 54
The real name of this restaurant seems to be *Le 70* after the year that PSG (Paris Saint-Germain football club) was founded. True to its name, this venue shamelessly maintains extreme 1970s décor with lime-green plastic-roofed booths and a glowing blue illuminated bar.

A key for all maps is on the inside front cover

**RUGBY BARS IN CENTRAL PARIS**

# Bars in central Paris

## Rugby bars

Arrondissement 1

### Le Sous Bock
49 rue St Honore; metro: Chatelet
01 40 26 46 61
09.00-05.00 daily; meals lunch & dinner
Former rugby player Frédéric Beurq
proudly displays his trophy and winning
ball in a case beside the entrance of his large
establishment. Though it appears to be quite
small from the front, there is a large seating
area at the back and another in the cellar.
For Rugby World Cup 2007, Frédéric is busy
reupholstering the seats in team colours: red
for Wales, blue for France, green for Ireland,
black for New Zealand.

### Café Oz
18 rue Saint Denis; metro: Chatelet
01 40 39 00 18
An Australian bar where rugby players from
the Sorbonne team drink. The huge wooden
chairs and booths resemble something out
of a medieval castle. There are large screens
and you can't miss the rugby posters. They
serve a large range of beer but the service
could be better.

FRÉDÉRIC BEURQ

Arrondissement 2

### Le Louis d'Or
3 rue de la Bourse; metro: Bourse
01 42 97 48 89
08.00-01.00 daily; meals lunch & dinner
tapas all hours
A devoted Biarritz supporter, Louis closed
the street to host a massive celebration when
they won the French championship.
On tap are two Basque beers, a blonde and
a dark. Tapas are also served Basque style
– plates arrive piled high with slices of
baguette topped with sausage, paté and
hot chillies.

### Kitty O'Shea's
10 rue des Capucines; metro: Opera
The most popular Irish bar in Paris has long
been a favourite with rugby players and
fans. Owner Brian Loughney is well-known
in rugby circles and members of the Irish
team have been spotted here, as have the
VISA rugby legends. Irish supporters are
sure to be here in droves throughout the
tournament.

### The Black Bear
161 rue Montmartre; metro: Bourse
A relative new-comer, this large bar is owned
by former rugby stars Jean-Pierre Rives and
Paperemborde. It is decorated with the usual
rugby memoribilia, with some unusual items
such as Eric Cantona's Manchester United
shirt and cricketer Ian Botham's pads. There
are plenty of large screens around the bar
and plenty of beer on tap.

LOUIS D'OR

## Arrondissement 6

### Eden Park
10 rue Princesse; metro: Mabillon
A cool and trendy rugby bar owned by the clothing company founded by French rugby players Franck Mesnel and Eric Blanc.

## Arrondissement 8

### Le Rugby Bar
2 rue Roquepine; metro: Saint Augustin
01 42 65 38 45
Open until 4am on match days, this is another shrine to rugby whose patrón hails from the south-west of France. Stade Francais supporters form the core of a large and varied crowd of rugbymen. Good beer and a central location make this venue well worth a visit.

## Arrondissement 15

### Au Metro
18 boulevard Pasteur; metro: Pasteur
01 47 34 21 24
Players from the French and Parisian teams often come to this rugby-themed bar right next to the Pasteur station. The owner Jean-Pierre Mourin is from rugby country in the French south-west but has brought his passion to Paris. Jean-Pierre will be keeping his bar open 24 hours during the semi-final and final games.

## Sports bars

## Arrondissement 4

### The Auld Alliance
80 rue François Miron; metro: St Paul
01 48 04 30 40
open till 02.00; food not served
A large Scottish pub with big screens and a selection of 150 pure Scottish malts.

JEAN-PIERRE MOURIN

## Arrondissement 6

### Cafe 'Le Conti'
1 rue de Buci; metro: Mabillon
01 43 26 68 13
07.00-05.00 daily; continous food service
Though not a rugby bar per se, Le Conti is a friendly sports bar with a tradition of welcoming English speaking fans. It has 3 screens, seating areas upstairs and a large outdoor section. Barman Arnaud speaks English and will give you a friendly *Hello*.

### Le Buci
52 rue Dauphine; metro: Mabillon
01 43 26 67 52
06.30-04.00 daily continous food service
This is a typical French style bar with most seating facing outwards onto the street and along the pavement. Inside are three screens showing rugby matches. Service is also typically Parisian – brusque but efficient.

## Arrondissement 9

### O'Sullivans Irish Pub
1 boulevard Montmarte; metro: Grands Blvds
01 40 26 73 41
12.00-05.00 Fri-Sat, 12.00-02.00 Sun-Thurs
One of the largest Irish bars in Paris with plenty of big screens and leather upholstered seating.

## Arrondissement 18

### Corcoran's Pub
110 boulevard Clichy; metro: place de Clichy
01 42 23 00 30
This Irish pub is always packed for rugby matches and attracts an international crowd that often spills out onto the pavement.

# La Seine

The first people settled on the banks of the Seine about 2,300 years ago, choosing a spot on the Île de la Cité well-used by travellers. It was a handy place to cross the river, with the island in the centre narrowing the waters.

Stand on Pont Neuf and wipe the city from your mind. Picture the once simple village. Then imagine the City of Light growing and spreading around it through the centuries – the huge edifice of Notre-Dame looming over the river, and later the royal palace rising on the right bank, which now houses the Musée du Louvre.

The river and its bridges may no longer be the lifeblood of the city as they once were, but they are still a magical part of Paris life. Find time to walk the banks of the river, and cross from side to side over the old and the newer bridges. Each has a story to tell, pieces of the mosaic that make up the city of Paris. Pont Neuf or New Bridge was built in 1607 and is now the oldest surviving

bridge across the Seine. It was opened by King Henri IV racing across it on his horse and was the first pedestrian bridge in Paris with no dwellings on it. Every summer, the right banks of the Seine from here to Île St Louis are turned into Paris Plage, a beach in the centre of the city. Word is the Plage has made Parisians more casual, to the point of no longer wearing ties in the summer heat.

Pont Alexandre III was built for the Paris Exposition of 1900 to provide a crossing from the left bank to the newly-built Grand Palais and Petit Palais. Cross towards the left bank for the best view of the Hôtel des Invalides and the Dôme Church under which is Napoleon's Tomb.

Other bridges, other views:
• Pont de la Concorde towards the place de la Concorde with the Egyptian obelisk at its centre;
• from the Trocadéro over the Pont d'Iéna during the day for the second-best view of the Eiffel Tower;
• the same bridge at night, when the tower is lit up.

PONT ALEXANDRE III

## On the river

The river was once the prime form of transport in Paris when everything clustered along its banks. Now it is an often neglected means of transport. Yet who would prefer being under the ground or stuck in traffic when they could be gliding along on the Seine?

A Parisian Batobus cruises the river from April till December, taking a relaxing thirty minutes or so to visit the eight stops from the Port de la Bourdonnais, near the Eiffel Tower, to the Jardin des Plantes, east of Notre-Dame at the Pont de Sully. Note that boats travel in an anti-clockwise circle, calling at places on the left bank first and then the right bank.

A *Bateau Mouche* is a huge boat that carries tourists along the river. Passengers are seated facing outwards for the best views of the sights lining the Seine. A Parisian wouldn't be seen dead on one of these cruises but in fact they are well worth doing and, as happens worldwide, a visitor will see more of a city in a few days than a local might in a year. There are regular daytime trips and special lunch and dinner cruises when the boats turn into romantic floating restaurants. People dress smartly for dinner and the cost is on the expensive side, but the food can be quite good.

*Bateaux Vedettes* have smaller boats with no food served on board. These older vessels have face-forward seating with commentary provided by tourism students.

**Bateaux Mouches**
01 40 76 99 99; www.bateaux-mouches.fr
**Bateaux Parisiens Notre-Dame**
01 43 26 92 55
**Bateaux Parisiens Tour Eiffel**
01 44 11 33 44
www.bateauxparisiens.com
**Bateaux-Vedettes de Paris**
01 47 05 71 29
**Bateaux-Vedettes de Pont Neuf**
01 46 33 98 38
www.vedettesdupontneuf.com
**Batobus**
01 44 11 33 99; www.batobus.fr

## LA SEINE

## Notre-Dame

place du Parvis-Notre-Dame
metro: Cité, St-Michel Notre-Dame
01 53 10 07 02
07.45-18.45 daily, free

Notre-Dame is the spiritual heart of France and the country's most important cathedral. Look up at the facade and you can well believe there's still a hunchback swinging around up there among the gargoyles, or that a king is about to be crowned inside.

The imagination that created *The Hunchback of Notre-Dame* belongs to the same man that launched the campaign to save the cathedral: Victor Hugo. The novel's hero is Quasimodo, a tortured bell-ringer at the cathedral who falls in love with the gypsy girl, Esmeralda. The hunchback is first under the control of the evil archdeacon, but Quasimodo is slowly transformed by the kindness

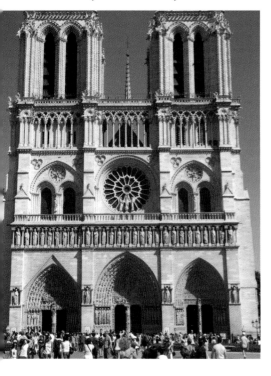

of Esmeralda to rebel against his evil master. In the end, Quasimodo makes the ultimate sacrifice for love.

Hugo's novel has endured for centuries, but even as the book was published in 1831, the cathedral had been crumbling into ruin for some time. Walls were in such poor repair they were hidden behind tapestries for the coronation of Napoleon and Josephine, a ceremony attended by Pope Pius VII. Hugo launched the campaign to save Notre-Dame and work began in 1841. It took 23 years to restore the cathedral.

Over the centuries many notable people have walked through the centre doors: Mary Queen of Scots was crowned Queen of France after her marriage to François II; Henry VI of England added the crown of France to his titles; and Charles I of England was married here. Walk through those doors and you are walking through the history of Europe.

Building Notre-Dame took 170 years from the time Pope Alexander III laid the foundation stone in 1163. Teams of master craftsmen laboured continously, sometimes through several generations of the same family. Look for the three great rose windows, in the north and south walls, and in the west wall over the entrance. The window in the north wall still has the original 13th-century stained glass. To the left of the entrance are the stairs to the towers, where 387 steps take you up to dramatic views over Paris.

In the square in front of Notre-Dame is the almost-hidden entrance to the **Crypte Archéologique**. Down below ground (many of Paris's most interesting places are below street level) are Roman remains, the remnants of medieval streets and a fascinating scale model showing the development of the city.

## Île de la Cité

metro: Cité

The 'island of the city' is just that: the
island where the city was born. Paris
owes its name to a Celtic tribe called the
Parisii, who settled here in 300BC. This
tiny island in the Seine is not only the
location of Notre-Dame, but also houses
the law courts at the Palais de Justice
and the police headquarters where the
famous fictional Frenchman (created by
a Belgian) Inspector Maigret was based.

The point of land on the west tip of
the island is called **square du Vert
Galand**. Sit in the sun on the point or
relax on a bench around a grassy area
lined with shady trees. Stairs lead down
from Pont Neuf. A Seine river cruise

departs from here and refreshments are
available at their kiosk. There is also
a fountain with drinking water where
you can fill your bottle.

At the western end of the island, visit
the **Conciergerie**, a Gothic palace
where Marie-Antoinette and others
were held prior to their dates with
Madame Guillotine during the French
Revolution.

Incongrously set inside the Palais de
Justice is **Sainte-Chapelle**, another
Gothic masterpiece. This one is a
visual symphony in stained glass: 15
stained-glass windows soar up towards
a vaulted roof, covered in stars, some
15m (50ft) above your head. Be aware
that a security check is required to enter
the Palais de Justice.

# La Tour Eiffel

Champs de Mars
RER: C Champ de Mars Tour Eiffel
metro: École Militaire
01 44 11 23 45 or 01 44 11 23 23 (recorded
information)
www.tour-eiffel.fr
lifts: 09.30-23.45 daily September- June

€11 to the top, less for lower levels only.
Last ascent will be earlier than closing time,
varying with the level and the time of year.
The steps close earlier.

TO AVOID QUEUES ARRIVE FIRST THING IN
THE MORNING, OR LATER AT NIGHT

When the Eiffel Tower was built in
1889 for the Universal Exhibition, many
people were appalled at the prospect of
a 320m (1050ft) high tower made of iron
girders filling the sky over the newly-
elegant Paris streets. Revered architect
Baron Von Haussmann had only just
completed his 18-year beautification of
Paris in 1870, and here was an engineer,
Gustave Eiffel, proposing to vandalise
the skyline by creating the world's
tallest building! *Sacre bleu!* Feelings were
summed up by the writer Maupassant
who said that he consented to dine at the
Eiffel Tower, only because it was the one
place where he didn't have to look at it.

Today, almost 120 years later, Gustave's
tower is still here, looking fabulous and
now *the* symbol not only of Paris but of
France. Recognised the world over, it was
chosen by the French state to mark the
arrival of the millennium on 1 January
2000, with a spectacular lightshow and
fireworks thought by many to have been
the best display in the world. For those
visiting Paris for the first time, the tower
is the one thing they have to see. Indeed,
as obvious and as touristy as it is, you
simply haven't been to Paris until you've
been to the top of the Eiffel Tower.

On the way up in the lift, you might mull
over some facts: These are the original

lifts that travel 100,000km each year, transporting people between the levels. Eiffel's precise engineering means the top of the tower doesn't sway more than about 12cm (4.5 in) even in very strong winds. This stability is largely thanks to the 2.5 million rivets that fasten the 18,000 metal parts – made to withstand the August heat which can increase the tower's size by 15 cm (6 in) on hot days.

If you get to the tower and the queues are really long, try climbing the 360 steps to the first level and joining the lifts there. If you're feeling fit, you can even walk another 700 steps to take you up to the second level. You must use the lifts to go to the top where you'll find various displays and a viewing gallery, from where on the proverbial clear day you can see for up to 80 km (50 miles).

## Musée du Quai Branly

206 quai Branly
01 56 61 70 00
10.00-18.30 Tues-Sun
late opening till 21.30 Thurs
Across the Seine and hidden behind a forest of trees is Paris' newest museum. It is devoted to the primitive arts and civilisations of Africa, Oceania, the East and the Americas. Designed by Jean Nouvel, the ultra modern building was comissioned by Jacques Chirac as his legacy to Paris.

## Arc de Triomphe

place Charles-de-Gaulle
metro: Charles de Gaulle Étoile
01 55 37 73 77
10.00-23.00 daily (closes 22.30 Oct-Mar)
€7

There's more to the grand arch than immediately meets the eye. Based on Emperor Constantine's arch in Rome, it was built to celebrate Napoleon's triumph at the Battle of Austerlitz on 2 December 1805. Each 2 December, the sun sets in line with the Champs-Élysée and throws the Arch's shadow down the street towards the Arc de Triomphe du Carrousel, in front of the Louvre, designed in perfect alignment with the Arc de Triomphe. In 1989, a third triumphal arch was added to the alignment: the Grande Arche at La Défense, in a new business district in the west of Paris, to make a trio of triumphal arches.

At the top of Arc de Triomphe is the Tomb of the Unknown Soldier, and a small but enjoyable museum telling the story of the arch and providing close ups of the shields and friezes covering the monument.

## Musée du Louvre

rue de Rivoli
metro: Louvre Rivoli
01 40 20 50 50 and
01 40 20 51 51 (for
recorded information
www.louvre.fr
09.00-18.00 daily
till 21.45 Wed & Fri
closed Tuesday, €8.50
free admission:
18.00-21.45 Fri &
first Sun of the month

### Tickets

Purchase your ticket in
advance (at least the
day before) and plan
to arrive early in the
morning or else late
on a Wednesday or
Friday. Tickets can be
obtained from:
Virgin Megastore
Carrousel du Louvre
(next to the Louvre)
99 rue de Rivoli

Once you've got
your tickets, pick up
a museum plan at the
Louvre's information
desk. This shows
you where the most
popular exhibits are to
be found, and marks
the museum entrances.

### Mona Lisa

The entrance nearest
to *Mona Lisa* is not the
main entrance beneath
the glass pyramid (you
can enjoy this on your
way out so don't let it
detain you) but at the
Porte des Lions. This
is on the south side of
the museum, west of
the Pont du Carrousel.
Then proceed directly
to the Salles des États
(room 6).

If you visited the Louvre every day for a year, and were
able to view one hundred pieces of art each day, you
would eventually see every object in the museum's vast
collection. The Louvre holds 35,000 pieces of art, spread
over four floors of a large palace. Each floor is divided into
three zones corresponding to areas or wings of the palace:
**Sully, Denon** and **Richelieu**.

The **lower ground floor** holds Islamic, Egyptian and part
of the Greek collection along with classical statuary from
French collections. On the **ground floor** is Near Eastern,
Oriental, Greek, Etruscan and Roman antiquities. The
**first floor** comprises Napoleon III's apartments, Egyptian
artefacts and an outstanding collection of Italian and
French Renaissance paintings (go to room 6 for the Mona
Lisa). The **second floor** displays Dutch and Flemish
masters together with French paintings from the
Baroque era.

There are so many highlights in the Louvre that it is hard
to know where to begin. Sculpture and paintings vie for

your attention in rooms packed with art. Even dividers between rooms have display cases tucked into them; one showcases a rare Etruscan bronze.

If you only want to spend a few hours and be sure to see the masterpieces, arrive early and be prepared to climb stairs. Begin in the Sully wing on the ground floor. This outstanding scuplture gallery includes the sensuous *Venus de Milo*, and the powerful *Winged Victory of Samothraki*.

Continue on the sculpture trail and visit Michelangelo in the Denon wing, then climb the steps to the first floor and the Italian Renaissance collection with Leonardo da Vinci's *Mona Lisa*. The artist carried the painting with him on his travels around Italy and it was

with him when he died in France. The subject has never been identified and Leonardo himself never considered it finished.

Much of the Louvre's spectacular collection of Italian art was acquired by Napoleon, who, together with his army, conquered the duchies of Italy, dismantled the Venetian Republic and kept the pope prisoner in the Vatican.

Cross the courtyard (by the Pyramid) and climb to the second floor of the Richelieu wing where you'll find an outstanding collection of northern European paintings including Jan Vermeer's exquisite *The Lacemaker*. This last alone is worth spending time with, instead of jostling for space in the crowds permanently gathered around Leonardo da Vinci's portrait. See the tinted panel for tips on how to see the *Mona Lisa* in peace for a few minutes, or even if you just want to beat the slow moving ticket queue.

Afterwards, relax at one of the museum's five cafés, or at Le Grand Louvre, the more formal restaurant underneath the pyramid. All of these eating places are closed on Tuesday.

| **Ground floor** | |
| --- | --- |
| Venus de Milo | Sully wing, room 12 |
| Winged Victory of Samothraki | |
| | Denon wing, Escalier Daru |
| Michelangelo | Denon wing, room 4 |
| **First floor** | |
| Mona Lisa | Denon wing, room 6 |
| Géricault | Denon wing, room 77 |
| Delacroix | Denon wing, room 77 |
| **Second floor** | |
| Vermeer | Richelieu wing, room 38 |
| Rubens | Richelieu wing, room 18 |
| Durer | Richelieu wing, room 8 |
| Rembrandt | Richelieu wing, room 31 |
| Watteau | Sully wing, room 36 |
| Fragonard | Sully wing, room 48 |
| Ingres | Sully wing, room 60 |

# Jardin des Tuileries

Jardin Des Tuileries (Tuileries Gardens)
rue de Rivoli
metro: Tuileries
07.30-19.00 daily
**Jeu de Paume**
12.00-21.00 Tues; 12.00-19.00 Wed-Fri
10.00-19.00 Sat-Sun; closed Mon
**Orangerie**
12.30-19.00 daily; until 21.00 Fri
closed Tues

The Tuileries gardens and palace were built as private gardens in 1564, for Catherine de Médici, the wife of King Henri II. A century later, in 1664, they were turned into more formal gardens and opened to the public. Today the public loves them, locals and visitors alike. The paths through the gardens are lined with lime and chestnut trees, and there are benches, a pond and quite a few sculptures including some by Henry Moore, Alberto Giacometti and Aristide Maillol.

As popular as the gardens are today, their history is dark. Where children play was once all bloodshed and death at the end of the 18th century. In 1792, at the climax of the French Revolution, citizens of Paris stormed the gardens and the royal Tuileries Palace and ransacked them. The protests and attacks went on from 20 June until 10 August, when King Louis XVI was dragged from the throne and the French royal family imprisoned and executed.

The Tuileries palace survived the Revolution, but was destroyed in 1871 during the brief months of revolutionary government known as the Paris Commune.

At the western end of the gardens, near place de la Concorde, are two important galleries. In the north corner is **Jeu de Paume** with exhibitions of contemporary paintings, sculpture and photography that are some of the best shows in Paris.

In the south, is the **Orangerie**, built around the large and precious canvases of Claude Monet's *Waterlilies*. The stunning gallery took six years to complete. The gallery also has the Walter-Guillaume Collection of paintings from 1870-1930, a short timespan in a small gallery, but which nonetheless manages to include Auguste Renoir, Pablo Picasso, Henri Matisse and Paul Cézanne.

## Musée d'Orsay

Better even than the Louvre, the Musée d'Orsay focuses on Western art in the explosive period from 1848 to 1914. For most people this means the Impressionists and post-Impressionists, and the museum does have a wonderful collection. Here you have some of Van Gogh's most powerful paintings, including his *Bedroom at Arles*, alongside Edouard Manet's controversial *Le Déjeuner sur l'Herbe* and *Olympia*, and large collections of works by Claude Monet, Auguste Renoir, Gauguin, Henri Toulouse-Lautrec and Paul Cézanne. Degas appears in both the sculpture and photography collections, this last amounting to over 10,000 items alone.

This is only the tip of the iceberg, as you discover when you wander round this converted railway station, full of light and space. The station was built in 1900 to provide easier, central access to the Paris Exposition, but it closed in 1939. It then stood unused until Orson Welles stumbled across it and used it as a location for his 1962 film version of Kafka's *The Trial*. In 1986 it re-opened as an exciting museum, using the vast space to great effect. It is exhilarating just to wander around, even before you start admiring the exhibits.

Be sure to visit the Art Nouveau rooms on the first floor. Here are some of the most exquisitely designed rooms you will ever see. Many are panelled in exotic woods. The galleries also include crystal and jewellery by Rene Lalique.

Almost every art movement from the period is represented, including the Romantics, the Art Nouveau movement, the School of Pont-Aven, the Realists, the Barbizon school and the Pointillists. It's one of those museums you just won't want to leave.

I rue de la Légion d'Honneur
RER: C Musée d'Orsay
metro: Assembée Nationale
01 40 49 48 14, or 01 45 49 11 11 (recorded information)
www.musee-orsay.fr
10.00-18.00 Tues-Wed, Fri-Sat
10.00-21.45 Thurs, 09.00-18.00 Sun
closed Mon; open at 09.00 Jun-Sep
€7

# Centre George Pompidou

rue Beaubourg
metro: Rambuteau
01 44 78 12 33
www.centrepompidou.fr
11.00-21.00 Wed-Mon, closed Tuesday
€7, museum

Now 30 years old, the Pompidou Centre still manages to look outrageous, like a punk who has never grown up. And like the punk movement, it created outrage when it opened in 1977. Architects Renzo Piano and Richard Rogers 'inside-out' building startled Paris, if not the world. Pipes that are normally hidden are exposed on the outside of the building in bold colours: blue for AC, green for water and yellow for the electricity supply. There's also an external escalator which zig-zags up the front of the building in a plexi-glass tube. And after three decades, the inside-out look still works.

### Musée de l'Art Moderne

The modern art collection is on the fourth and fifth floors with the entrance on the fourth. The fifth floor is used for temporary exhibits while the lower floor exhibits works from 1905-1960. Highlights include *L'Atelier au Mimosa*

by Pierre Bonnard, *Acrobates en Gris* by Fernand Léger, *Le Rêve* by Henri Matisse, Pablo Picasso's *l'Arlequin*, and Rene Rousseau's *Snakecharmer*, paintings by Jackson Pollock and a superb collection of sculpture by Alberto Giacometti and Constantin Brancusi, including his atelier.

There is a cinema, temporary exhibition spaces, library, performance spaces and a large art bookshop. Take the outside escalator up to the top floor for the views over the city, access is free. The Georges restaurant on the sixth floor has superb French-Asian fusion cuisine and unbeatable views.

The outrageous punky aesthetic also applies to statues in the fountains in **place Igor Stravinsky**, beside the Pompidou, inspired by the composer's ballet, *The Firebird*. There is a terrace alongside the fountain with several brasseries that serve good quality salads, omelettes, and other simple French dishes. An excellent stop for lunch.

## Les Halles

### Forum des Halles

101 porte Berger
metro: Châtelet-Les-Halles
01 44 76 96 56
10.00-19.30 daily, closed Sunday

Once known as *'L'estomac de Paris'*, les Halles was the city's largest fresh food market, and for 800 years was the hub for all food distribution in Paris. But the importance and stature of the market was the source of its own demise, as it brought major traffic problems to the centre of the capital. In the 1960s the market buildings were demolished and eventually made way for a metro station and a multistorey shopping mall with 180 shops. Here you'll find a La Redoute outlet and other French and global chains. There are restaurants and cinemas on five levels and underneath it all is Châtelet-Les-Halles, said to be the world's busiest subway station. In addition there is a large swimming and fitness complex.

### Saint Eustache

The beautiful rosette window is the highlight of this large church with a history of helping poor people from the market – today it supports aids sufferers. Madame de Pompadour and Cardinal Richelieu were baptised here.

### Centre Sportif Suzanne Berlioux

10 place de la Rotunda, Les Halles
11.30-22.00 Monday-Friday
09.00-19.00 Saturday-Sunday
10.00-22.00 Wednesday

**LE MARAIS**

## Le Marais

Many guidebooks dismiss the Marais district, on the grounds that it has been discovered by tourists (you know – people who buy guidebooks), but for us the Marais remains one of the best areas for walking and eating. Here you'll find a fascinating cultural mix that includes Kosher restaurants and the Paris gay quarter. There are numerous restaurants, bars and tiny lanes with food shops to drool over. Le Marais has a genuine character. We love it.

### Place des Vosges

metro: St Paul, Chemin Vert

This beautiful square is the heart of the Marais and measures exactly 140m per side. It was first built by King Henri IV in 1612 on the site of the Hôtel des Tournelles. The layout of the square, with its integrated design of elegant matching housefronts built over arcades, was quickly and extensively copied throughout Europe. Place des Vosges became a model for urban living and was *the* place to live for the aristocracy, the literati, and anyone who was considered at all important in 17th century Paris.

When the royal court moved to Versailles in 1686, place des Vosges lost its allure and deteriorated. Eventually it became a slum and remained so until it was restored in the 1960s. Today it is once again one of Paris's most sought-after addresses. People who have lived here over the years include Molière, Cardinal Richelieu and Victor Hugo, whose house at number 6 is now a museum, **Maison de Victor Hugo**.

Other museums worth visiting in the area include the unmissable **Musée National Picasso**, the historical **Musée Carnavalet**, **Musée de l'Histoire de France**, **Musée**

PLACE DES VOSGES

**Cognacq-Jay**, **Musée d'Art et d'Histoire du Judaïsme** and the offbeat magic museum, **Musée de la Curiosité**. Paris's love for photography is expressed at the excellent **Maison Européenne de la Photographie**, which hosts an annual festival in October that is well worth a visit.

Food lovers should check out **rue St Antoine** for everything from goat's cheese and chocolate tarts to horsemeat. **Rue des Rosiers** is a lively street with plenty of takeaways. If you're looking for a brasserie try **place du Marché Sainte Catherine**. The best shopping is on (and just off) **rue des Francs**.

PLACE DU MARCHÉ SAINTE CATHERINE

## Musée National Picasso

Hôtel Salé, 5 rue de Thorigny
metro: St Paul, St Sebastien Froissart
01 42 71 25 21
www.musee-picasso.fr
09.30-18.00 daily in Sept. (closed 17.30 Oct.)
closed Tues; €5.50

If you only know Pablo Picasso (1881-1973) from his Cubist and more outlandish paintings, a visit here will show you that the man himself was like one of his own Cubist portraits – with many different sides. Don't dismiss the museum because you think you don't like Picasso's work. Pay a visit and you'll see thousands of items in the world's largest collection of his work, donated to the French state by the Picasso family in lieu of death duties.

The light and airy building is a work of art in itself – complete with furniture and chandeliers designed by Alberto's brother, Diego Giacometti. The mansion dates from the 17th century, when it was commissioned by a salt-tax collector, hence the name *Hôtel Salé* (Salt House).

Picasso's work is displayed in roughly chronological order, giving you a chance to appreciate the remarkable speed at which his talent developed. He was an accomplished artist from a very early age so it is no wonder he turned to experimentation. Don't miss the arresting self-portrait, done when the artist was poverty-stricken in 1901 and which grips you with its unflinching stare. In addition to paintings and sketches, there are also collections of Picasso's work in ceramics, sculpture and photography. The ceramics are especially good, whimsically showing the artist's sense of fun. Works from Picasso's own collection are on display, including those by his great friend Matisse. There is also a gift shop worth visiting, so leave yourself some extra time to browse the shelves .

PLACE DES VOSGES

## Saint Germain

The *rive gauche*, or left bank, of the Seine is the intellectual, literary and music pulse of Paris, with cafés, jazz clubs, bookshops and the ghosts of Picasso, Sartre and Scott Fitzgerald haunting the boulevards.

Boulevard Saint Germain makes an elegant arc as it stretches for 3km through the left bank and neighbouring Latin quarter, from pont de la Concorde to pont de Sully, passing through Saint Michel. The most famous street of them all owes its elegance to Baron Haussmann, Napoleon's architect who completely rebuilt Paris. He transformed the narrow medieval streets into the wide tree-lined boulevards we enjoy today.

Near Saint Germain des Prés, strung together like pearls on a necklace, are three of the most famous cafés in Paris. At number 151 is Brasserie Lipp, once the haunt of French politicians such as Georges Pompidou, Francois Mitterrand and Charles de Gaulle. Number 172, Café de Flore, is an art deco delight, favoured by intellectuals. It was here in the 1940s that Jean-Paul Sartre and Simone de Beauvoir would hold court. Across the street at number 170 is Les Deux Magots, the

café preferred by artists and writers, which appears in Hemingway's books *A Moveable Feast* and *The Sun Also Rises.* Scott Fitzgerald, Oscar Wilde, Paul Verlaine and André Breton have all drunk coffee or something stronger at the Magots, and it was here that Pablo Picasso first met his muse Dora Maar in 1937.

Just off the boulevard along the rue de l'Ancienne-Comédie is Le Procope, the oldest café in Paris, founded in 1686. The roll-call of names here is grander than any of them, ranging from Voltaire and Balzac to Napoleon Bonaparte, Victor Hugo and Benjamin Franklin. It's now a restaurant and you can still dine in the glamour of its 18th-century décor. Just be prepared for 21st-century prices.

There are some good sports bars and restaurants along rue de Buci and off rue du Four. The two streets join at Boulevard Saint Germain near the Mabillon metro. Follow rue du Four westwards to the lively network of lanes around rue de Canettes where there are bars frequented by 'Les Bleus' and the All Blacks. North of boulevard Saint Germain are Le Conti and Le Buci, on opposite corners of a lively intersection of pedestrianised streets.

# Rue Mouffetard

One of the oldest and best food markets in Paris is open daily except Sunday afternoons. If you want to stock up for a picnic, or replenish your self-catering fridge, this is the street for you.

Boulevard Saint Germain runs across the top of rue Mouffetard, though at that point the road is named rue de la Montagne. At this end, the street does not look very interesting, but you will be rewarded if you make the effort to walk up and over the hill to rue Mouffetard and its markets. Here you will find fantastic French bakeries, wine and cheese shops, charcuterie (deli's) and restaurants to rest your weary feet. The absolutely best iced tea can be found at Le Mouffetard, 116 rue Mouffetard.

As the saying goes: all roads lead to Rome, even this one. Rue Mouffetard began life as a Roman road, the main one leading south from Paris to Lyon, and beyond Lyon to Rome. The street was residential back in the 13th century, and many of the existing houses date from the 17th century. They can be hard to appreciate as many of the ground floors have become shops and cafés, and the street is almost always packed with people. To appreciate the buildings you'll need to find somewhere safe to stand and stare up to the upper floors, and beyond those to the original mansard roofs.

At number 1 place de la Contrescarpe, there used to be the Maison de la Pomme de Pin, the Pine Cone Club. In the 16th century this was also a café, frequented by Rabelais and other writers. On the square these days it's more likely to be a mix of tourists and students from the nearby university.

## Jardin des Plantes

place Valhubert, metro: gare d'Austerlitz
07.15-sunset daily, free

In 1626 the physicians to King Louis XIII planted a medicinal herb garden on the left bank of the Seine, and 14 years later the gardens were opened to the public. They are still open and remain a popular place for Parisians to relax. The garden serves as a plant research centre, with some 10,000 different species. These include an *Acacia robinia*, the oldest tree in Paris, planted in 1636. Mere striplings by comparison are a cedar of Lebanon from 1734 and a Sophora of Japan, planted in 1747. This first flowered in 1777 and is still flowering over 200 years later. It is a humbling and uplifting experience to gaze at these venerable trees and think of the events that have happened around them – wars and revolutions, and still they stand.

### Muséum d'Histoire Naturelle

57 rue Couvier; 01 40 79 54 79
metro: gare d'Austerlitz
10.00-18.00 Sun-Mon, Wed-Fri
10.00-20.00 Sat, closed Tues
Grand Galerie €7; other galleries €5

The museum is made up of several galleries, but the best is the **Grande Galerie de l'Evolution**. Set in a 19th century glass and steel builing, it is to natural history what the Musée d'Orsay is to art. On the ground floor, dozens of animals stride across an African savannah, showing how the human imagination can transform what are basically stuffed animals into an uplifting experience. Above the savannah exhibit hangs a huge whale skeleton, adding to the dramatic effect. The basement is dedicated to life in the oceans. On upper floors, displays concern the issues facing the natural world with thought-provoking exhibits including a population counter, increasing rapidly every second.

JARDIN DE CÉLESTE

## Jardin de Céleste
### Musée du Moyen Age

6 place Paul-Painlevé; metro: Cluny
09.15-17.45 Wed-Mon; closed Tues

A quiet medieval garden set on one of the busiest corners in Paris. There are several box plantings, each planted to a theme, one with medicinal herbs, one with plants from the Bible, one with fragrant plants. Formerly known as Musée Cluny, the museum houses the *Lady with the Unicorn* tapestry.

## Jardin du Luxembourg Luxembourg Gardens

rue de Vaugirard, metro: Jussieu
dawn-dusk daily, free

As a contrast to the traffic-filled boulevards and smoky cafés and bars, the Jardin du Luxembourg provides the left bank with some much-needed breathing space. Locals make use of it too, especially in summer when the grass is covered with lounging bodies, getting hot yet still looking cool. It's a legal requirement for every citizen of Paris to look cool at all times.

At the north end of the Jardin is the Palais du Luxembourg, which houses the French Senate. It was built in 1615-27 for Marie de Médicis, the widow of King Henri IV who had died in 1610, the style chosen to remind her of her native Florence to give her some comfort. In 1622 Marie de Médicis summoned Rubens to come to Paris and to paint two cycles of work for her new palace, one showing events in her own life and the other events in the life of her dead husband. Rubens painted 24 canvases under rather difficult conditions (Marie was a demanding subject and employer), most of which are now to be seen in the Louvre.

There's a café, fountains, trees, tennis courts and plenty for children to do, including donkey rides. The grounds are also liberally sprinkled with sculptures, including work by Ossip Zadkine, whose studio, now the Musée Zadkine, is close by. You're not recommended to try what Ernest Hemingway says he did in the gardens during his poverty-stricken early Paris days: shoot pigeons for the pot.

**Le Musée du Luxembourg** Luxembourg Museum
19 rue de Vaugirard
01 42 34 25 95 19
www.museeduluxembourg.fr
metro: Saint-Sulpice
RER B: Luxembourg
11.00-19.00 Tues-Thurs
11.00-20.00 Mon, Fri-Sat
09.00-19.00 Sun, Hols
€10
Good quality temporary exhibits, recently there have been a Titian and a René Lalique exhibit.

MUSÉE DU LUXEMBOURG

# Montmartre

The district that most visitors see on a quick trip is a far cry from Montmartre's Bohemian past, when showgirls, poets and painters rubbed shoulders (and much else besides). Today dancers are more likely to be from eastern Europe and painters earn their crust by sketching tourists in the place du Tertre as opposed to creating works that will end up in museums. But get away from the obvious and with a bit of effort you can still conjure up a feel for Montmarte as it was when Pablo Picasso worked as a waiter, and Henri Toulouse-Lautrec painted can-can girls.

Utrillo and Renoir are just two of the artists who used to live in Le Manoir de Rose de Rosimond, now the **Musée de Montmartre**. It's a good place to start to get an overview of the area's history, although the house is more interesting than the contents. The house overlooks one of Montmartre's little eccentricities – the only vineyard in Paris. In the middle of the 18th century, this whole area was covered in vines and Paris had a great reputation for its wine. Today there are just 2,000 vines, producing 1,000 bottles of wine a year, more for fun and charity than for serious consumption.

## Musée de l'Érotisme

72 boulevard de Clichy
metro: place de Clichy
01 42 58 28 73
www.musee-erotisme.com
10.00-02.00 daily; €7

Sex in the Pigalle and Montmartre districts these days is much more in your face, so to speak, than it was 100 years ago, when '*a glimpse of stocking was something shocking*'. Now, as Cole Porter said, anything goes. It certainly does at the Erotic Museum, although it is a far from sleazy place. The interior is well-lit with modern decor, and it is as serious

MONTMARTRE STEPS

about its subject matter as any other Paris museum. This private collection was opened in 1998 when the owner put on display the 5,000 erotic items collected on his travels. More objects have been added since and the exhibits provide a fascinating journey of global sexual practice, with paintings, photos, sculptures, automata, ceramics, toys, drawings, dolls. Don't go if you are easily shocked, but if you're fairly broadminded, your mind is likely to be even broader after your visit. And don't miss the gift shop for some very unusual souvenirs.

## Basilique du Sacré-Coeur

35 rue de Chevalier-de-la-Barre
metro: Anvers
01 53 41 89 00; 06.00-22.30 daily
crypt open 09.00-19.00 daily
free admission to church

Sacré-Coeur has been likened to a wedding cake. It is certainly distinctive, and at the front you will have one of the best views of Paris.

The church is actually less than a hundred years old, consecrated in 1919. It was built by two Catholic businessmen who vowed that they would build a church and dedicate it to the Sacred Heart of Jesus, if the country was spared in the Franco-Prussian war. The church welcomes all faiths and inside you even see a Jewish symbol.

It is possible to climb almost to the top, the second-highest point in the city after the Eiffel Tower, thanks to Montmartre's elevation, or you can descend to the crypt for an audio-visual display on the history of Sacré-Coeur. There are several ways to reach the church from place St Maladon: you can ride the funicular, climb aboard a tourist train, or use the steps.

BASILIQUE DU SACRÉ-COEUR

## Cemeteries

It may seem goulish, but in Paris many people pay a visit to one or more of these three famous cemetries: The **Cimetière de Montmartre** has a mix of history, nature and fame. Here lies Louise Weber, better known as *La Goulue,* one of the first can-can dancers at the Moulin Rouge and subject of Toulouse-Lautrec's most popular posters. Stendhal is here; the grave bears his real name, Henry Beyle. Others include Offenbach, Nijinsky, Degas, Berlioz and François Truffaut.

**Père-Lachaise** is one of the world's great cemeteries, and Paris' largest. Pick up a free map at the newsstand by the main entrance and stroll down its avenues. Everyone who was anyone is here: Oscar Wilde, Maria Callas, Marcel Proust, Isadora Duncan, Edith Piaf, Gertrude Stein. There is a surprisingly lighthearted atmosphere and you may find a group picnicking over the remains of Jim Morrison.

**Cimetière du Montparnasse**, has a delightful sculpture on the grave of Charles Pigeon, inventer of the gas lamp, showing him and his wife sitting in bed reading by the light of his invention. Samuel Beckett has a simple tomb, in keeping with the reticence of the man. Jean-Paul Sartre and his beloved companion Simone de Beauvoir lie together in a joint grave.

### Cemeteries opening hours
08.00-18.00 Mon-Fri, 08.30-18.00 Sat
09.00-18.00 Sun; free admission

### Cimetière de Montmartre
20 ave Rachel at rue Caulaincourt
01 53 42 36 30; metro: place de Clichy

### Cimetière du Père-Lachaise
boulevard de Ménilmontant; 01 55 25 82 10
metro: Père Lachaise

### Cimetière du Montparnasse
3 boulevard Edgar-Quinet; 01 44 10 86 50
metro: Raspail

# Restaurants

There is every kind of restaurant in Paris from the six-Michelin starred Alain Ducasse establishments to simple take-away falafel joints. Chances are you'll be able to find a good meal for the price you want to pay. Avoid the very touristy lanes of Saint Michel in favour of Le Marais or St Germain.

Restaurants are listed by districts (*arrondissements*) then by price: from the most expensive to the least. Some bars are included here but for rugby bars see pages 26-27. For the price guide see Travel Basics, page 287.

If you're looking for a simple meal at a reasonable price, head for a brasserie, or a bistro. They usually serve salads, omelettes, steak frites and a daily special or two, and generally offer good value for money. Find one that smells good and settle in for a nice meal. Salads in France tend to be large and can be a meal in themselves, but be aware that small pieces of offal are often served with a country campagne, or terroir salad – don't be afraid to ask.

## Arrondissements 1-2
(Louvre and Bourse)

### La Fontaine Gaillon
place Gaillon; metro: Opéra
01 47 42 63 22
12.00-14.30, 19.00-23.30 Mon-Fri
booking required
credit cards accepted
€€€€
Just off the avenue de l'Opéra is an elegant restaurant owned by screen legend and gourmand, Gérard Depardieu. Open in 2004, it is set in a historic building that was once owned by Cardinal Richelieu and later contained the classic restaurant, Pierre. La Fontaine Gaillon was decorated by actress Carole Bouquet and Séverine Courcoux, who restored the Fountain d'Antin and the facade to make one of the finest outdoor dining terraces in Paris. Inside, are five

comfortable dining rooms decorated in taupe and cream with plush burgundy and mocha seating. Chef Laurent Audiot's speciality is fish and there is much to choose from on the menu as well as daily specials; try sea-bass tartare with anchovies and herbs, raviolo of sea scallops with truffle sauce, or try a Depardieu creation like *terrine de lapin à gelée* made at the actor's Anjou vineyard, together with a glass of Cuvée Jean Carmet, made by the actor Jean Carmet, using Depardieu's grapes. Pricy but delicious French cooking and you never know when the famous owner will make an appearance.

### Chez Georges
1 rue du Mail; metro: Sentier
01 42 60 07 11
lunch and dinner Mon-Sat
booking required
credit cards accepted
€€€
Much of the clientele is from the nearby stock exchange and it is a favourite of politicians and diplomats including Bill Clinton. Chez Georges serves classic French sauces in a traditional style with a menu that includes steak *béarnaise* and sole *meunière* together with a list of market-fresh daily entrées. The wine list is extensive and caters to all price ranges, decor is elegant with leather seating and white tablecloths, service is excellent if a touch formal.

### Kinugawa
9 rue Mont Thabor; metro: Tuileries
01 42 60 65 07
12.00-14.30, 19.00-23.00 Mon-Sat
booking advised
credit cards accepted
€€€
An excellent Japanese restaurant near the Tuileries with warm yellow walls and a relaxed atmosphere. It has the best sushi bar in Paris and it is rumoured that Catherine Deneuve is a customer. The beef with ginger and teriyaki salmon are delicious.

### Willi's Wine Bar
13 rue des Petits-Champs; metro: Pyramides
01 42 61 05 09
12.00-14.30 and 19.00-22.30 Mon-Sat
booking recommended
some credit cards
€€
At the north end of Jardin du Palais Royal is one of the best wine bars in Paris – and it's owned by an Englishman. Parisians flock here, and your only problem may be getting a table. The quality of the food, though

inexpensive, is above average for a wine bar. Try the peppered house foie gras followed by steak, which is always good. The dining room has a high, oak-beamed ceiling and the walls are covered in the owner's collection of art that's been used on wine labels. Vast list of wines by the glass.

### Koetsu
42 rue Sainte Anne; metro: Pyramide
01 40 15 99 90
book on weekends
€€
There is a assortment of noodle bars and small Japanese restaurants on this street serving sushi, sashimi and yakatori. Koetsu is a bit more upscale than the others and portions can be on the small side. It's a good bet if you're having sushi or sashimi, the fish is served fresh and succulent, and the yakatori is well-prepared.

### La Taverne Henri IV
13 place du pont-Neuf; metro: pont Neuf
01 43 54 27 90
09.00-16.00 Mon-Sat and 18.00-21.00 Mon-Fri
booking not necessary
no credit cards
€
This is Maigret's *Brasserie Dauphine* – located just round the corner from the police inspector's office. Author Simenon was a regular here and it is more wine bar than restaurant, though they do serve snacks. La Taverne retains a 16th century atmosphere despite a recent makeover.

## Arrondissement 3
(Pompidou, Le Marais)

### L'Ambassade d'Auvergne
22 rue du Grenier-St-Lazare; metro: Rambuteau
01 42 72 31 22
12.00-14.00 and 19.30-22.30 daily
booking recommended
credit cards accepted
€€€
This country-style restaurant serves regional cooking from the Auvergne, an isolated region of France known for its pork. Decorated with heavy oak beams, hanging hams and ceramics plates, this restaurant serves rustic dishes like pork stew with cabbage and country sausage with *aligot* – a cheese and mash combo that is a house speciality and accompanies almost everything except dessert. The desserts are often unusual, such as rhubarb soup with fresh mint. There's a good regional wine list.

### Les Caves Saint-Gilles
4 rue Saint-Gilles; metro: Chemin Vert
01 48 87 22 62
lunch and dinner daily
booking advised at weekends
no credit cards
€€
A friendly Spanish tapas and wine bar not far from place des Vosges. The assorted hot and cold tapas plates are large enough to share. Bullfighting posters line the walls and tables are arranged rather close together. The sangria is delicious and reasonably priced.

LES CAVES SAINT-GILLES

**FOOD & DRINK**

PLACE DU MARCHÉ SAINTE CATHERINE

## Arrondissement 4 (Le Marais)

There are numerous restaurants in this arrondissement and you can usually get a table if you're willing to wander through the streets following your nose. The place du Marché Sainte Catherine, just off rue Saint Antoine, has five restaurants where you can have a good meal with wine for around €25. Choose from two French bistros, an Italian trattoria, a sushi bar and a Russian eatery. If you're just looking for a quick takeaway falafel there are several on rue des Rosiers, a pedestrianised (except for scooters) lane that can become quite crowded with people strolling and munching.

### Bofinger

5-7 rue de la Bastille; metro: Bastille
01 42 72 87 82
12.00-15.00, 18.30-01.00 Mon-Fri
12.00-01.00 Sat-Sun
booking suggested
credit cards accepted
€€

If you want to experience a classic Parisian brasserie, come here to the west side of place de la Bastille. The Art Nouveau decoration of shining brass, gleaming wood, leather seats and a sweeping staircase under an ornate domed ceiling dates back to the mid-19th century, and it feels like it hasn't changed. The same goes for the waiters and for the menu, which is made up of staple brasserie dishes such as foie gras, oysters, poached haddock, steak, ice cream: nothing innovative but everything satisfying.

### Aux Vins des Pyrénées

25 rue Beautreillis; metro: St Paul, Bastille
01 42 72 64 94
12.00-15.00, 19.00-23.00 Mon-Sat
booking advised or go early
credit cards accepted
€€

A large friendly restaurant decorated like an old cellar with posters on the walls. It's located just at the edge of the Marais and fills up by nine in the evenings. Like the name suggests, they serve good regional cooking and wine from the Pyrenees. The cheerful (and mostly female) staff are usually willing to speak a little English, and they're very pretty too. The beef carpaccio is superb, roast meats are well-prepared and there's often a choice of interesting daily specials. If you're looking for something vegetarian – try the *millefleur avec chèvre & courgette* (courgette and goats cheese in layers of puff pastry). Be sure to have the chocolate mousse for dessert.

### Auberge de Jarente

7 rue de Jarente; metro: St Paul
01 42 77 49 35
lunch and dinner Tues-Sat
booking usually not necessary
credit cards accepted
€€

Just off place du Marché Sainte Catherine is a cosy little Basque restaurant on two levels. The seating area is on the tiny ground floor with the kitchen in the cellar below. They specialise in hearty Basque cuisine and make an excellent cassoulet. If you're after something lighter, try the gambas or the smoked duck and chervil salad. There is usually a two-three course fixed price meal that is very good value and the wine list has beautiful Sancerre for €24.

### L'As du Falafel
32 rue des Rosiers; metro St Paul
open day and night till late; closed Sat
cash only
€
The falafel served here is the best on the street. The deluxe version comes on a plastic plate and is a deal at €6.

L'AS DU FALAFEL, RUE DES ROSIERS

### The Pure Malt
4 rue Caron; metro: St Paul
01 42 76 03 77
open till 02.00
Scottish fans will feel right at home in this small bar near the place des Vosges. Like the name implies, the bar stocks over 100 varieties of Scotch wisky.

## Arrondissement 5

### La Tour d'Argent
15-17 quai de la Tournelle
metro: Maubert Mutualité
01 43 54 23 31
12.00-13.15 Wed-Sun, 19.30-21.00 Tue-Sun
booking essential
credit cards
€€€€
One of the top restaurants in Paris is on the left bank of the Seine, across from Île Saint Louis, with views of Notre-Dame. This Parisian institution has been here in

one form or another since 1582. The dining room is located on the 5th floor of a historical building, with one of the best wine cellars in Paris below street level. What happens on the other floors? That's something to contemplate as you enjoy *duck à l'orange*, invented here in 1892 and with over one million served since then. It's the obvious choice, but it is superb, and when in Rome...

### L'Atelier Maître Albert
1 rue Maître Albert; metro: Saint Michel
01 56 81 30 01
12.00-14.30, 19.00-23.30 Mon-Wed,
till 01.00 Thurs-Sat
booking advised
credit cards accepted
€€€

On the edge of Saint Michel and just across the river from Notre-Dame, is one of chef Guy Savoy's restaurants. The decor is modern with a black facade, stone surfaces and an open rotisserie. Here the speciality is grilled meats and fish, cooked to perfection and reasonably priced. There is a fixed price menu at €45 for three courses: salad, mains and dessert. The menu isn't large but everything is prepared with great care. Service is relaxed but efficient and the wine list has something for every budget. Those who love their meat and potatoes should look no further. Chef Laurent Jacquet is a rugby fan and many players stop in for a visit. There is also a bar where you can just have a drink and a snack.

L'ATELIER MAÎTRE ALBERT

### La Fourmi Ailée
8 rue du Fouarre; metro: St-Michel Notre-Dame
01 43 29 40 99
12.00-24.00 daily
booking not required
credit cards accepted
€

A cosy restaurant located close to the tourist sights. This former bookshop, around the corner from the famous Shakespeare & Co., is now a tea room serving delicious pastries as well as full meals. The lighting is soft and low and books still line the walls.

### Comptoir des Arts
100 rue Monge; metro: Censier Daubenton
01 45 35 28 34
11.00-23.00 daily
booking not required
credit cards accepted
€

A simple French bistro near the markets of rue Mouffetard. There are several moderately priced restaurants nearby if this one is full. Salads start at €6, beefsteak and chips is a deal at €11.

### Le Mouffetard
116 rue Mouffetard; metro: Censier Daubenton
01 43 31 42 50
open daily
€

Located at the food market end of rue Mouffetard, this is a small café with chairs spilling out onto the pavement. It isn't cheap, but they serve the best iced tea you'll ever have, complete with fresh sprigs of mint.

## Arrondissement 6
(St Germain des Prés)

There are plenty of restaurants along rue de Canettes, rue Guisarde, rue Mabillon and there's the Eden Park rugby bar on rue Princesse. North of Boulevard Saint Germain are the more touristy streets near rue de Buci. It is always lively here and a good place to begin the evening with an aperitif and a bit of people-watching. Then go to rue Cannettes or queue for steak and chips on rue St Benoit, another street lined with restaurants for all budgets.

Afterwards, go dancing at Le Pousse au Crime on rue Guisarde and rub shoulders with the rugby crowd.

### Alcazar
62 rue Mazarine; metro: Odéon
01 53 10 19 99
12.00-15.00, 19.00-00.30 daily
booking suggested
credit cards accepted
€€€

A stylish yet casual Terence Conran bar and restaurant, in the heart of the left bank. The designer-sleek minimalist interior buzzes with chic locals and even after several years it remains one of the places to meet and be seen. Enjoy a cocktail in the bar before going on to the dining rooms. The menu includes items as simple as sandwiches or steak, in addition to more contemporary French cuisine such as chicken stuffed with foie gras or sea bass.

### Le Cherche Midi
22 rue du Cherche Midi; metro: St-Placide
01 45 48 27 44
lunch and dinner daily (opens 20.00 for dinner)
booking advised; non-smoking
credit cards accepted
€€€

A mid-priced Italian restaurant where patrons squeeze together elbow-to-elbow while the owner (from Solerno) insults you – its all part of the charm. The homemade basil pesto is excellent, full of flavour and with lots of garlic. Entrées are priced around €12 for pasta, €18 for mains and this is one of the few restaurants in the area open on Sunday. Beware of the homemade *Limoncello*.

RUE GUISARDE

### Le Relais de l'Entrecote
20 rue St-Benoît; metro: St-Germain des Prés
01 45 49 16 00
12.00–01.00 daily
bookings not taken
credit cards accepted
€€
One of a chain with a simple concept: serve only steak and chips, salad and dessert for €30 per person with wine. There is a starter salad and steak with frites which is prepared either rare or medium and is served with a delicious sauce. Dessert is included and there are several choices. The house wine is good or you may upgrade to a very reasonable bottle of Burgundy. Arrive early to avoid a queue, but if you have to wait, it shouldn't be too long as people don't linger.

### Le Port Dauphine
18 rue Dauphine; metro: Odéon
01 43 54 53 16
booking not required
credit cards accepted
€€
Located near Pont Neuf with a nice loft upstairs. A set menu for three courses at €19.00 is good value although cheap and cheerful sauces sometimes mask a cheaper cut of meat. Service is good.

### La Boussole
12 rue Guisarde; metro: Mabillon
01 56 24 82 20
lunch and dinner Mon-Fri, all day Sat-Sun
booking not required
credit cards accepted
€€
*La Boussole* means compass, and the cuisine here features exotic spices and international influences. The fixed price plats-du-jour is €14.50 with a choice of seafood or beef.

### O'Neil
20 rue des Canettes; metro: St-Germain des Prés
01 46 33 36 66
12.00–02.00 daily
€
An artisan brewery and restaurant that is good value, especially during happy hour when pints of beer are half price. O'Neil's serves grilled steak, sausages and salads, a house specialty *Les flammekueches* is akin to a thin pizza, but served on a crêpe.

### Le Pousse au Crime
rue Guisarde
22.00–04.00 Wed-Sun
Late night dance club frequented by the French rugby team.

O'NEIL

## Arrondissement 7 (Eiffel Tower)

### Tribeca
36 rue Cler; metro: École Militaire
01 45 55 12 01
09.00–23.00 Mon-Sat, 09.00–17.00 Sun
book on weekend evenings
credit cards accepted
€€
It can be difficult to find a good restaurant near the Eiffel Tower and Tribeca succeeds admirably. A lively spot day or night, with an excellent kitchen and reasonable prices (€8 starter, €12 main course). They serve traditional French dishes with a modern touch and also offer risotto and pizza. Portions are generous and the service is friendly yet efficient. A stylish yet unpretentious neighbourhood restaurant that also serves great coffee. A real gem.

### Café des Lettres
53 rue de Verneuil; metro: rue du Bac
01 42 22 52 17
lunch and dinner Mon-Sat
closed Sunday evenings
booking not necessary
credit cards accepted
€€
A literary cafe located two blocks behind Musee d'Orsay on the street where poet Serge Gainsbourg once lived. They serve good homestyle Swedish cuisine in a relaxed atmosphere. Most of the staff speak English.

**FOOD & DRINK**

### Les Deux Musées
5 rue de Bellechasse RER C: Musée d'Orsay
01 45 55 13 39
08.00-20.00 daily
credit cards accepted
€
If you're in need of refreshment after a visit to Musée d'Orsay, this cafe/brasserie is just behind the main entrance and has a more friendly staff than the others on the street.

## Arrondissement 8 (Elysées)

### Alain Ducasse au Plaza Athénée
Hôtel Plaza Athénée; 25 avenue Montaigne
metro: Franklin D. Roosevelt
01 53 67 65 00
19.45-22.15 Mon-Fri; 12.45-14.45 Thu-Fri
booking essential
credit cards accepted
€€€€
As the first man ever to earn six Michelin stars for his two flagship restaurants in Monaco and Paris, Alain Ducasse has earned all the accolades that come his way. The dining room is simple and elegant, and the service friendly but impeccable. Ducasse does not believe in the kind of intimidating atmosphere that some gourmet temples create, and with 55 staff serving 50 covers you receive every attention without them being over-fussy. It costs the earth, of course, but some of his dishes are legendary, like the truffle soup or the signature starter of langoustines and caviar. This alone costs €130, though entrées are in the €65-95 range.

### Cinq
Hôtel George V; 31 avenue George V
metro: George V
01 49 52 71 54
07.00-10.00 Mon-Fri, 07.00-10.30 Sat-Sun
12.00-14.30 Mon-Fri, 12.30-14.30 Sat-Sun
18.30-23.00 daily
booking for lunch and dinner essential
credit cards accepted
€€€€
Cinq opened in 2000 and within three years had earned its three Michelin stars. The room is a mix of elegant greys and golds, always with a huge stunning floral arrangement in the centre, one of the hotel's notable features. But it's the food that has propelled this into being one of the city's best dining experiences. Try morel mushrooms stuffed with crab and lobster, or turbot with a pumpkin and grapefruit marmalade, and you'll know why diners love it here.

### Pierre Gagnaire
6 rue Balzac; metro: Charles de Gaulle Étoile
01 58 36 12 50
12.30-14.00, 19.30-22.00 daily
booking essential
credit cards accepted
€€€€
Originally from Montpellier, Gagnaire has brought the passion and sunshine of the south to the art deco elegance of the dining room at his restaurant near the Arc de Triomphe. There are several menu options, some of them priced very reasonably given the superb standard of food on offer, especially at lunchtime when you have the best chance of getting a table. There are market menus, seasonal truffle menus and naturally a *dégustation* menu, but whichever you choose make sure you get the grand dessert Pierre Gagnaire, a 7-dish miniature dessert *dégustation*. Then call a cab.

## Arrondissement 9
(Opéra and Pigalle)

### Chartier
7 rue du Faubourg-Montmartre;
metro: Grands Boulevards
01 47 70 86 29
11.30-15.00, 18.00-22.00 daily
bookings not taken
some credit cards
€
One of the great bargains – and great eating experiences – in Paris is at Chartier. It opened in 1896 as a working man's café, and it still has its turn-of-the-century décor and has been declared a national monument. You'll probably have to queue but that's all part of the Chartier experience. Once inside you'll be rubbing shoulders with your neighbours and tucking into no-nonsense cooking like steak and chips or *boeuf bourguignon*, and the simple but very drinkable house wine. Then the waiter will scribble your bill on the paper tablecloth, though there's no pressure to leave despite the endless queues.

## Arrondissement 11
(Bastille, edge of Marais)

### Au C'Amelot
50 rue Amelot; metro: Chemin Vert
01 43 55 54 04
12.00-14.00 Tue-Fri, 19.00-22.00 Tue-Sat
booking recommended
some credit cards
€€
The stone-walled dining rooms and wooden beams give a homey feel to the place, and this

atmosphere matches the food. The menu is simple, based on what the chef finds at the market that day, with only two options for each course. There's usually a soup to start, then maybe fish followed by wild boar or another meat choice. Service is friendly.

### Bistro Mélac
42 rue Léon Frot; metro Charonne
01 43 70 59 27
09.00-late, Tue-Sat, closed: Sun-Mon
bookings not taken
€€
Twenty-five years ago Jacques Mélac planted some vines in his cellar. They have thrived and there's even one growing in the bar. He harvests his own grapes and also collects grapes from his friends to produce their own vintage: all 35 bottles. The Bistro serves hearty food from Aveyron such as *aligot* (mashed potatoes with garlic and a particular local cow's cheese). Wines are personally chosen by Mélac, partly for taste and value, but also because he likes the winemakers. A sign on the wall reminds customers that 'water is reserved for cooking potatoes'.

## Arrondissement 15-16
(Montparnasse)

### La Villa Corse
164 boulevard de Grenelle; metro: Cambronne
01 53 86 70 81
09.00-02.00 Mon-Sat, bar open
12.00-14.00, 19.00-23.00 Mon-Sat, food service
booking advised for lunch or dinner
credit cards accepted
€€€
A good Corsican restaurant, decorated in Mediterranean style, arranged around a central bar with comfy leather seating. Chef Henri Boutié serves delicious food – some favourites are: a mushroom fricassee starter, ravioli in cream sauce, grilled mullet, wild boar with chestnuts, lamb casserole.

### Zébra Square
3 place Clément Ader; metro: Mirabeau
01 44 14 91 91
08.00-02.00 bar open
12.00-14.00, 19.00-23.00 food service
booking advised
credit cards accepted
€€€
Depending on when you visit, Zébra Square can either be very good or too trendy for words. Food is generally good and the duck with figs is a sublime experience.

## Arrondissements 17-18 (North)

### Le Relais de Venise
271 boulevard Pereire; metro: porte Maillot
01 45 74 27 97
bookings not taken
credit cards accepted
€€
Another variation of the set menu concept serving only steak and frites. For €22 you get a salad, steak and chips (with a second helping) wine and dessert.

### Bistro des Dames
18 rue des Dames; metro: place de Clichy
01 45 22 13 42
12.00-14.30, 19.00-02.00 daily
open all day Sat-Sun
book for the garden on Sunday
€€
A quiet little bistro with a pleasant garden. The interior is cave-like so come on a warm day. The *gazpacho* and *tortilla jambon* is good, but it's not cheap at €13.00 for a main course. The large salads are fresh but beware, the *salade des dames* is served with (raw) duck. *Bourgogne Aligote* is only €3.50 for a glass.

## Pont des Beaux Arts

Each warm Thursday evening Parisians gather for a picnic on the wooden bridge. The atmosphere is congenial as people spread their blankets down on the warm wood, pour a glass of wine and dig into their picnics.

## Life is a Cabaret

The spectacular cabarets of Paris have a special place in the history of the city. Shows are entertaining but expensive, and an evening could easily cost more than €100 per person if there is a compulsory drinks purchase. Some Paris night-time tours may offer better prices, enquire at the Tourist Office.

### Folies Bergère

32 rue Richer; metro: Grands Boulevards
01 44 79 98 90
On 30th November 1886 the curtain went up on the first show featuring costumed female dancers. It was only a few years later, when the craze for striptease reached Paris, that the clothes came off. In 1926, Josephine Baker made her debut wearing a skirt made of bananas that caused a sensation. In 1961 she was awarded the Légion d'Honneur. Today the Folies are more of a theatre than cabaret, though the show running at press time was *Cabaret*.

### Moulin Rouge

82 boulevard de Clichy; metro: Pigalle
01 53 09 82 82
www.moulinrouge.fr
The giant red windmill on the edge of Montmartre is as Parisian as the Eiffel Tower. Both date from 1889, and the Universal Exposition in Paris (for which the tower was built). This was where Henri Toulouse-Lautrec found his models – dancers would earn extra money by posing for him. But there was a catch since the diminutive artist regularly fell deeply in love with his models. Today, these paintings can be seen on the walls of Musée d'Orsay. Moulin Rouge is the home of the *can-can*, another Parisian icon, which is still the main attraction of its shows. Anyone going to the Moulin Rouge and not seeing a can-can would be bitterly disappointed... how many know that it was actually invented in London by an Englishman, Charles Morton, in 1861?

## Lido

116 bis avenue des Champs-Élysées
metro; George V
01 40 76 56 10
www.lido.fr

The Lido is relatively new, having only started in 1946. By 1955 the Lido had opened in Las Vegas, and its shows today mix that Vegas pizzazz with Parisian flair, with the help of its own famous troupe of dancers, the Bluebell Girls. Exceptionally tall (at least 5' 10") and the epitome of the Parisian showgirl, many of them, in fact, are originally from England.

The troupe was first formed by Margaret Kelly in 1932. The first 24 girls danced between films at a London Paramount cinema, and it wasn't until the 1950s that the troupe moved to Paris and the Lido. The new producers requested the Bluebells dance topless but Ms Kelly took some convincing. It was only when the girls themselves insisted they really didn't mind dancing topless, that she agreed.

## Crazy Horse Saloon

12 avenue George V; metro: George V
01 47 23 32 32
www.crazyhorse.fr

In 1960 Alain Bernardin, a former antique dealer and painter, wanted to put some more passion into the existing show. He was familiar with the world of surrealism and the avant-garde, where people like Andy Warhol and John Cage were doing challenging work. Bernardin was also fascinated by the American west, and aware of what was happening in the extravagant shows being staged in Las Vegas. He wanted to combine these elements and produce spectacular shows which highlighted the beauty of the female nude. So, that's what he did, and what the show continues to do. It has a reputation for putting on the most spectacular productions with dazzling computer-controlled lighting effects, and much more nudity than the other famous Paris cabarets. The current production is aptly named *Taboo*.

### A feather in their cap

There's a story behind every detail of the lavish cabaret costumes of the Paris showgirls. The feathers in the headdresses of the girls at the Moulin Rouge come from the specialist feather supplier Nicole Février, who since 1928 have supplied feathers to everyone from the legendary American dancer Josephine Baker to current Las Vegas shows and the fashion designer Jean-Paul Gaultier. The feathers come mainly from cocks, ostriches and pheasants, arriving from all over the world to the workshop on the rue du Mail. Here they are brushed, washed, boiled, beaten, dyed and finally tested to see if they can stand up to the heat generated by the powerful stage lights.

# Shopping

Paris was made for shopping, whether your interest is food, fashion or just plain fun. There are still plenty of quirky one-off shops, in among the names like Prada, Armani, Gaultier and Lagerfeld. For every gourmet temple there's a funky street market or little patisserie to tempt you. It's become a cliché to describe cities as being made up of villages, but it is true of Paris where each neighbourhood still has its own street market. Some areas have designer chocolatiers and others have horse-meat shops. It's all here.

Most shops are open 10am to 7pm and closed on Sundays.

## High fashion

Paris is still the centre of the fashion industry, with its spring and autumn fashion shows grabbing the attention of the world's media. Top designers Dior, Yves Saint Laurent, Jean-Paul Gaultier, Vivienne Westwood, John Galliano, Sonia Rykiel, Karl Lagerfeld and Louis Vuitton all have their flagship stores in Paris. Window-shopping at these shops isn't easy, as many take a minimalist approach to exterior decoration, and you have to pass security guards to enter the inner sanctums before seeing what's on sale. Sales staff can tell your budget at a glance.

The two best streets for designer shops are: **avenue Montaigne,** from Champs-Élysées to pont d'Alma, most of the big names are here: MaxMara, Valentino, Chanel, Calvin Klein, Prada, Jil Sander, Nina Ricci and Emanuel Ungaro. From avenue Montaigne it's only a short walk to the other essential address for the fashion-conscious: **rue du Faubourg-St-Honoré,** here you'll find designer accessories, perfumes, jewellery and luggage, not to mention wine shops, food stores, art galleries and antique shops. And the Presidential Palace – it's that kind of street.

### Agnès B
6 rue du Vieux Colombier; metro: St Sulpice
01 44 39 02 60
This shop is part of a large French chain that has several branches in Paris. Their styles are trendy, yet wearable and affordable.

### Isabel Marant
1 rue Jacob; metro: Mabillon
01 43 26 04 12
Isabel designs clothing and accessories with a timeless quality that you can wear and wear.

### A P C
3-4 rue des Fleurus; metro: St Sulpice
01 42 22 12 77
Popular amongst young Parisians, this shop sells fabulous clothes and great accessories.

### Maria Luisa
2 rue Cambon; metro: Concorde
Tucked away on a side street behind a nondescript exterior is this shop featuring a great selection of avant-garde clothing including Alexander McQueen. There's also a branch on rue du Mont-Thabor selling accessories, and Manolo Blahnik.

## French lingerie

The French make the most beautiful lingerie and Paris has the very best shops, for you or for someone special.

### Alice Cadolle
14 rue Cambon; metro: Concorde
255 rue Saint Honoré; metro: Tuileries
This is the family that invented the brassiere. They have been in business since 1889 and styles are classical but sexy, with ready-to-wear items and a personal fitting service. Clients have included Mata Hari, Brigitte Bardot and Catherine Deneuve.

### Fifi Chachnil
26 rue Cambon; metro: Concorde
231 rue Saint Honoré; metro: Tuileries
This designer has done costumes for stage, film and pop videos and her style is the more blatantly pin-up look of the 1950s and 1960s, using bright colours. Fifi also produces a line of flattering swimwear.

## Rugby shops

### Eden Park
192-194 and 202 rue de Courcelles
10 rue de Buci; metro: Saint Germain des Près
The large flagship shop on rue de Courcelles is a must-visit for all rugby fans. Eden Park was founded by two French rugby players, Franck Mesnel and Eric Blanc, who have designed a line of quality clothing for men, women and children. There is also a rugby bar on rue de Princesse.

### Rugby World Cup 2007 Official Store
32 avenue de l'Opera; metro: Opéra
This is your one-stop shop for official branded clothing and accessories.

**VISA**

w.eden-park.com

# Eden ✺ Park

**RUGBY** COLLECTION

**SHOPPING**

## Department stores

09.30-19.00 Mon-Fri, 09.30-20.00 Sat
till 21.00 Thurs

### Le Bon Marché
24 rue de Sèvres; metro: Sèvres-Babylone
01 44 39 80 00
The only department store on the Left
Bank and considered by many to be the
best in Paris, with all the best designers.

### Galeries Lafayette
40 boulevard Haussmann; metro: Opéra
01 42 82 36 40
A gigantic department store located
directly opposite the Opera with three
buildings: Coupole (women and children),
Homme (men) and Maison (home).

### La Samaritaine (closed)
19 rue de la Monnaie; metro: Pont Neuf
01 40 41 20 20
A Parisian landmark, the shop has been
closed since 2005 and is not due to re-open
anytime soon.

### Printemps
64 bd Haussmann; metro: Opéra
01 42 82 50 00
A contemporary general department store.

### Collette
213 rue Saint Honoré; metro: Tuileries
01 55 35 33 90
10.30-21.30 Mon-Sat
A purely Parisian concept selling books,
art and clothing in beautiful surroundings.

## Accessories

### Il pour l'homme
209 rue Saint Honoré; metro: Tuileries
Just down the street from Collette is this
shop with all those accessories men love.
This is the place to buy your Zeiss binoculars
and leather-bound hip flasks.

### Marie Mercié
23 rue St Sulpice; metro: Mabillon
01 43 26 45 83
11.00-19.00 Mon-Sat
They design every type of hat imaginable, if
you want a hat, you'll it find here.

### Jamin Puech
61 rue d'Hauteville; metro: Bonne-Nouvelle
01 40 22 08 32

Beautiful bags for all occasions from
bohemian to trendy. Worth the extra effort of
a trip to the 10th arrondissement.

## Perfume

### Musée de la Parfumerie Fragonard
9 rue Scribe; metro Opéra
01 47 42 04 56
09.00-17.30 daily; free
39 boulevard des Capucines
01 42 60 37 14
09.00-17.30 Mon-Sat
Here you'll learn the history of perfume-
making, which is a fascinating story, and
how a good perfume is created. If you
make a purchase in the gift shop you can be
confident you're buying the real thing and
not just over-priced scented water.

### L'Artisan Parfumeur
99 rue Rivoli; metro: St Paul
01 42 96 21 44
This boutique was founded by Jean Laporte
in 1976 and offers a limited range of specially
created fragrances. You are sure to find a
scent for yourself or for a gift.

### Maitre Parfumeur et Gantier
84 rue de Grenelle; metro rue du Bac
01 45 44 61 57
10.30-18.30 Mon-Sat
They sell the essence that goes into the
making of all perfumes (vanilla, rose, musk
etc.) and will give advice on creating your
own personal fragrance.

16 and 23 avenue de la Motte Picquet (7th)
One of the best chocolatiers in Paris, his chocolates have been compared to fine wines, because of the complexity of their taste. Over-exaggeration? Try one.

### Christian Constant

37 rue d'Assas; metro: Vavin
Rivalling Hévin is Christian, who uses exotic flavours like cardamom. At his tea room next to the shop you may indulge yourself with drinks that combine chocolate, jasmine, green tea and crème brûlée.

### Debauve and Gallais

30 rue des Sts Pères; metro: Sèvres-Babylone
33 rue Vivienne; metro: Pyramides
They have been around since the early 19th century when they sold chocolate for medicinal purposes. You need no such excuse to sample their treats.

## Bread

### Lionel Poilâne

8 rue du Cherche-Midi; metro: St Sulpice
In France even bread-makers are revered, and none more so than Lionel. He opened his bakery in 1932, and it's more popular now than ever. Restaurants boast of having his bread on their tables and queues form every day, especially for a fresh batch of his most famous loaf, the pain Poilâne.

## Cheese

### Barthélemy

51 rue de Grenelle; metro: rue de Bac
01 45 48 56 75
closed midday and Sun-Mon
Those who love French cheese should make sure to pay a visit to this fantastic shop.

## Food markets

### Marché d'Aligre

rue d'Aligre; metro: Bastille
every afternoon
South-east of place de la Bastille is a very expensive indoor market where you can buy everything from wild boar and pheasants to saffron and other pricey spices. Outdoor is a more regular street market, and a flea market, and there are also some great bakers and other food shops around. One of the best wine bars in the area is Le Baron Rouge, at 1 rue Théophile-Roussel.

### Marché Richard-Lenoir

boulevard Richard Lenoir; metro: Bastille
Thursdays and Sundays
An afternoon farmers market with wine and other products from Île-de-France.

## Food

### Place de la Madeleine

When food lovers die and go to heaven it will be like place de la Madeleine in the chic 8th arrondissement. The best collection of food shops in Paris surrounds a central church and spill out into nearby streets. Shops are often devoted to one type of produce: only honey, or cheese, or chocolate, or truffles – one just sells caviar. On the square itself are two of the most wonderful food shops in Paris: **Fauchon** and **Hédiard**. Fauchon is the Louvre of food shops, with eye-catching and mouth-watering window displays. Hédiard is more traditional, established in 1854 and selling spices, teas, exotic coffees, caviar and a cellar of 3,000 different wines. Heaven indeed.

### Chocolate shops

Parisians take chocolate seriously, though not as seriously as do the chocolatiers themselves. There are awards for the best chocolates, books of chocolate recipes and societies for people with a passion for chocolate.

### Jean-Paul Hévin

flagship shop: 3 rue Vavin; metro: Vavin
231 rue Saint Honoré; metro: Tuileries

61

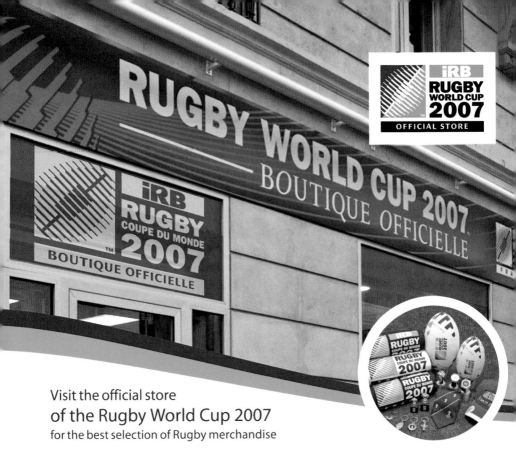

Visit the official store
## of the Rugby World Cup 2007
for the best selection of Rugby merchandise

The store is located in the Opéra district in the heart of Paris. The whole store is dedicated to Rugby World Cup 2007, selling all the official licensed products for the event and the participating teams.

### Products :

National team replica kits, T-shirts, polo-shirts, jackets, caps, berets, knitted hats, scarves, ties, backpacks, balls, watches, pins, key rings, card holders…
About 350 different products, something for everyone.

**Location :** *32, avenue de l'Opéra – 75002 PARIS.*
Ⓜ *Metro Stops Opéra / Pyramides – Lignes 2, 7, 8, 14.*
🄴 *RER Stop Opéra – Ligne A.*
🄱 *Bus Stops Opéra – Lignes 22, 52, 53, 66, 197.*

### Contact:

*Rugby World Cup 2007 Official Store / 32, avenue de l'Opéra – Paris – FRANCE.*
*Phone : +33 (0)1 40 07 55 17 – Fax : +33 (0)1 40 07 57 39 - rwcboutique@orange.fr*

## Eclectic

### Le Prince Jardinier
37 rue de Valois; metro: musée du Louvre
01 42 60 37 13
French gardening chic – Louis Vuitton claims
this is where he buys his gardening shirts.
A simple linen shirt is around €60 and a
matching garden hat will cost €35.

### Au nom de la Rose
46 rue du Bac; metro: rue du Bac
01 42 22 22 12
A theme shop devoted entirely to roses
with everything from fresh bouquets to
embroidered towels.

### Deyrolle
46 rue du Bac; metro: rue du Bac
01 42 22 30 07
An eccentric shop selling stuffed animals.

## Antiques

### Hotel Drouot
9 rue Drouot; metro: Le Peletier
01 48 00 20 20
A 16-room venue that holds sales daily
except Sunday. It attracts many of Paris's
top dealers and collectors who come to buy
paintings, sculpture, furniture, jewellery
and wine.

## Second-hand books

### Bouquinistes
the Seine, Pont de la Tournelle to Pont Neuf
The name *bouc* means goat, referring to the
skin once used in bookbinding. There have
been stalls selling a variety of books and
printed material along both sides of the river
for 300 years.

### Shakespeare & Co
37 rue de la Bucherie; metro: St Michel
01 43 25 40 93
noon-midnight daily
An English bookshop that has become a
Paris institution. They also sell new books.

## Shopping arcades

### Caire
2 place du Caire; metro: Réaumur-Sébastopol
This passageway opened in 1798 was
inspired by Napoleon's Egyptian campaign.
Today it houses an interesting selection of
clothing shops.

### Colbert/Vivienne
16 rue des Petits-Champs; metro: Bourse
One of the most opulent shopping arcades
in Paris was built in 1823. Shops here are on
the expensive side.

### Galerie de la Madeleine
9 place de la Madeleine; metro: Madeleine
A 19th century arcade with interesting
boutiques and food shops.

## Flea markets

If you're looking for something a little less
expensive than the latest Prada handbag,
Paris has plenty of flea markets where you
can hunt around for discards, seconds,
fabrics, antiques or just plain old junk. Many
designers check out the flea markets looking
for ideas or unusual fabrics to inspire them.
Alongside the food market on rue d'Aligre is
a little flea market (Tue-Sun) where you can
find fabrics and funky junky clothes.

**VISA**

## Golf and Sport

Paris has plenty of sporting opportunities not too far outside the city. One of the prettiest places to visit is Chantilly, a centre of horse-racing and also known for its delicious whipped cream. The Musee Chateau Conde is a surprisingly good art gallery with many stunning paintings including Raphael's *Three Graces*. It is set in luxurious English-style gardens where you may enjoy raspberries with Chantilly cream.

### Golf

**Le Golf National**
2 avenue du Golf; 78280 Guyancourt
01 30 43 36 00
RER C7 St Quentin-en-Yvelines
gn@golf-national.com
www.golf-national.com
Just outside the town of Versailles, Le Golf National is France's premier golf course and is ranked fourth among European courses. The venue for the French Open, it nonetheless stays true to the nation's spirit of égalité and is open to all. The complex includes the championship course, an 18 hole course, a nine hole course, a six hole pitch and putt, full practice facilities, the National Golf Academy and a Novotel. It is also the headquarters of the French Golf Federation. No buggies are allowed on the courses, but caddies are available. Practice facilities include a huge 150 bay driving range, putting and chipping greens. Professional coaches offer private lessons and five-day courses. Stay on-site at the Novotel with a view of the 18th green, or opt for luxury accommodation in nearby Versailles.

**Chantilly Golf Club**
allée de la Menagerie; 60500 Chantilly
03 44 57 04 43
RER D1 Orry-la-Ville-Coye
golfchan@club-internet.fr
Chantilly is a private club but welcomes visitors, although access is restricted to members and their guests at weekends.
booking is strongly advised
The Chantilly Golf Club is one of the more traditional clubs in the Paris area, and its Vineuil course is ranked third in Europe. Designed by famous golf architect Tom Simpson at the beginning of the century, the Vineuil course still retains its original character. The lengthy layout with well-separated fairways stretches through the Apremont forest in beautiful surroundings. First class accommodation is available at the Domaine de Chantilly, a golf resort with a luxury hotel and its own course extending through formal French gardens and only one kilometre away from Chantilly golf club. Alternative accommodation might be at the nearby Chateau de Montvillargenne, a Rothschild mansion which is now a luxury hotel and gourmet restaurant.

**Compiègne Golf Club**
avenue Royale; 60200 Compiègne
03 44 38 48 00
SNCF Compiègne
golfdecompiegne@9business.fr
www.golf-compiegne.com
A little to the north of Paris and founded in 1896, Compiègne is one of the earliest golf courses to be built in France, and one of the only two golf courses to have ever been the venue of the Olympic Games golf event. You shouldn't miss the opportunity to play on this vintage course, set in beautiful wooded surroundings. The club is public, and has a warm and welcoming clubhouse with an

LE GOLF NATIONAL

English style bar and restaurant. There are also three tennis courts. Accommodation is available at the Château de Bellinglise, a lovely Renaissance castle offering privileged access and reduced green fees at Compiègne.

### Golf du Domaine de Mont Griffon
95270 Luzarches; SNCF Luzarches
01 34 09 20 00
montgriffon@wanadoo.com
www.golfhotel.paris.com
The vast and recently-built Domaine de Mont-Griffon resort extends across 250 hectares of parkland. The 18-hole Lakes course provides not only a technically challenging game, but also beautiful views of the Ysieu valley. There's also a golfing academy and some of the best and most up-to-date practice facilities in Europe.

### Disneyland Paris
1 allee de la Mare-Houleuse; Magny-le-Hongre
01 60 45 68 90
RER A4 Marne-la-Vallée-Chessy
dlp.nwy.golf@disney.com
Eurodisney's golf course was conceived following the Disney philosophy of providing amusement and entertainment. The course can be played in any combination of its three nines: Wonderland, Neverland and The Hundred Acre Wood courses, all named after Disney themes.
The use of buggies is obligatory and walking on the course is not allowed. The impressive clubhouse overlooks the Wonderland course, but lacks the spirit of a real golf club. Accommodation is available at any of the seven hotels at Disneyland resort which total no less than 5,700 rooms, ranging from 2 to 4 star, each with its own theme and atmosphere. Golf Getaway packages are available and include accommodation at the Newport Bay Club hotel and a choice of Theme Park entrances or green fees for each day of your stay, so that golfers and their families can both have fun either on the fairways or at Disneyland.

### Golf Club de Bondoufle
91070 Bondoufle; RER D4 Evry
01 60 86 41 71
The course has been laid out to provide players with the widest possible range of golfing challenges. It offers an unusual feature, in that there is a choice of five tee positions per hole, so that the approach and the difficulty of each hole can be tailored to the player's needs. There is water on eight holes and plenty of bunker action; there are also extensive practice facilities. A hotel, restaurant and bar are all to be found on site.

## Racing

### Longchamp
route des Tribunes; Bois de Boulogne
01 44 30 75 00
metro: Boulogne – Pont de Saint-Cloud
www.france-galop.com
France's most prestigious racecourse hosts the annual *Prix de l'Arc de Triomphe* as part of its 31-weekend calendar. This year it will be held on 7th October 2007, the race attracts the best horses from around the world. The Prix is the world's premier race for three year-olds over twelve furlongs. There are two restaurants at the course and any number of bars and outlets for snacks; children enjoy a free crèche and pony rides.

### Chantilly
16 avenue du Général Leclerc; 60631 Chantilly
01 44 62 41 00
RER: D1 Orry-la-Ville-Coye
One of France's oldest racecourses, Chantilly hosted its first meeting in 1834. Set on the edge of an extensive forest and overlooked by the impressive chateau and its beautiful formal gardens, it's a fabulous venue for a day's flatracing. Chantilly is the self-proclaimed 'horse capital of the world,' and next to the course is the fascinating Living Museum of the Horse, housed in spectacular 18th century stables and holding regular shows of horse training and horsemanship.

## Karting

### Racing Kart de Cormeilles
Aérodrome de Pontoise; 95650 Boissy l'Aillerie
01 307 328 00
SNCF Pontoise
www.rkc.fr; rkc95@wanadoo.fr
Paris's biggest and best karting venue is northwest of the city; built on an old aerodrome with three kart tracks of differing lengths and abilities, and karts of different speeds and sizes. Training sessions are available. There is also a health spa with masseurs and a bar overlooking the track.

### Fun Kart Paris Sud
118-122, rue Léon Geffroy; 94400 Vitry-sur-Seine
01 468 232 00
RER C2/4/6 Les Ardoines
www.fun-kart.com
Much closer to the centre of the city, and right next to an RER station (just turn left out of the station car park) is this indoor kart venue. There's a 400m track with lap timing, and a bar with a view of the action.

# Paris has many interesting places to visit that are within an hour's drive of the centre. Versailles and Giverny are two of the most popular for adults. For kids, its a choice of Asterix or Disneyland.

## Château de Versailles

Château de Versailles
Versailles
01 30 83 76 20
www.chateauversailles.fr
09.00-18.30 Tues-Sun
last admission 18.00
closed Mon
palace €8, gardens free

**Getting there**
Take the RER C5 line.
The journey takes
about 40 minutes and
the Palace of Versailles
is a short walk from
the RER station of
Versailles-Rive Gauche.

One look round the opulent palace and you know immediately why there was a French Revolution. It was commissioned by King Louis XIV (the Sun King) because he was jealous of the splendid château Vaux-le-Vicomte, built by his finance minister, Nicolas Fouquet. Located near Melun, south of Paris, Vaux-le-Vicomte is actually a nicer place to visit than Versailles.

The King did not do things by halves. He hired the team that built Fouquet's château and told them to build something that was a hundred times bigger. The result was Versailles, so vast that it needed a household of about 20,000 people to look after the house, the royal family and their guests. Work began in 1668, and took some 14 years to complete. Louis was so delighted that he decided to move the royal household out of Paris and make Versailles his permanent home. It also had the advantage of being far away from his hungry and disgruntled citizens in Paris.

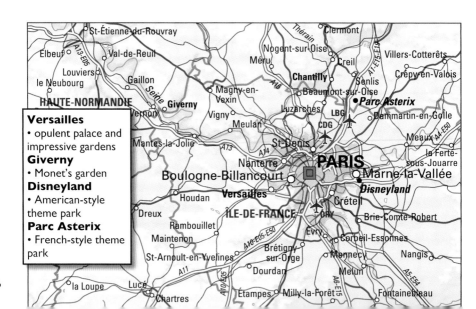

**Versailles**
• opulent palace and impressive gardens
**Giverny**
• Monet's garden
**Disneyland**
• American-style theme park
**Parc Asterix**
• French-style theme park

Years passed and in 1789 the French Revolution was gaining momentum – King Louis XVI was forced to leave Versailles and return to Paris. Four years later both King and Queen were dead, and forty years after that Versailles was surrendered to the state.

Visitors must join a guided tour and be shepherded around a set route. Once the tour has begun, it is not possible to turn around, slow down, or stop. What you see is impressive, especially the **Hall of Mirrors** which stretches for 233ft (70m) along the rear of the main palace. Its ceilings groan under the weight of enormous chandeliers, and the large windows fill the room with light which is reflected back by all the mirrors. The windows provide gorgeous views of the gardens and it is torturous not to be able to stop and gaze out for awhile,  but, you are forced to keep moving. However, one cannot travel to Versailles without seeing the interiors. Arrive early in the morning to join the first tour and take the rest of the day to enjoy what is really special about Versailles – the gardens.

The gardens were designed by the noted landscape artist, André Le Nôtre (1613-1700). Le Nôtre, like his father before him, was head gardener at the Jardin des Tuileries, where the royal palace was located. He planned the gardens at Vaux-le-Vicomte, which attracted the attention of Louis XIV. Le Nôtre's work at Versailles was his most ambitious. The formal gardens make good use of water with numerous fountains. The **Fountain of Latona** dominates the area immediately behind the palace. Latona was the mother of Apollo, the Sun God, and the gardens made full use of such imagery to flatter the Sun King. Further on is the Grand Canal, where the King and Queen used to hold lavish boating parties.

At the far end of the grounds is the **Grand Trianon**, built by Louis XIV in 1687 to escape the pressures of life at the palace and where he could also entertain his mistress, Madame de Maintenon, who he would eventually marry six months after the death of his wife. In 1768 Louis XV added another building, the **Petit Trianon**. Both of these are more pleasant than the main palace.

## Giverny

84 rue Claude Monet
Giverny
02 32 51 28 21
www.fondation-monet.com
09.30-18.00
Tues-Sun
last admission 17.30
closed Mon
€5.50

### Getting there

Take a train from Paris-St-Lazare station to Vernon, for a 45 minute journey.
At Vernon, a bus meets arriving passengers to take you the roughly 4 miles (6 kms) to Monet's Gardens.

The world's obsession with Claude Monet is such that the peace of the gardens can be spoiled by crowds, especially at weekends. Claude Monet's house and garden, which inspired him to the point of obsession, are still more or less as they were when the artist lived here from 1883 till his death in 1926. The most oft-painted bridge was built in a Japanese style and reflects the artist's own interest in Japanese art. His collection of 32 Japanese woodblock prints are still on the walls of his house, and the rooms are decorated as they were. Monet's studio has also been restored, and now contains the shop. The whole property was donated to the French Académie des Beaux-Arts by the artist's son.

Monet was born in Paris in 1840 and moved to Le Havre when he was five. He spent his youth and teenage years drawing caricatures of local people in charcoal, and selling them. Soon he would meet the artist Boudin, who would inspire him and give him a love of nature and of painting in the open air. He returned to Paris where he joined a studio and met artists including Sisley and Renoir, who shared his view of the world. Monet moved to England to avoid the Franco-Prussian war, and there was influenced by J.M.W. Turner, who was an impressionist before the term was invented. Today, Monet's work makes him the most popular artist on earth, beating Picasso.

THE BRIDGE AT GIVERNY

## Disneyland

Marne-la-Vallée
01 60 30 60 30
10.00-18.00 Mon-Fri, 09.00-20.00 Sat-Sun
adult day-pass €39, children 3-11 day-pass
€29, under-3s free

If you've got children then there's no doubt what the major attraction is in Paris. Not the *Mona Lisa,* not even the Eiffel Tower, but Disneyland. Don't fight it, they'll want to go. Allow them at least a full day, arriving early and leaving late, as the resort is big and queues can be long for popular rides and attractions. Some rides are worth taking twice. With over 12 million visitors per year, it is the most popular theme park in Europe. The Disneyland Resort Paris (they changed the name from EuroDisney some time ago) is just like the Disney resorts in the USA, with the possible exception that the food is better and you'll see more adults enjoying a glass of wine with their meal.

The resort is divided into five different 'lands': Fantasyland, Discoveryland, Frontierland, Adventureland and Main Street USA. The special effects on most of the rides are fantastic, especially on the two most popular: Pirates of the Caribbean and Indiana Jones and the Temple of Doom (located in Adventureland). In Discoveryland is the Space Mountain ride which hurtles you at enormous speeds through pitch blackness, with only the sound of people's screams for company.

MONTAGNE, PARC ASTÉRIX

### Getting there

Take the RER A, which links with Gare de Lyon, Châtelet-Les Halles and Charles de Gaulle-Étoile metro stations. It takes about 40 minutes to get to Marne-la-Vallée/Chessy: the stop right outside Disneyland.

## Parc Astérix

60128 Plailly
10.00-19.00 daily
see website for calendar;www.parcasterix.fr

Located 30km to the north of Paris and with its own exit from the A1 autoroute is a Gaulish village. Here they welcome invading visitors with a French-style theme-park. It's the antidote to Disneyland and it's as French as a theme park can be – including better food and wine.

Asterix's home village and Roman camp are faithfully reproduced from the original comic books. Children of all ages will love the costumed staff with their winged helmets. Rides include the Menhir Express log flume, Grand Splash boat-ride and the wooden rollercoaster *Tonnerre de Zeus* – one of the best in Europe.

# This small working-class city will host England, USA, South Africa, Georgia and Namibia.

Lens is a former coal mining town with distinctive pyramid-shaped slag heaps that can be seen for miles around. These existing 'pyramids' may have been a factor in the selection of Lens for the new satellite Louvre gallery.

Since a large part of the artworks in the Louvre are in storage, it was decided to build an extension to the gallery and to locate it in the post-industrial region north of Paris. Lens won the bid out of six cities that competed for the project, including Calais, Boulogne and Valenciennes. The reason given for the choice was to connect sport with culture. Lens has a well-established football team that has a large fan base and generates considerable revenue from corporate hospitality, though they don't often win many games. Le Louvre-Lens, scheduled to open in 2009, will be constructed on fallow land near the stadium and will be linked to it with a pedestrian walkway.

Much of Lens was built by a coal mining company to accommodate employees. In World War I the city was completely destroyed by the Germans, who flooded the mineshafts in 1915 in an attempt to destroy the French economy. They also cut the ropes in the mine shafts to stop French spies from navigating through the tunnels. The coal company drained and restored the mines after the war and also rebuilt Lens in a modern style, unlike neighbouring Arras. Coal mining activity decreased from 1945-1970 and

today there is virtually no industry left.

Place Jean-Jaurès is the town's central square with shops and restaurants. Unlike neighbouring Arras and Lille, Lens has no reputation as a tourist town and does not yet have the quality of hotels and facilities that one might expect. Opposite Gare de Lens station are a couple of two star hotels and there is one three star hotel near the stadium. Directly opposite the station are a few of bars and restaurants. To reach the stadium, turn left outside the station. It is a 15 minute walk.

ST-LEGER CHURCH: PLACE JEAN-JAURÈS

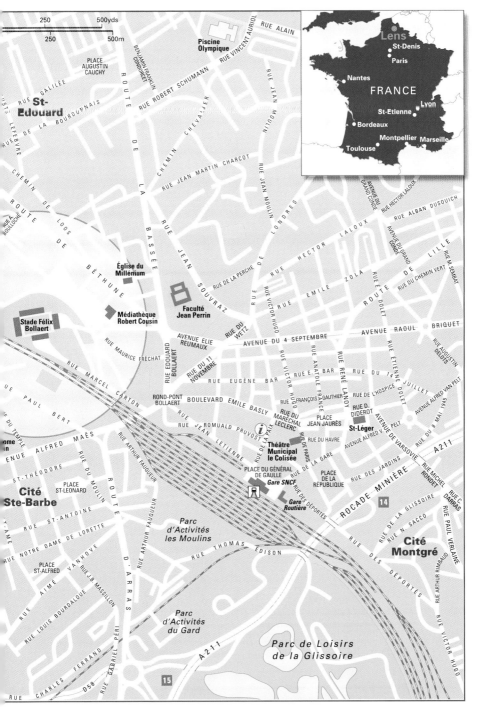

250    500yds

250    500m

RUE ALAIN

Piscine
Olympique

RUE VINCENT AURIOL

PLACE
AUGUSTIN
CAUCHY

BENJAMIN FRANKLIN
CONDORCET

ROUTE

RUE JEAN MOULIN

St-Denis

Paris

Nantes

FRANCE

Lyon

St-Etienne

Bordeaux

Montpellier  Marseille

Toulouse

RUE GALILÉE

St-
Edouard

RUE ROBERT SCHUMANN

RUE DE LA BOURDONNAIS

CHEMIN  CHEVALIER

RUE LEFEBVRE

DE

LA

BASSÉE

RUE JEAN MARTIN CHARCOT

CHEMIN DE LOOS

ROUTE

DE

BOULLOCHE

RUE À

BÉTHUNE

Église du
Millénium

RUE JEAN

SOUVRAZ

RUE DE LA PERCHE

RUE VICTOR HUGO

RUE  EMILE

HECTOR

LONDRES

LALOUX

AVENUE DU GRAND CONDÉ

RUE HECTOR LALOUX

RUE ALBAN DUSOUICH

AVENUE DU GRAND CONDÉ

DE

LILLE

RUE M. SERBAT

ZOLA

ROUTE

DOLET

RUE DU CHEMIN VERT

BRIQUET

Stade Félix
Bollaert

Médiathèque
Robert Cousin

Faculté
Jean Perrin

RUE MAURICE FRÉCHAT

RUE MARCEL CARTON

RUE ÉDOUARD BOLLAERT

RUE DU 11 NOVEMBRE

AVENUE ELIE
REUMAUX

RUE DU
WETZ

AVENUE DU 4 SEPTEMBRE

RUE EUGÈNE  BAR

RUE VICTOR HUGO

RUE A. E. BAR

RUE ANATOLE FRANCE

AVENUE RAOUL

RUE RENÉ LANOY

RUE  DU  14

RUE ÉTIENNE DOLET

JUILLET

RUE AUGUSTIN DELOTS

ROND-POINT
BOLLAERT

BOULEVARD EMILE BASLY

RUE FRANÇOIS GAUTHIER

RUE DE L'HOSPICE

RUE ALFRED VAN PELT

U E  PAUL  BERT

RUE JEAN ROMUALD PRUVOST

RUE DU
MARÉCHAL
LECLERC

PLACE
JEAN JAURÈS

RUE D.
DIDEROT

St-Léger

AVENUE DE VARSOVIE

RUE DU 8 MAI 1945

A 211

ENUE  ALFRED  MAËS

RUE JEAN LÉTIENNE

RUE DE LA PAIX

Théâtre
Municipal
le Colisée

RUE DE PARIS

RUE DU HAVRE

AVENUE ALFRED V. PELT

RUE MICHEL RONDET

ST-THÉODORE

PLACE
ST-LÉONARD

ROUTE DU MOULIN

RUE ARTHUR FAUQUEUR

PLACE DU GÉNÉRAL
DE GAULLE

Gare SNCF

Gare
Routière

RUE DE LA GARE

PLACE
DE LA
RÉPUBLIQUE

ROCADE  MINIÈRE

RUE DES JARDINS

RUE C.
D'ARRAS

Cité
Ste-Barbe

RUE ST-ANTOINE

RUE NOTRE DAME DE LORETTE

VANHOVE

RUE JB MASSILLON

D'ARRAS

Parc
d'Activités
les Moulins

RUE THOMAS  EDISON

RUE DES DÉPORTÉS

14

RUE DE LA GLISSOIRE

RUE N. SACCO

RUE PAUL VERLAINE

Cité
Montgré

PLACE
ST-ALFRED

RUE AIMÉ

RUE LOUIS BOURDALOUE

RUE GABRIEL PÉRI

FERRAND

Parc
d'Activités
du Gard

A 211

RUE DES DÉPORTÉS

RUE ARTHUR RIMBAUD

RUE VICTOR HUGO

RUE CHARLES

D58

Parc de Loisirs
de la Glissoire

15

RUE

**STADE FÉLIX-BOLLAERT**

## Getting to the stadium

**Nearest airport**
Lille-Lesquin, 8km outside Lille.

**Car**
Autoroute A1 from Lille and then follow the signs. Drivers should use public carparks around the city and walk or take a bus to the stadium.

**Eurostar**
Take the Eurostar to Lille. Change to the Lens train which departs from Gare Lille Flandres, a 5-minute walk from the Eurostar terminal.

**Train**
Gare SNCF de Lens is located in the town centre and is a 15-minute walk to the stadium.

## Getting around Lens

Lens is such a small city that it is easy to walk everywhere. There is a StopBus service that circulates through the town with stops at the train station and the stadium.

**Tourist Office**
26 rue de la Paix
03 21 67 66 66
09.30-12.00, 13.30-18.30
Mon-Sat
info@tourisme-lenslievin.fr
www.tourisme-lenslievin.fr

**Parking in Lens**
Obtain a free parking disc from the Tourist Office and you can park free all around town where you see blue markings – time limit 90 mins. Other carparks in the town are free.

## Stade Félix-Bollaert capacity 38,285

| Matches | Date | Pool |
|---|---|---|
| England v United States | 8 September, Sat | A |
| South Africa v Tonga | 22 September, Sat | A |
| Georgia v Namibia | 26 September, Wed | D |

## The stadium and around

avenue Alfred Maes
03 21 13 65 44

This is an English-style stadium with four stands. The Lens football team motto '*sang et or*' (blood and gold) is emblazoned across the stadium. In 2009, one stand will be demolished, to be rebuilt with a casino, shopping mall and covered passage to Le Louvre-Lens.

The stadium is named after Felix Bollaert, the director of coal mines in the region, who commissioned the project. Behind the scenes, several of the VIP rooms are decorated in a coal-mining theme with old lamps, coal walls, coal trucks and a cloakroom that is an imitation of a miners' changing area. VIP seating is combined with no individual boxes for groups. The stadium takes in considerable revenue from its hospitality rooms, which are decorated according to theme: African, Italian, Mexican, South Seas – all very kitsch.

There is a McDonald's and other fast food establishments located adjacent to the stadium.

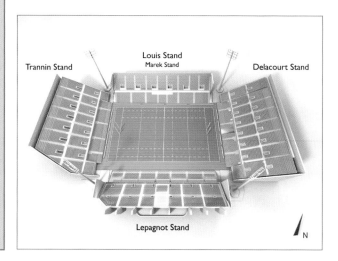

Trannin Stand · Louis Stand · Marek Stand · Delacourt Stand · Lepagnot Stand · N

# Sports bars

### Le Distingo
13 rue de la Paix
03 21 42 38 17
A friendly bar located two blocks from the train station with a big screen and sandwiches.

### Le Leffe
22 place du Général de Gaulle
03 21 42 13 58
This bar/brasserie is ideally located directly opposite the train station. They also serve food; main courses average around €10.

### Au Carrefour des Artistes
72 rue René Lanoy
03 21 43 57 97
Located a bit further away, off place Jean-Jaurès this large artists' bar will be showing matches on the big screen.

### Irish Tavern
6 avenue Raoul Briquet
03 21 78 79 20
A geniune Irish pub serving Irish beer and food with big screens showing Rugby World Cup 2007 matches.

### Le MacEwans
10 avenue Raoul Briquet
03 21 28 44 88
Another Irish bar serving a choice of beer and showing rugby matches on a big screen.

### Hôtel Espace Bollaert
13 C route de Béthune
03 21 78 30 30
There is a bar/dining room on the ground floor of this three star hotel located in the large grounds next to the stadium.

### Brasserie Saint Germain
26 route d'Arras; 62160 Aix Noulette
03 20 72 24 24
open for tastings14.00-18.00 or by appointment

This small artisan brewery is owned by two brothers, Vincent and Stéphane Bogaert. Vincent is a keen rugby player and runs a small club that plays in Folkstone each year.

The name of the beer, Page 24, relates to a quote from Abbess Hildegarde that the secret to brewing beer could be found on page 24 of a certain book - a page which was blank. When asked what this means, Vincent laughs and says, 'The secret to brewing beer lies in the heart of the brewer, it cannot be written down'. Vincent must know something because his blonde beer won a gold medal at the Salon Agricole de Paris in 2006.

On the wall is a Brewer's Star, which looks exactly like a Star of David. Some say the two are connected and that King David was himself a brewer. Whatever its origins, the Brewer's Star is a symbol of purity affixed to the bottom of barrels to indicate that the brew is completely free of additives. The six points of the star represent the six aspects of brewing most critical to purity: water, hops, grain, malt, yeast and, of course, the brewer.

STÉPHANE AND VINCENT BOGAERT

FOR LOCATIONS OF
CEMETERIES, PLEASE
SEE MAP IN BEYOND
LENS SECTION

**Loos-en-Gohelle**
03 21 69 88 77
open
located 10 minutes drive
north of Lens

**Canadian Memorial
at Vimy Ridge**
03 21 50 68 68
10.00-18.00 daily
free admission
located south of Lens

**Notre-Dame de
Lorette**
03 21 45 15 80
open

**Faubourg-d'Amiens**
Arras
always open

**Battlefield tours**

**Lens and Arras
Tourist Offices**
The two towns have
joined forces to offer a
tour that includes all the
battlefields listed here as
well as those in Arras and
Artois. Contact either the
Lens or Arras office.

**Salient Tours**
06 86 05 61 30
afternoon tours
guided tours in English
€35 per person.
A private tour operator
offering a variety of
battlefield tours.

# World War 1 Battlefields

The region around Lens saw some of the fiercest fighting of World War I. German troops established themselves on the tops of the slag heaps and on the higher ground of Vimy Ridge. From these positions they were able to see for miles around and anticipate Allied troop movements. Underground tunnels became key to taking the enemy by surprise to achieve victory.

After the war, the British made the decision to bury their dead where they had fallen and as a result the region has a great many British cemeteries, together with those who fought alongside: Canadians, Australians, Indians, New Zealanders. Maps of the battlefields and cemeteries can be obtained from any local Tourist Office.

The French decided to gather their dead together into one large cemetery at **Notre-Dame de Lorette**, on a hilltop just outside Lens.

LOOS MEMORIAL AND DUD CORNER CEMETERY

## Loos-en-Gohelle

The largest British cemetery in the area commemorates the Battle of Loos in 1915 when the British liberated part of the village. The Loos Memorial surrounds Dud Corner Cemetery. On the walls of the memorial are recorded the names of Fergus Bowes-Lyon, brother of the Queen Mother and John Kipling, son of Rudyard Kipling. John Kipling had very poor eyesight and was persuaded to enlist by his father who was concerned about his own reputation. John soon died and Rudyard later wrote that he regretted his decision to send his son into battle.

## The Canadian Vimy Memorial

This gigantic limestone monument can be seen for miles around. It was erected in memory of the 66,655 Canadians who died in the First World War (just over 10% of the young country's population). The sculpture and surrounding 100-hectare park is entirely maintained by the Canadian government and is manned by history students. In the park is a visitor centre that details the battle and you may walk through restored trenches and tunnels.

Walter Seymour Allward took 11 years to build the giant sculpture from 11,000 tonnes of concrete and 6,000 tonnes of limestone. The sorrowing cloaked figure of a woman represents Canada, mourning her dead. Carved on the walls are the names of the 11,000 who were missing in action. At the base of the steps are the Defenders: groupings of figures

known as *Breaking of the Sword* and *Sympathy for the Helpless*. At the top are figures representing Peace, Justice, Truth, Knowledge, Gallantry and Sympathy. Around these figures are shields of Canada, Britain and France.

Vimy Ridge is the highest point in the area and was in the firm control of the German forces for three years. Originally the hilltop was flat – the undulating landscape you see now was created by bombs to provide cover for Allied troop movements. Tunnels were constructed to provide secrecy and aid in planning for the final assault, planned for a snowy April 9, 1917. Rehearsals were conducted for months during the planning of the attack. On the day, under the cover of artillery barrage, all four Canadian divisions stormed out of the secret tunnels to take the German forces by surprise. By mid-afternoon they had captured the crest of the ridge and in three days the entire hill was in Canadian control.

### Faubourg-d'Amiens Cemetery

The official memorial for the Battle of Arras which was one of the first victories for the Allies in World War I. The enclosure bears the names of 35,942 soldiers who died.

The extensive network of chalk tunnels beneath Arras and the surrounding area were extended and used to assemble Allied troops. To aid soldiers in navigation through the tunnels, each tunnel was named after an Allied city and positioned in a logical way relative to other tunnels, for example, Manchester was located north of Birmingham.

FOOD & DRINK

LE PAIN DE LA BOUCHE

## Restaurants

See page 287 for price guide.

### L'Arcadie II
13 bis, rue Decrombecque; 03 21 70 32 22
daily for lunch; Tues, Thurs, Sat for dinner
€€€
An elegant restaurant on a small side street
that serves excellent cuisine. There is often a
set menu, with wine, that is good value. The
homemade foie gras is very good, the fish
and meat courses are well-prepared. Save
room for a dessert, the cheesecake is divine.

### La Vylla
15 rue Diderot; 03 21 67 10 10
lunch and dinner daily; closed Sunday
€€€
A new trendy restaurant located just near
the Saint-Léger Church. The presentation
is interesting and they are trying to vary
traditional recipes, but it can seem a bit
pretentious and it takes forever to be served.

### La Cantine
103 rue Jean Létienne; 03 21 42 56 43
lunch and dinner daily; closed Sunday
€€
This warm and cosy Italian restaurant is
conveniently located opposite the train
station. It fills up with locals at lunch who
come for the delicious daily specials.

### Le Pain de la Bouche
41 bis, rue de la Gare; 03 21 67 68 68
lunch and dinner daily; closed Sunday
€€
An *Estaminet* is a restaurant serving Flemish
regional food. This is the best in Lens serving
specialities such *faluches* (soft pizza), *potée de*

*pois cassés* (thick pea stew), and *coq à la bière*
(poultry cooked in beer). All smell and taste
delicious. The atmosphere is friendly and the
decor old-fashioned, with memoribilia.

### Aux Arts
105 rue Jean Létienne; 03 21 70 12 95
open daily til 01.00
€
This bar/brasserie serves light meals and is
the only place in Lens with WiFi.

### Le Brussel's Café
78, rue René Lanoy; 03 21 43 50 50
open daily til 01.00
€
A popular establishment with a large screen.

### Maître Patigoustier
42 place Jean-Jaurès; 03 21 28 24 21
07.30-20.00 Thurs-Sun
Patissier Jean-Claude Jeanson has created a
special pyramid shaped chocolate in honour
of Le Louvre-Lens. The restaurant is very
popular for lunch, tea and chocolate. Take a
box of delicious chocolates home with you.

JEAN-CLAUDE JEANSON

# Golf and other sports

The canals and man-made lakes in the region provide plenty of opportunities for boating, rafting and kayaking on both flat and white water. In addition there are several world-class golf courses, fishing lakes and hiking trails.

## Golf

### Golf d'Arras
rue Briquet Taillandier; 62223 Anzin-St-Aubin
03 21 50 24 24
This championship course is located only five minutes away from Arras town centre in the Scarpe valley. It is a relatively flat par 72 course, 6738 yards long, with many lakes and water features, and has hosted the Ladies French Open (Evian Tour) in 1996, 2000 & 2001, and the French Professional Championship (Challenge Tour) 1997-1999.

### Golf de Bondues
Château de la Vigne; Bondues 59910
8km north of Lille
03 20 23 20 62
There are two courses located here: the Hawtree and the Trent-Jones. Hawtree is an English design (quite flat and a little short for big-hitters), while Trent-Jones is American, with plenty of water and large bunkering. Of the two, the Hawtree is the better course.

### Golf du Touquet, La Mer Course
avenue du Golf; Le Touquet 62520
03 21 06 28 00
The La Mer course is set in an area of unspoilt and often mountainous sand dunes. Small trees and bushes line many of the fairways, with the large dunes also creating superb contouring for each hole. The course can take quite a pounding from its many visiting golfers, but generally the greenkeepers maintain quality. On the 17th green and 18th tee (on a clear day) you may glimpse the sea.

### Aa Saint-Omer Golf Club
chemin des Bois, Acquin-Westbécourt
Lumbres St Omer 62380 (A26)
03 21 38 59 90
The course landscape is in the valley of the river Aa. In 2003 it hosted its first European Tour event – now an annual occurrence. There are splendid views over surrounding countryside from the clubhouse and more elevated positions on the course. The greens are not large but the slopes can be steep. An enjoyable course with many international visitors.

# River sports, canoeing

### White Water Stadium
rue Laurent Gers, Saint-Laurent Blangy
03 32 73 74 93
www.eauxvivesslb.fr.st
An outdoor leisure and water sports centre built on former industrial wasteland in the heart of the Val de Scarpe nature park. There are flat water and white water activities including canoeing, kayaking and rafting. Lessons are available and this is where the French national team does their training.

WHITE WATER STADIUM

### Biache-Saint-Vaast Water Sports Park
03 21 73 35 08
Canoe centre

### Canal du Nord Centre
Marquoin Canoe Centre
03 21 59 10 63
Canoe centre

### Le Grand Marais
Ecourt-Saint-Quentin
03 21 73 50 00
Small boat rentals and outings

## Fishing lakes

### Etang de Cesar
Etrun; 03 21 22 39 22
closed Thurs

### Domaine des Cascades
Wancourt; 03 21 58 25 34
open daily

### Moulin de Roy Fish Farm
Rémy; 03 21 22 30 61

## Swimming

### Piscine Olympique - Lens
rue Robert Sherman; 03 21 28 37 35
08.30-13.00, 14.00-19.30 Mon-Sat
09.00-13.00 Sun; €2.60 adult, €1.90 child
A modern, Olympic-size swimming pool.

# Arras and Lille are an ideal choice for your base to attend matches in Lens or even Paris. Each city has a selection of hotels and good rail links from Gare Lille Flandres to Paris (1 hr) and to Lens (40 minutes).

Lens does not yet have many activities for tourists, but nearby are two attractive cities, Arras and Lille, with plenty of sights for the visitor to enjoy. Lille is larger and more lively with good shops and markets. Arras is smaller, but very pretty, centred around two interconnecting squares of buildings with Flemish/Dutch style facades. Both cities have interesting art galleries and large markets at the weekends.

**Arras**
• faithfully restored Flemish town
**Lille**
• vibrant city with great shopping and busy restaurants

## Arras

The original 16th century Flemish city was largely destroyed in the First World War. It was faithfully restored in the 1930s and, at first, residents were dismissive – they considered the buildings were not authentically old and were therefore an illusion, or fake. They also wanted to put the memory of the war behind them. Lately though, the citizens of Arras have regained their pride in the restoration, acknowledging its architectural value. With this new pride has come a curiosity about the First World War and the contribution of Arras residents to the Allied victory.

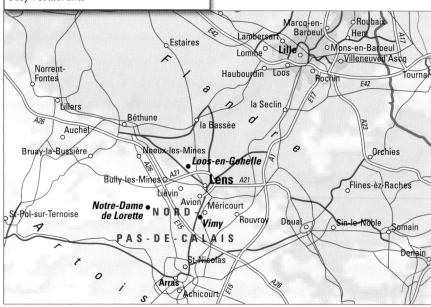

BUILDINGS ON THE GRAND PLACE, ARRAS' OLDEST HOUSE IS SECOND FROM LEFT

The town is organised around two central squares: the Grand'Place and place des Héros, with the town hall and Belfry. Both squares have spaces for parking on street level but these are often full, so it is best to use the large carpark underneath the Grand'Place. Arras comes alive on Saturday mornings when there is a large market in Grand'Place, place des Héros and place de la Vacqerie. The town hosts a film festival every autumn and a traditional Christmas market every year. Most hotels in Arras are located in place de la Gare, directly opposite the station.

**Tourist Office**
Hôtel de Ville
place des Héros
03 21 51 26 95
Located on the ground floor of the Belfry.
Take the lift (+43 steps) to the top of the Belfry for a fantastic view.
The tunnels can only be visited by guided tour

## First World War Tunnels

Beneath the Arras Belfry is a network of tunnels used by the Allies during the First World War. These tunnels played a key part in the Battle of Arras, a well executed maneouvre that proved a turning point for the Allies. The tunnels are well-lit (though damp), and are illustrated with photographs of soldiers engaged in routine activities: making tea, queuing for meals, sharing a laugh. These simple, moving images bring home the humanity of the young men who fought so courageously.

## Musée des Beaux Arts

22 rue Paul-Doumer
Entrance is via the abbey courtyard
03 21 71 26 43
09.30-12.00, 14.00-17.30, closed Tues
€4

The Fine Arts Museum is set in the huge Saint-Vaast Abbey, the largest complex of religious architecture in France. It was founded in the 7th century, and completely rebuilt in the 18th. The Abbey was rebuilt three times in its history but was one of the few buildings in Arras to survive the First World War bombings. Bullet holes dating from the confict can still be seen in the exterior walls and represent one of the ways of identifying what is old and what has been rebuilt. After the war, the Louvre donated works of religous art to rebuild the collection.

### The collection

In the entrance is a striking bronze lion which once stood atop the Belfry in place des Héros. On the **ground floor** are archaeological exhibits with artefacts discovered in Arras from the 4th century onwards. Also on this level is the main collection of medieval sculpture including the *Angels of Saudemont*, two exquisitley carved angels with large golden wings. Arras was once an important centre for tapestry. One of the few remaining pieces depicts Saint Vaast taming a bear, a miracle that brought the people of Arras back to Christianity.

On the **first floor** are painting and ceramics galleries. There are several works by Camille Corot, from the 19th century school of Arras, and Jules Breton who found inspiration in the daily lives of the peasants of the region. The stunning collection of ceramics exhibits many pieces of *Porcelaine d'Arras*, with its distinctive fine blue design on white porcelain known as *Bleu d'Arras*.

# Restaurants

See page 287 for price guide.

SANDRINE AND LAURENT DUBURQUOY

### La Faisanderie
45 Grand'Place, 03 21 48 20 76
open lunch and dinner daily
€€€
Sandrine and Laurent Duburquoy are your
charming hosts in this lovely restaurant
tucked away in a converted hay cellar. Chef
Laurent does wonders with salmon - on the
night we dined he served it four different
ways. Also delicious are the light and fluffy
prawn pancakes, *blinis de crevette grises*. If
the *soufflé chaud au chocolat* is on the dessert
menu be sure to order it, and you won't want
to share.

### La Clef des Sens
60-62 place des Héros, 03 21 51 00 50
10.00-23.00 daily
€€€
This is a friendly brasserie decorated in
the French *belle-epoque* style with plenty of
brass and wood. There is a large menu with
something for everyone, as well as daily
specials including very fresh fish. Service
is prompt and the wine list is considerable.
Sommelier Sebastien Reymbaut has chosen
some excellent wines from neighbouring
Touraine and Sancerre. Unusually, he has
also stocked a large selection of malt whisky.

SÉBASTIEN RAMPTEAU

# Sports bars

### Au Troquet Bar
rue des Trois Visages
This small bar is located just off place des
Héros, on a side street near the Belfry.
Owner, Mr Bastien, nicknamed *Babasse*, is
a big rugby fan and will be showing the
matches on his large screen television.

BABASSE

### Cap Horn
place des Héros
The bar is under the arcades on the north
side near the town hall. It is popular with
the Arras rugby team as the owner's son is
one of their players.

### Dan Foley's
place des Héros
Those in search of real Irish beer need look
no further.

### La Feria
rue de la Housse
A small bar with a good atmosphere.

### L'Elysée
boulevard de Strasbourg
This is a quiet, classy bar located close to the
train station.

### Ould Shebeen
boulevard Faidherbe
An Irish bar owned by a formidable
landlady.

### Le Dakota Bar
boulevard Faidherbe
A sports bar with large screens that is
popular with the younger crowd and comes
alive at night.

ARRAS FOOD & DRINK

## Lille

**Tourist Office**
Palais Rihour, place Rihour
03 59 57 94 00
www.lilletourism.com
09.30-18.30 Mon-Sat
10.00-17.00 Sun

**Bus tour**
A 50 minute tour in
English departs hourly
from the Tourist Office.
10.00-18.00 May-Oct
€9.50 adult
€7.50 cons

**Walking tours**
Tours in English every
Saturday at 14.30 depart
from the Tourist Office
Duration: 2 hours
€7,50 adult, €6,50 cons

A walk through Vieux Lille
with an overview of the
city's heritage, history and
lifestyle through its main
sites and monuments.
Very entertaining and
lively commentary with
interesting facts you may
not know.

The city was named Europe's Capital of Culture in 2004 and has since become a very popular short break destination. It has excellent shopping and lively restaurants, many serving Flemish cuisine. The Tourist Office here is very proactive and sponsors a many large city-wide festivals. In 2006, the festival theme was India and the entire city took part – large elephants lined the main street, Gare Lille Flandres was decorated to resemble an Indian palace and special Indian dishes were offered in the restaurants. In 2009 the festival theme will be Eastern Europe.

As you leave the Eurostar station (Lille Europe) you will be struck by the vibrancy of an ultra-modern city. Opposite the station is a huge indoor shopping centre called (confusingly) Euralille. Here you will find 140 shops including all the modern French and international chains: Carrefour, La Redoute, Sephora, Zara etc. Just past Euralille is Gare Lille Flandres where you can catch the train to Lens.

The train station is on the edge of **Vieux Lille**, the charming old town with its Dutch and Flemish architecture and large squares. These were constructed before the 16th century and were the first in France – there were no squares in the rest of France until the 17th century. Main sights include place du Général de Gaulle (Grand'Place), Vieille Bourse, Cathédrale Notre-Dame de la Treille and Palais Rihour.

All of these are located within walking distance and a walking tour is recommended to learn about the city's heritage. The street between place Rihour and Grand'Place is very good for late night eating as many of the restaurants serve food up to 4am. La Chicorée is open 24 hours. Lille is a surprisingly lively city, especially at weekends, so it is advised to book if you're going out to eat on Saturday night. The city is reputed to have the best school of journalism in France and is the third largest university city, with 36% of the population under 25.

## Bars in Lille

### Rugby bar

**Le Flanker**
36 place de la Gare
(nr Gare Lille Flandres)
03 20 21 00 01
food 12.00-14.00, 19.00-24.00
This bar is co-owned by Nicolas Fischer, a former hooker for Lille who now plays regularly in a veteran team. One of the waitresses plays in the French Women's national team. There is an enormous, cinema-sized screen that spans two floors in height. Rugby memorabilia fills the display cases along the walls. They serve hearty food and service could be non-stop during Rugby World Cup 2007.

NICOLAS FISCHER, LE FLANKER

## Other sports bars

**Tir Na Nog**
30 place Philippe Lebon
03 20 54 66 69
One of the best Irish bars in Lille is easy to find, off rue Solférino, near the church of Saint Michel, south of the Palais des Beaux Arts.

**Café OZ Australian Bar**
33 place Louise de Bettignies
03 20 55 15 15
This is a modern sports bar by day, and turns into a trendy cocktail bar by night.

**Le Sherwood**
40 rue Masséna
03 20 14 38 86
Located on a busy street with many other pubs and cheap and cheerful restaurants, near Les Halles Centrales, off rue Solférino. Large screens showing all kinds of sports.

**L'Irlandais**
106 rue Solférino
03 20 57 04 74
Your typical Irish bar serving the expected Irish beer.

**Scotland Fire**
rue Solférino
A large Scottish bar located next to L'Irlandais serving a selection of malt whisky.

**Les 3 Brasseurs**
22 place de la Gare
03 20 06 46 25
A microbrewery located opposite Lille Flanders station that also serves good *Flammekuche* (an Alsatian speciality similar to pizza).

## Getting around

Lille has a large, efficient, integrated transport system with the first driverless metro trains in the world. Stations are modern and clean with good signage. The bus network is useful for travelling around Vieux Lille.

**Tickets**
• **Ticket Zap**
1 journey, 3 stops, 60c
• **City Pass**
travel on all metro, trams and buses and includes city bus tour, entrance to all principal museums and attractions, also discounts on entertainment tickets
   day pass €18;
   2 day pass €30
   3 day pass €45
(3 day pass includes travel on regional trains and an Arras town hall Belfry and tunnel tour)

**Bicycle hire**
The flat landscape of Lille makes it an ideal city for cycling and many of the locals prefer this mode of transport. Bike racks are numerous and conveniently located, crime is relatively low, and bikes can be taken on trams and the metro.
• **Ch'ti vélo,**
10 av Willy Brandt near Gare Lille-Flandres
03 28 53 07 49.
07.30-19.30 Mon-Fri;
09.00-19.30 Sat-Sun

VIEILLE BOURSE

## Place du Général de Gaulle

Grand'Place was renamed after Lille's most famous son, Charles de Gaulle, born in 1890. In the centre is a statue of a goddess who commemorates the siege by the Austrians in 1792, when the citizens of Lille held off 35,000 troops. She holds a cannon fuse in her right hand and is shown as having a large forehead. Apparently this represents the stubborness of women in Northern France. When the statue was moved, a time capsule from 1850 was discovered. It contained a pessimistic prediction of the future and some French coins.

## Vieille Bourse (Old Stock Exchange)

The Italianate exterior uses the three building materials typical of Lille: grey sandstone, yellow limestone and red brick. The two lions holding the Fleur-de-Lys represent that Lille belonged to the Netherlands. The Flemish lion frequently appears on buildings in Lille, as does the ram's head – symbolising the Golden Fleece. In the courtyard you will find second-hand booksellers and chess players. It is open afternoons from 1pm except Monday.

## Rue de la Bourse and Rang du Beauregard

Fourteen three-storey private houses from the 17th century are so uniform that the only way to tell where one house ends and another begins is to look at the angel capitals on the upper storeys – two together signify a dividing wall. Look closely at the buildings in these two streets and you will discover indentations and even cannonballs embedded in the walls. These date from the siege of 1792, when residents would keep damp hay in their lofts so that the enemy's red-hot cannonballs would not set their homes on fire

## Place aux Oignons

*Oignons* derives from '*donjon*', meaning a tower in the middle of a castle. Lille was a centre of weaving and from the 1720s the ground floor of houses were of double-height to accommodate the looms. As a consequence, the cellar a underneath was only 2m high. Whole families lived in such cramped quarters with an infant mortality rate of 75%.

## Notre-Dame de la Treille

place Gilleson; 03 20 55 28 72
10.00-12.00, 14.00-18.00 Mon-Sat

In 1870 a competition was held to build what was planned as France's greatest neo-Gothic cathedral. Three designs were submitted: two by English architects, one by a French firm. The French bid won the competition but apparently the building soon began to sink and an English architect had to take over the project.

The most interesting part of the church is the facade which dates from 1999. Cables that suspend the slab are interwoven and represent a trellis (*treille*), as well as representing the connection and interdependency of human beings on each other. Georges Jeanclos, was himself a holocaust survivor and he designed the entrance as a symbol of human suffering and forgiveness. He was diagnosed with cancer but was determined to finish his work and died just two weeks after it was completed. The enormous marble facade appears to be opaque from the outside but, at sunset, it glows with a beautiful pink light as you view it from inside the cathedral.

## Palais des Beaux Arts

place de la République; 03 20 06 78 00
14.00-18.00 Mon, 10.00-18.00 Wed-Thurs
10.00-19.00 Fri, closed Tues
€5

Lille's premier gallery exhibits an outstanding collection of Flemish painting. The complex is made of two buildings: one 19th century, and one strikingly modern with a café on the ground floor.

Peter Breughel the Younger's charming *Bethlehem Census* is on the ground floor and there are also works by Peter Paul Rubens, Claude Monet and Edouard Vuillard. *Vanity* by Alfred Agache is a stunning work.

MUSÉE DES BEAUX ARTS

## Restaurants

Flemish food tends to be on the sweet side and beer is often used in cooking – *carbonnade à la Flamande* is beef cooked in beer, onions and brown sugar. Flans are on most local menus and *moules-frites* is the only food served during the annual 24-hour market *La Braderie*. Beware of the red beer made out of cherries, it tastes of cough syrup. Restaurants that specialise in regional cuisine are known as *Estaminet* and many can be found on rue de Gand. Book ahead at weekends.

See page 287 for price guide.

JEAN-LUC GERMOND, LE SEBASTOPOL

### Le Sebastopol
1 place Sébastopol; 03 20 57 05 05
lunch and dinner Tues-Sat; lunch Sunday
booking required; www.restaurant-sebastopol.fr
€€€€
Chef-owner Jean-Luc Germond, is President of Les Tables Gourmandes and a Maître Cuisinier de France, and has 1 Michelin star. The *Musée et Gourmandise* is a 7 course lunch including wine that is good value at €65. Everything is excellent, not to be missed.

### A L'Huitriere
3 rue des Chats Bossus; 03 20 55 43 41
closed Sun eve
€€€€
Decorated with a mosaic façade by Meheut Mathurin, this elegant dining room overlooks the cathedral gardens and the food is flawless, if expensive.

### Brasserie Alcide
5 rue des Débris Saint Etienne; 03 20 12 06 95
€€€
This is the place to have your *moules-frites*, preceded by the freshest oysters.

### Les Compagnons de la Grappe
26 rue Lepelletier; 03 20 21 02 79
€€
Set in a charming courtyard behind the Bourse, this French style bistro and wine bar places an emphasis on wine that is matched by their excellent food.

### Estaminet Chez La Vieille
60 rue de Gand; 03 28 36 40 06
€€
Flemish cuisine served in a friendly atmosphere. The giant salads are delicious and they serve an excellent quiche.

### Meert
27 rue Esquermoise; 03 20 57 07 44
This traditional patisserie with a lavish oriental interior specialises in *gaufres*: sweet waffles filled with Bourbon vanilla cream. They were a favourite of Charles de Gaulle.

### La Part Des Anges
50 rue de La Monnaie; 03 20 06 44 01
An unpretentious wine bar set on a lively shopping street that stocks a large variety of clarets from the best producers in Bordeaux and also a good selection of Chablis.

ESTAMINET CHEZ LA VIEILLE

# Shopping

Lille is a fantastic city for shopping with many original boutiques clustered close together in the old town. Walking through the shopping lanes is a pleasure and you'll be sure to find something special. It is especially good for clothing: women's lingerie and men's shirting. Shops are open till 7pm on Saturday night but beware, they are all closed on Sunday.

### Eden Park

7-9-11 rue de la Monnaie, 03 28 36 53 90
Established in 1987 by French rugby players Franck Mesnel and Éric Blanc who added a pink bow tie to their club kit for the French Championship final match. The chain is known for its quality wearable fashions with a strong rugby theme.

NODUS

### Nodus

6 bis rue de la Monnaie, 03 20 06 86 58
Up-to-the-minute stylish shirts and ties for men. Starting at €84 they do not come cheap, but are irresistible. The colour combinations of their striped range are inspired.

### Exopotamie

48-50 rue Esquermoise, 03 20 06 50 77
They have a wonderful selection of reasonably priced accessories; jewellery, bags, scarves

### Mise au Green

4 place du Lion d'Or, 03 20 55 54 84
Great clothing for men especially if you are of rugby build. Plenty of choice up to XXL.

### Paul Chausseur

38 rue de la Monnaie
03 20 31 62 58
Stylish shoes – mostly women's and some men's.

### Guillaume Vincent (Chocolatier)

12 rue du Curé St Etienne
03 20 42 98 43
A new concept in the art of the chocolatier, Guillaume Vincent uses the finest pure cocoa butter to produce seasonal selections of the most exquisitely decorated chocolates, each one like a tiny work of modern art. The surface decoration is applied with cocoa butter colour and all production takes place on the premises.

### Philippe Olivier

3 rue du Curé St Etienne
03 20 74 96 99
There are always queues outside this pungent cheese shop. They stock cheeses from all over France but specialise in more than 30 varieties from the Nord-Pas de Calais region. Try Maroilles, fantastic baked in a tart.

## Market

### Wazemmes

place de Nouvelle Aventure
metro: Gambetta
This enormous Sunday morning market is south of the centre. Different areas of the market clustered around the church of St. Pierre and St. Paul display a whole range of goods: antiques, bric-a-brac, homeware, material, clothes and flowers. Fresh produce can be found in the market hall itself. Stop here to pick up wonderful cheeses and local delicacies to take home. Many cut-price shops in the neighbouring streets are open and there are plenty of cafés.

**VISA**

# Nantes, situated on the Loire and Erdre rivers, will host three of the opening matches.

The Wales v Canada game will be a tough one for Canada; Cardiff is twinned with Nantes and the Welsh will be here in full force, even bringing their own wine. Canadians have a centuries-old connection with Nantes going back to the days of the Acadian deportations. Members of the Canadian team have recently been spotted at the Webb Ellis bar.

After the game, take time to stroll along the charming narrow lanes of the medieval quarter around the place du Bouffay, or window-shop in the elegant

LANES IN THE MEDIEVAL QUARTER

19th century streets off the place du Commerce. These squares are at the heart of the two distinct centres of Nantes. Another fun place to have a drink is the LU (Lieu Unique) centre. The distinctive landmark was once a biscuit factory owned by Lefèvre-Utile. Today it has been transformed into a lively cultural centre with bars, restaurants, theatre and an exhibition space.

Nantes is vibrant and prosperous, with most of its population under forty. It is the second largest university city in France (after Paris) and is a centre for biotechnology research.

**Château de Bretagne**
- the castle of the Dukes of Brittany

**Musée des Beaux Arts**
- eclectic collection

**Trentemoult**
- a colourful artists' community

**River Erdre**
- relaxing lunch and dinner cruises

**Musée Jules Verne**
- the author's home is now a museum

## Getting to the stadium

**Nearest airport**
Nantes Atlantique
A small airport south-west of Nantes. Car hire is directly across from the terminal.

**Car**
Autoroute A11
There will be no parking near the stadium, so drivers should use public carparks in the city, available and well-indicated, and travel to the stadium by public transport.

**Train** (TGV)
Gare de Nantes
2 hours from Paris.

**Tram**
Line 1 departs from place du Commerce and stops outside the stadium.

## Getting around Nantes

**Tourist Office**
nantes-tourisme.com
Metropole, Cathedrale
33 02 40 20 60 03

**Pass Nantes**
All-in pass covers public transport and entrance to over 20 sights.

**Tram**
The system has 3 lines: line 1 east-west, line 2 north-south, and line 3 north-west from the centre.
Single tickets €1.20

**Ferries**
There are two ferries: One makes 7 stops along the river Erdre from St Felix-La Jonelière, the other crosses the Loire to Trentemoult.

REMEMBER TO PURCHASE YOUR TRANSPORT TICKETS WELL IN ADVANCE OF THE MATCH TO SAVE TIME QUEUING.

### Stade de la Beaujoire   capacity 38,285

| Matches | Date | Pool |
|---|---|---|
| Wales v Canada | 9 September, Sun | B |
| England v Samoa | 22 September, Sat | A |
| Wales v Fiji | 29 September, Sat | B |

## The stadium and around

Route de Saint-Joseph: 02 40 30 11 22

La Beaujoire is a small, more intimate stadium with seats situated very close to the pitch. It is home to the local football club in Nantes, traditionally a football-supporting city where rugby is gaining in popularity. The tram takes about 20 minutes and stops just outside the stadium. Once you're here there isn't much to do beyond watch the match.

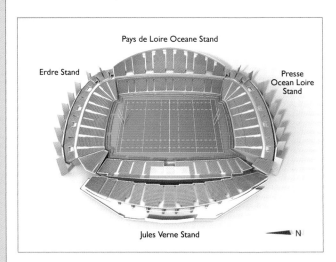

Pays de Loire Oceane Stand

Erdre Stand

Presse Ocean Loire Stand

Jules Verne Stand

N

## Bars near the stadium

The only bar is located in the Brithotel.

**Brithotel Amandine**
45 blvd des Batignolles
02 40 50 07 07
www.brithotel.fr
Rugby World Cup 2007 matches will be broadcast on large screens.

**Les Etoiles du Stade**
boulevard de La Beaujoire
(in the stadium)
02 28 23 03 00
booking advisable
The restaurant is reserved for VIPs only on match days. On other days the restaurant will be open and will have big screens showing Rugby World Cup 2007 games.

## Rugby bar

### Webb Ellis and Co
6 rue Santeuil
02 40 69 75 89
17.00-02.00 Mon-Tues
12.00-02.00 Wed-Fri
13.00-02.00 Sat
A rugby stronghold located
two streets west of place du
Commerce, owned by Ludovic
Mocard. The bar is decorated
with flags, souvenirs and
relics from around the world
collected over the past 15
years. Ludovic proudly serves
products from all countries
represented in his rugby
memorabilia: beer from Wales,
whiskies from Canada, wines
from Argentina and South
Africa.

Ludovic is planning a multitude of events around Rugby
World Cup 2007 together with Nantes town hall. He is
also planning to extend his opening hours during the
tournament.

---

## Other sports bars

### L'Autre Bar
19 rue Carmes (n/w of place du
Bouffay)
02 40 47 90 12
09.00-20.30 Mon-Wed
09.00-22.00 Thurs-Sat
Friendly modern bar, the
place to go for a late afternoon
aperitif.

### Café du Gaz
5 allée des Tanneurs
02 40 48 29 02
20.00-02.00 Mon-Sat
Located 10 minutes north of
place du Bouffay is this large
bar with pool tables.

### Molly Malone
33 rue de Verdun
02 40 08 05 20
A traditional Irish pub located
off place Saint Pierre. Parking
nearby.

### John Mac Byrne
21 rue des Petites Ecuries
02 40 89 64 46
14.00-02.00 Mon-Sun
Irish pub one block east of
place du Bouffay.

### Le Rabelais
3 rue du Bouffay
02 40 35 12 13
11.00-02.00 Tues-Sat
15.00-02.00 Sun, Mon
Well located just off place du
Bouffay.

### Spoon Café
13 place du Commerce
02 40 35 69 22
09.00-02.00 daily
A traditional French brasserie
with tables spilling out into the
square. Arrive early for a seat
on match days.

### Place du Commerce
This lively square in
the centre of Nantes,
promises to be a
gathering place for
rugby fans before
and after the match.
At press time there
were plans being
made for large
screens.

# Boat trips

## L'Erdre

The two and a half hour cruise up the Erdre glides along green riverbanks passing several large châteaux. The river is calm and peaceful and the journey very relaxing. Board the boat at quai de la Motte-Rouge just north of the centre. The graceful single-arched metal bridge was built in 1885.

The 18km route travels north passing many grand châteaux once owned by dukes and other noble families. Today many of these have been converted into faculty buildings for Nantes University and one or two are now hotels.

The recorded commentary on board is in French, but maps are available with

CHATEAU DE LA DESNERIE

sights along the route described in English, Italian, Spanish and German.

The boat turns around at the charming riverside town of Sucé, a popular spot for a Sunday walk. This is a pleasant stop before or after a match at La Beaujoire which is located nearby.

Lunch and dinner cruises are also available on the Erdre. A four-course meal is available with a choice of menu and wine. There is also a non-alcoholic option and a child portion. The food is surprisingly good, served with fresh ingredients and delicate sauces. Service is friendly and attentive.

**Bateaux Nantais**
Quai de la Motte Rouge
(tram line 2, Motte Rouge)
02 40 14 51 14
www.bateaux-nantais.fr
12.00-15.00 lunch, 20.00-23.00 dinner
€50-80 per person
€15 per child, €10 cruise only

VIEW OF TRENTEMOULT

## La Loire

For a delicious riverside lunch (or dinner) catch the ferry at Gare Maritime for the 15 minute journey along the Loire to Trentemoult. The Loire river is quite broad at Nantes and can be choppy. The boat travels at speed so this is not a cruise, but it is a good opportunity to see the Nantes skyline and appreciate its historical importance as a port city.

Nantes was once a large port before the river silted up and the industry moved to St Nazaire. The large riverfront warehouses once used for shipbuilding are being regenerated into artists' studios. One such project is the 'Isle of Nantes Machines', an ambitious scheme to build massive kinetic sculptures in the shapes of elephants and huge amphibious creatures. Contact the Tourist Office to arrange a visit.

> **Navibus**
> Tram station :
> Gare Maritime to
> Trentemoult
> single journey: €1.20
> free with Pass
> Nantes
> departs every 20 min
> 07.40-19. 40 daily
> 07.40-24.00 Fri-Sat

## Trentemoult

What was once a fishing village has evolved into a colourful, quiet artists' community set in a park. It is now becoming popular with the Nantais who come here to frequent the excellent riverside restaurant, La Civelle.

It is also possible to drive here.

## Château des Ducs de Bretagne

1 place Marc Elder
09.00-20.00 daily, closed Tuesday
€6.00

Dominating the Nantes riverside and old town is the Château, a castle that is both a military fortress and a residential palace. Henri IV signed the Edict of Nantes here in 1598, granting Protestants rights to their religion.

The castle was the birthplace of Anne de Bretagne (Anne of Brittany) in 1477. Nantes was historically the eastern border of Brittany, a region that maintained its independence from France until Anne was crowned Queen of France. In fact, Anne is the only woman to have been twice crowned Queen of France: in the deal to surrender Brittany to France was a clause that if Anne was to outlive her first husband, King Charles VIII, she would marry his successor – which she did by marrying Louis XII. Anne bequeathed the castle to Nantes.

Restorations have taken three years and are scheduled for completion in early 2007. Visitors will be now have access to the many sumptuous rooms of the residence that were previously closed.

## Musée des Beaux Arts

10 rue Georges Clémenceau
02 51 17 45 00
10.00-18.00 daily, open till 20.00 Thursday
closed Tuesday

It is unusual to find an excellent art collection in a relatively small French city and this gallery has several unexpected masterpieces. The paintings are well displayed in a beautiful 19th century building filled with natural light from the central skylight.

On the first floor are works by artists who just pre-date the Impressionists. The gallery has many impressive portraits by Jean-Auguste Ingres, an extremely successful painter of society and the artist that young Impressionists loved to vilify. Georges de la Tour, a master of light, is represented as is the master of colour, Gustave Courbet.

The contemporary gallery has works by Pablo Picasso, Henri Matisse and Marc Chagall and a surprisingly comprehensive collection of Vassily Kandinsky.

## Jules Verne Museum

4 rue de Clisson
09.00-20.00 daily, closed Tuesday

This house on the hill was Verne's family home and is filled with his research, library, journals and more.

## Jules Verne (1828-1905)

Born in Nantes, Jules Verne was 11 when he stowed away on a boat. Sent home in disgrace, he vowed to travel only in his imagination.

Verne studied law in Paris and began writing opera librettos and plays. His first novel, *Five weeks in a Balloon*, was inspired by his studies in African geography and modern scientific inventions. It was first written as a treatise and was rejected by many publishers until one suggested Verne rewrite it as an adventure story. As a novel it proved a huge success and Verne's career was made. The author anticipated many of the scientific advancements of the 20th century including submarines, helicopters, guided missiles and air conditioning.

**Selected bibliography:**
Journey to the Centre of the Earth (1864)
20,000 Leagues Under the Sea (1870)
Around the World in 80 days (1873)
A Captain at Fifteen (1878)

## Acadians

A couple of streets to the left of the Jules Verne museum is a stunning mural that depicts a group of Acadians arriving in Nantes. These people were Canadians of French origin forced off their land in 1755 by the English and put onto boats destined for France.

Their story is a sad one, many did not survive the journey and those who did were not welcome in Nantes. Having lived several generations in Canada, working the land and developing their own customs, the Acadians were never integrated into the life of Nantes. Social programs had to be instituted to feed them because no one would offer them employment. In 1785, over 1,500 Acadians seized the opportunity to move to Louisianna where they came to be known as 'Cajuns'.

# FOOD & DRINK

## Local Cuisine

Nantes is officially located in Western Loire but has long been considered part of Brittany, a region known for seafood and crêpes – be sure to try both while you're here. The local scallops, known as Coquilles St Jacques, are especially good: juicy and tender. Another speciality, Dublin Bay prawns, are very large, like langoustine. Beware, local oysters can be salty and a little tough. The local speciality crêpe is *la gallette curé Nantais*, served with local cheese and Muscadet wine.

## Local Drink

Cider is the traditional beverage of Brittany and it is served dry or sweet. It is the perfect accompaniment to a crêpe.

Most wine served in Nantes is produced in Anjou, known for making a quality rosé. The Loire valley produces white wines from Chenin Blanc (Vouvray) and Sauvignon Blanc (Touraine) grapes.

Generally a Touraine will be crisp and best with seafood while Vouvray tends to be a little sweeter, perfect as an aperitif or with salads. Muscadet is the local white wine – drink with oysters.

Whisky is growing in popularity and Nantes has several 'whisky clubs' that have formed that conduct 'tastings' at local restaurants. Whisky is proving so popular that two new whisky distilleries have opened nearby in Brittany.

## Restaurants

See page 287 for price guide.

### Near the stadium

**Manoir de la Régate**
155 route de Gachet
02 40 18 02 97
lunch and dinner daily
closed Monday, Saturday lunch, Sunday dinner
booking required
credit cards accepted

€€€€
This is a charming and comfortable restaurant located north of the city, near to the stadium. The terrace offers a view of château de la Gascherie and the park.

**Auberge du Vieux Gachet**
route de Gachet, Carquefou
02 40 25 10 92
lunch and dinner daily
closed all day Mon, dinner Wed and Sun
€€€
Head chef Walter Lescot serves well-prepared French dishes in a large country house with old fashioned stone walls and 2 large fireplaces. The setting is pastoral on the banks of the river Erdre.

### In the centre of Nantes

**L'Atlantide**
16 quai E Renaud, 4th floor (nr Musée Naval)
02 40 73 23 23
12.00-14.30 Mon-Fri, 19.30-22.00 Mon-Sat
closed Sunday
booking required
credit cards accepted
€€€€
Chef Jean-Yves Gueho has secured one Michelin star for his innovative seafood dishes combining traditional Breton recipes with exotic spices and flavours. Specialities include lobster salad with a yellow wine sauce, Breton turbot with oriental sauce, langoustines with Thai basil. The nautical-themed interior was decorated by Jean-Pierre Wilmotte, a renowned restaurant designer.

**La Cigale**
4 place Graslin
02 51 84 94 94
07.45 breakfast, 11.45-0.30 continuous service
book for large parties
credit cards accepted
€€€
This beautiful Art Nouveau restaurant has been a Nantes institution since its founding in 1895 by Emile Libaudière. Seafood is plentiful with a fresh oyster bar available during lunch and dinner. The food is not as impressive as the decor, but La Cigale is a pleasant place for a long leisurely lunch.

**L'Embellie**
14 rue Armand-Brossard (nr place du Cirque)
02 40 48 20 02
lunch and dinner daily
closed all day Sun and Mon dinner
credit cards accepted
€€
Chef Yvonnick Briand's menu is dependent

on what's available in the markets. Fresh fish is served daily and he is so particular about his foie gras that he has his own smokehouse for salmon and duck. French West Indian spices feature prominently in his creations. For dessert try pineapple croquant with rum-laced creole ice cream.

### La Ciboulette
9 rue St-Pierre
02 40 47 88 71
closed Sunday
€€
The fixed price lunch and dinner menus are a bargain in this neighbourhood restaurant, located on a side street close to the cathedral.

### L'Île Mysterieuse
13 rue Kervégan (on Île Feydeau)
02 40 47 42 83
closed Sun, Mon
€
One of the best crêperies in Nantes and the place to try *la gallette curé Nantais.*

### Café La Perle
10 rue Port au Vin
02 40 48 51 94
11.30-21.00 Mon-Sat
A friendly bistro that is a little run-down, but well located near place du Commerce.

LA CIVELLE

## Outside the centre

### La Civelle
Trentemoult; 02 40 75 46 60
lunch and dinner daily, booking advised
credit cards accepted
€€€
Spacious and modern with contemporary art on the walls and a riverside patio, La Civelle is popular with locals. The seafood is excellent as are the large salads. Service is friendly.

# Shopping

Shops are open from 10am-7pm, but some smaller family-run businesses close for lunch. Shops are closed on Sundays.

### Eden Park 〔⭗〕
15 rue Rubens
02 40 08 00 08; www.eden-park.tm.fr
Established in 1987 by French rugby players Franck Mesnel and Eric Blanc who added a pink bow tie to their club kit for the French Championship final match. The chain is known for its quality wearable fashions with a strong rugby theme.

### Passage Pomeraye
A multi-level Art N ouveau wrought-iron and glass-covered shopping centre near place du Commerce. Shops here are more expensive than in the lanes in the medieval quarter.

### Les Caves du Beffroi
12 rue de la Paix (west of place du Bouffay)
02 40 47 04 12
A shop selling every type of wine produced in the Loire as well as an outstanding selection of Bordeaux and Burgundy. They also sell Breton cider, whisky and locally made beer.

### Librairie Coiffard
7-8 rue de la Fosse; 02 40 48 16 19
Guidebooks and novels in English.

### Gautier Debotté
• 9 rue de la Fosse (off place Royale)
02 40 48 23 19
• 3 rue de Budapest; 02 40 48 18 16
• 2 rue des Hauts Pavés; 02 40 20 05 81
This chain of pâtisseries is a Nantes institution serving delicious chocolate and pastries.

### Devineau
2 place Ste Croix (nr place du Bouffay)
The Devineau family established this small chain of shops in 1803. Here you'll find the prettiest items for your table or window, including fine white linens decorated with swans and cranes, sheer fabrics that shimmer in the light.

### Régine Duchayne
10 rue de la Fosse (off place Royale)
02 40 48 26 28
If you're female and you want pampering look no further than this combination parfumerie and aesthetician. Enjoy a facial followed by a guided scent tour through their stock of rare essences and perfumes.

**VISA**

# Golf and other sports

Western Loire boasts the famed La Bretesche and La Baule golf clubs, but these are only two of the many beautiful courses in this region. And there are miles of beautiful coastline, enabling you to take in the stunning scenery as well as the golf.

LA BAULE INTERNATIONAL BARRIÈRE CLUB

## Golf Courses

### Nantes

**Nantes Golf Club**
44360 Vigneux de Bretagne
02 40 63 25 82; www.golfclubdenantes.com
restaurant closed Monday:
This is a testing course, criss-crossed by the river Cens. Set in parkland around the Château de Buron, it has generous fairways. The friendly clubhouse ensures a warm welcome and there is a good restaurant overlooking the terrace.

### Anjou

**Angers Golf Club**
Moulin de Pistrait, 49320 St Jean des Mauvrets
02 41 91 96 56; www.golfangers.com
A short distance from historic Angers near Brissac-Quince, this interesting parkland course is bordered by ancient trees and water hazards. The clubhouse is located in an old mill. Practice area available.

**Anjou Golf & Country Club**
route de Cheffes, 49330 Champigné
02 41 42 01 01; www.anjougolf.com
This international course covers a large area of tranquil, undulating countryside with lovely old trees and hedgerows, punctuated by numerous lakes and water hazards. A covered practice area is available for a pre-round warm up, and there is a swimming pool (in season) for a quick dip afterwards.

### Cap d'Atlantique

**La Baule International Barrière Club**
Domaine de Saint-Denac, 44117 Saint-André-des-Eaux; 02 40 60 46 18

www.lucienbarriere.com
This magnificent course is set around the national park of La Grande Brière and offers excellent facilities for golfers of all standards, with three courses from 9 to 18 holes able to meet the needs of everyone from beginners to those in search of a real challenge. The thatch-roofed clubhouse overlooks the course and there is an outdoor swimming pool, restaurant, covered practice area and two putting greens.

**La Bretesche Golf Club**
Domaine de la Bretesche, 44780 Missillac
02 51 76 86 86; www.golf-bretesche.com
The course is set in a forest with many holes running through dense woodland, making accuracy off the tee very important. The closing holes run around the lake and château, providing an unforgettable view.

**Pornic Golf Club**
49 boulevard de l'Océan, Sainte-Marie/Mer
44210 Pornic
02 40 82 06 69; www.formule-golf.com
A course where the first five holes are set in hilly and wooded landscape with wide fairways, whilst the later holes are like a links course with undulating fairways, water hazards and very well defended greens.

**Savenay Golf Club**
44260 Savenay
02 40 56 88 05; www.formule.golf.com
restaurant closed Monday
This is a spectacularly beautiful course on the edge of La Brière marshes and close to the beaches of La Baule. It has a varied terrain with chestnut woods, open valleys and water.

## Cycling

### La Loire à Vélo

www.loire-a-velo.fr

The Loire à Vélo is the name of what is planned to be a 500 mile continuous cycle trail stretching from St-Brévin-les-Pins (near La Baule) to Cuffy (near Sancerre). The trail is a signposted and safe itinerary along minor roads and cycling tracks beside Europe's last untamed river, a region that has been included in the UNESCO World Heritage List. Cycle through historic towns, on paths beside châteaux overlooking the river, along the edges of gardens and vineyards.

Parts of the trail are already open and new sections are being developed. There is a 100-mile itinerary between Angers and Tours, and another, shorter trail between Bois and Orleans has recently been completed.

Route maps are available at Tourism Offices, or download a handbook complete with maps from the excellent website available in English, French, German and Dutch languages. The website offers advice on cycle hire and local accommodation.

Existing cycle trails around La Baule are plentiful throughout the beautiful Guérande Peninsula, with tracks marked out for cycling or horseriding.

### Cycle Hire

**Angers**
• Espace 2 roues, 45 rue Beaurepaire
02 41 87 69 46
• Office de Tourisme, place Kennedy
02 41 23 50 00

**La Baule**
• M. Chaillou, 3 place de la Victoire, 02 40 60 07 06
• Rent La Baule, 23 avenue G. Clemenceau
02 40 11 17 00

**Guérande**
• Motos Cycle Diffusion, 5 place Kerhilliers
02 40 24 91 44

### Boating and sailing

**Angers**
• Angers Canoeing Club-Boating Centre
75 av. du lac de Maine, 02 41 72 07 04

**La Baule**
• Club Holywind Royal, Plage Benoît
02 40 60 51 96
• Latitude, Baie de la Baule; 06 03 15 23 04

## Spa/Thalassotherapy

### La Baule
• Relais Thalasso La Baule
28 boulevard de l'Ocean
08 20 90 32 44
08.00-13.00, 14.00-19.00 daily
Hydrotonic centre, slimming, massage, facials, post natal and beauty treatments.

• Thalgo La Baule
6 avenue Marie Louise
02 40 11 99 99
08.30-19.00 Mon-Sat, 8.45-12.45 Sun
€90-136
Restore and revitalise with one of their 'taster packs' that introduce you to a variety of treatments. These include: insomnia, anti-stress, back-pain, stop smoking, obesity.

### Pornichet
• Thalassotherapie Centre Daniel Jouvance
66 boulevard des Océanides
02 40 61 89 98
09.00-13.00, 14.00-18.00 daily
Slimming, massage, rejuvenating, well-being, calming, back treatments, mens treatments... all using natural products from the sea.

## Horse riding

### La Baule
• Centre Equestre et Poney-Club de La Baule
5 av. de Rosières; 02 40 60 39 29
### Guérande
• Les Rosières Equitation, Les Rosières
02 40 62 12 56

## Pétanque

In Nantes you can either watch or play with the locals, rendezvous at the foot of the steps of the Cours Saint André behind the château.

# Anjou is a wine and châteaux area located one hour east of Nantes. One hour's drive west of Nantes is the coastal area of Cap d'Atlantique.

**Angers**
• capital of Anjou
**Château d'Angers**
• the French built this fortress to keep out the English
**Château de Brissac**
• largest fortified castle in France
**La Baule**
• miles of beach with soft white sand
**La Brière**
• protected marshland good for birdwatching
**Guérande**
• salt marshes, famous for *Fleur de Sel*

**Anjou** is a wine making region known for its rosé and white wines. There are 1,200 grand châteaux and stately homes in Anjou, a testimony to the power and wealth of the ruling dynasty. This is the land of Eleanor of Aquitaine and King Henry II of England who are buried together with their son, Richard I, in the Abbey of Fontevraud. Anjou châteaux combine the virtues of fortified buildings with the need for a comfortable home and some, like Château de Brissac, are still family residences.

The flat marshlands and beaches of **Cap d'Atlantique** are a sports lovers paradise. In addition to miles of sandy beach, La Baule has a world-reknowned golf course and several spas. Historically part of Brittany, this region was under the firm control of the English who were based in the fortress town of Guérande. Le Croisic is a French-style Padstow with a row of restaurants along the waterfront.

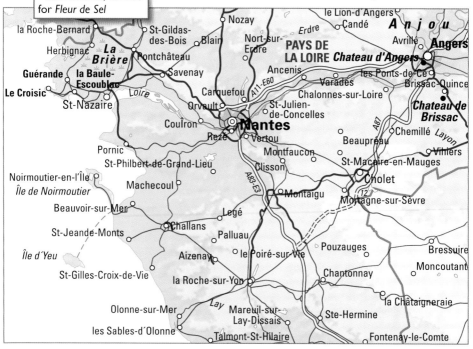

# Angers

Angers is located on the river Maine just north of the Loire. It is a pretty town with many public gardens and pleasant shopping streets.

Angers, capital of Anjou, is dominated by a large castle. It is from here that the Plantagenets created an empire that stretched from Scotland to the Pyrenees. Gardens are allowed to grow a little wilder here, more English in style than is common in France.

## Château d'Angers

The largest fortified castle in France was built in the 13th century, by Louis IX and his mother, Blanche of Castile, after Anjou was returned to the French crown. The fortifications cover half a square mile with 17 towers. English Protestants were tossed over the ramparts during the French-English wars.

## Apocalypse Tapestry

Also known as the 'Star of Anjou', it is the largest woven artifact in the world. This tapestry tells the history of the medieval world and casts the English King Henry as the devil with many heads. The tapestry was lost until 1845 when a monk found it warming the rumps of horses in the stables. It had been cut into 40 pieces. The cloth has since been restitched and is displayed in a special building.

## Château de Brissac

The tallest château in France reaches seven stories and is set in 70 hectacres of parkland. Still a family home after 500 years, the living rooms have personal photographs on the piano. Regrettably, a photograph of the Marquis with the Queen Mother has been stolen. The château sells its own wine, hosts events and rents suites.

## Château Brézé

Located south-east of Angers (off map) is this château with the largest system of secret underground passages in Europe. It was once the home of the late Comtesse de Colbert who was the first woman to be president of a French rugby team.

CHÂTEAU DE BRISSAC

SAILLÉ

### Parc de Brière

This is the second largest marshland in France after Le Camargue and has been a protected area since 1970. You can explore the marshes aboard a chaland (flat bottomed boat). Once on the boat, it is very quiet and peaceful – excellent for bird watching.

**L'Arche Brièronne**
Bernard Deniaud, port de Bréca
02 40 91 33 97
April - October daily
45 minute barge trip
€7.00 adults, €6.00 children

### Guérande Salt Marshes

Salt and fish are still a very important part of the local economy. The salt produced here is considered a delicacy and there are several varieties – the most special is called Fleur de Sel.

### La Baule

A popular resort for Parisians, La Baule has miles of soft honey-coloured sand beaches, with quaint houses that give the town a unique character. La Baule is so laid-back that you will feel the tension leave your body soon after your arrival. If you require more relaxation there are several spas and golf courses nearby.

Whether you like your seaside calm or wild, there is something for everyone: La Baule faces south onto a calm and sheltered bay. Drive around the point towards Le Pouliguen and you will find a rocky coastline dotted with tiny coves and inlets reminiscent of the Cornish coast.

# Guérande

In the heart of the salt marshes is this medieval fortress town with a labyrinth of small lanes. Guérande's ramparts are 1,434m long with four gates: Saint Michel to the east, Vannetais to the north, Bizienne to the west and Saillé to the south. Salt was an important source of income for the medieval city as was the peat harvested from the marshes.

Geoffrey, Duke of Brittany (1158–1186) was the third son of Henry II and Eleanor. Guérande was Geoffrey's English stronghold and remained independent until Brittany's union with France in 1532. The fortifications were strengthened and rebuilt in 1343 after Spanish troops led by Charles de Blois destroyed the town when they attacked the heir to Brittany, Jean de Monfort.

### Musée du Pays de Guérande
porte Saint-Michel, 02 28 55 05 05
10.00-12.00 and 14.30-19.00 daily
closed Monday morning
Inside the Saint Michel gate is a museum made up of three floors and two towers. On display are costumes and furniture made using materials unique to the region. Included in your admission is a walk on a portion of the ramparts. Just inside the gate, on your right, is an excellent crêperie.

LANES IN GUÉRANDE

### Le Croisic

A resort and fishing village in the style of Padstow in Cornwall. Several excellent restaurants line the waterfront.

Fishing is still a thriving industry because nearby are found the delectable scallops known as *Coquilles Saint Jacques*. Local restaurants serve them in a variety of ways beyond the typical scallop shell – try them stuffed in a crêpe or grilled with butter sauce.

QUAY AT LE CROISIC

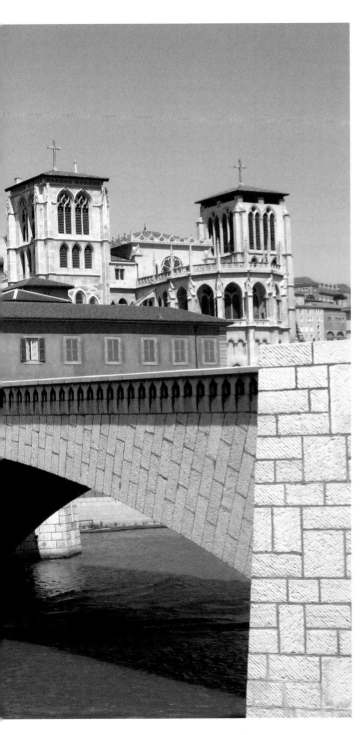

LYON

RIVER SAÔNE, CATHÉDRALE AND NÔTRE DAME

# Lyon vies with Marseille to be France's second city but it prides itself on being the first city, gastronomically speaking.

The Rhône and Saône rivers converge in Lyon. Sandwiched between them is *La Presqu'île* ('almost an island'). This narrow strip of land is the heart of Lyon and is alive with bars, cafés, and shops. La Presqu'île has two grand squares: place Bellecour and place des Terreaux, linked by a pedestrianised shopping street, rue de la République. During Rugby World Cup 2007, these two squares will be the best place for a beer before the match or to find big screens and sports bars.

Croix Rousse, up the hill to the north, is where the city's silk-weavers used to live. West across the Saône is Vieux Lyon, the wonderfully atmospheric medieval quarter of the city, today a UNESCO World Heritage Site. From here you can take the funicular up to Fourvière, with its Roman remains and Gallo-Romaine museum. Further up the hill is the distinctive Basilica of Nôtre-Dame overlooking the city.

Lyon has plenty of good museums and historical sights but what the city is really known for is the food. Whether you choose to dine at a simple *bouchon* or at the flagship restaurant of a great chef, you are sure to have a good meal in Lyon – enjoy!

### Getting around Lyon
Lyon has a good metro, bus and tram system. Tickets are valid for one hour on all services. Single tickets cost €1.40, day ticket €4.20 a carnet of 10 tickets €11.50
### Lyon City Card
day pass €18, two days €28, three days €38 Unlimited use of public transportation system, free or reduced entry to sights and activities.
### Tourist Office
• Gare Routière • place Bellecour

### La Presqu'île
• the lively centre of Lyon
### Vieux Lyon
• the medieval old town
### La Croix Rousse
• silk-weavers' historic area
### Fourvière
• take the funicular up to the Basilica
### Musée Lumière
• dedicated to the brothers who invented cinem

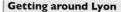

LES ANNÉES BAR, QUAI ROMAIN ROLLAND

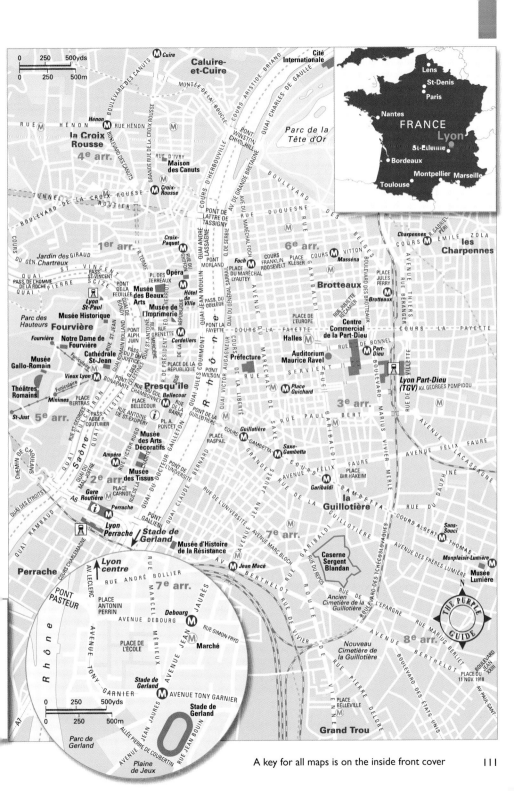

A key for all maps is on the inside front cover 111

## Getting to the stadium

**Nearest airport**
Saint-Exupéry airport is 30km southeast of the city centre. There are shuttle bus services every 20 minutes into the centre, stopping at the two main railway stations, Gare de la Part-Dieu and Gare de Perrache. Both have metro stations.

**Car**
Carparks near the stadium will be reserved for press and VIPs. Drivers should use public carparks around the city and walk or take a bus to the stadium.

**Bus**
Number 96 runs from the bus depot at Gare Perrache to Stade de Gerland and beyond. The stop at Piscine de Gerland is closer to the stadium main entrance.

**Tram**
Lyon has a new and small tram network, but at present there is no line near the stadium.

**Metro**
The metro is the best way to get to the stadium. Take Line B south to Stade de Gerland.

**Train**
Both of Lyon's main stations have a metro stop with easy connections to the stadium.

REMEMBER TO
PURCHASE YOUR
TRANSPORT TICKETS
WELL IN ADVANCE OF
THE MATCH TO SAVE
TIME QUEUING.

## Stade de Gerland capacity 41,044

| Matches | Date | Pool |
|---|---|---|
| Australia v Japan | 8 September, Sat | B |
| Argentina v Georgia | 11 September, Tues | D |
| New Zealand v Portugal | 15 September, Sat | C |

## The stadium and around

30 allée Pierre de Coubertin
04 72 76 01 70

The proud home of the Olympique Lyonnais soccer team, four times French champions, was opened in 1926. It was designed by renowned local architect Tony Garnier (1869-1948). Garnier was born and is buried in Lyon's Croix Rousse district and was one of the leading French architects of his day. Over 80 years later, the 41,000 seat stadium has retained Garnier's basic design, except for the canopies over the corner sections added for the 1998 FIFA World Cup. The redesign must have inspired the Olympique Lyonnais team – they went on to win the French championship four years in a row (2002-2005).

Rugby isn't a big sport in Lyon, but the stadium has hosted international matches and several French championship finals. It may also become home to the newly resurgent Lyon Olympique Universitaire Rugby team, if Olympique Lyonnais see through their plans to build themselves a new soccer stadium.

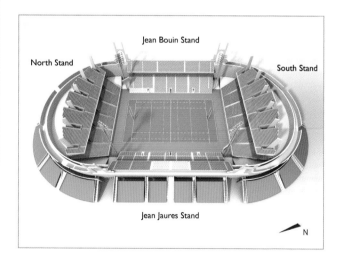

## Bars near the stadium

**Brasserie Rive Gauche**
24 allée Pierre de Courbertin
04 78 72 62 37
www.larivegauche-restaurant.fr
09.00-19.00 daily, food served at lunch
phone ahead on match days
credit cards accepted
€€
In a pleasant park close to the stadium is the brasserie/bar where Olympique Lyonnais players come to relax after training or a match. The menu is simple with plenty of steak options, a dish of the day (such as *escalope de saumon)* and sandwiches. The house wine is inexpensive.

**Ninkasi Ale House**
267 rue Marcel Mérieux
04 72 76 89 00
An industrial brewery located near the stadium with a large open space around the bar and a range of beers brewed on site.

## Bars in the centre

**Albion Pub**
12 rue Sainte Catherine (north of place des Terreaux)
04 78 28 33 00
17.00-03.00 daily, happy hour 17.00-21.00
This Scottish pub is one of the oldest in Lyon. They serve over 30 varieties of single malt whiskies and have eight different beers on tap. There's a giant screen in the sports bar, and two dart boards as well as other games.

**Ayers Rock**
2 rue Désirée (northwest of Opera)
08 20 32 02 03
Aiming to be a little piece of Oz in Lyon, Ayers Rock has in fact won an award for being the most authentic Australian pub in France. Boasting flamboyant barmen and surfing memorabilia, it attracts a busy and youthful international crowd.

**Down Under**
12 rue Griffon (close to Hotel de Ville)
04 78 27 35 86
A large Australian bar on two floors with a giant screen for sports. Well-priced Australian beer is on draught and authentic food is also available (including kangaroo steaks).

**St. James Pub**
19 rue Saint Jean
04 78 37 36 70
Situated on the cobbled streets of the fifth arrondissement in the heart of Lyon, they have large screens and will be showing rugby.

**Johnny Walsh's**
56 rue Saint George
04 78 42 98 76
Owned and managed by an ex-pat Irishman, who is often to be found playing his guitar along with the band. Staff are either British or Irish and the Irish brew is the best you'll find outside of Ireland. A real 'local'.

**The Shamrock**
15 rue Sainte Catherine
04 78 27 37 82
Irish bar with sports screens and plenty of Irish beer on tap.

PLACE BELLECOUR LOOKING UP AT NOTRE DAME

## La Presqu'île

This is the centre of Lyon with shops, bars, cafés, restaurants, markets, banks and museums. The area has three squares: place Carnot in the south, place Bellecour in the centre and place des Terreaux in the north. This district has many of Lyon's fine museums and galleries including the Musee des Beaux Arts and the Musée des Tissus, two special museums worthy of a visit.

### Place Carnot

An organic food market is held here every Wednesday evening from 4pm-7pm and on Sunday mornings from 5am-1.30 pm.

### Place Bellecour

The most grand of the three squares is the city's traditional location for large gatherings and home to the Tourist Office. It's one of the largest squares in Europe and features a large equestrian statue of Louis XIV in the centre.

### Place des Terreaux

Surrounded by bars and restaurants this square is the true heart of Lyon. The town hall is on the northeast corner and this is likely to be where large screens will be placed during the Rugby World Cup 2007, but it's best to check beforehand.

The stunning fountain in the centre was made by the same man who sculpted the Statue of Liberty, Frédéric Bartholdi. On the south side of the square is the Musée des Beaux-Arts.

## Musée des Beaux Arts

Palais Saint-Pierre, 20 place des Terreaux
04 72 10 17 40
10.00-18.00 daily 10.30-20.00 Fri
closed Tue and holidays
some rooms close at lunchtime
€6

Lyon's main museum has the most important collection of art outside the Louvre. The ground floor has antiquities from Greece, Rome and Egypt: paintings and sculpture are exhibited on the first floor.

The Egyptian collection on the first floor is outstanding, with vast temple walls, mummified remains, carved gold jewellery and vases decorated in colours so vivid they look completely modern.

On the second floor, in **Room 9,** is Rembrandt's *The Stoning of St Stephen*. In **Room 19** are amusing satirical busts of local politicians and celebrities, made by Honoré Daumier (1808-79). Daumier was a genius at caricature with a special affinity for the poor and downtrodden and an ability to poke fun at the rich and powerful. Tiny busts of characters such as *The Timid*, *The Stupid* and *The Gourmet* are all still hilariously funny.

Give yourself plenty of time to explore the collection which includes paintings by Camille Pissaro, Alfred Sisley, Paul Gauguin, Claude Monet, Edouard Manet, Edgar Dégas, Pierre-Auguste Renoir, Pablo Picasso, Marc Chagall, Georges Braque and Francis Bacon. Take a break among the statues and greenery in the pleasant courtyard.

MUSÉE DES BEAUX ARTS

## Musée des Tissus (Fabric Museum)

34 rue de la Charité
04 78 38 42 00
www.musee-des-tissus.com
10.00-12.00, 14.00-17.30
closed Monday and holidays
€4.60

There are several small museums in Lyon but this is the most outstanding collection. Naturally Lyon's own silk-weaving industry features prominently, but this is just a part of a large collection of fabric from all over the world. Exhibits include textiles from ancient Greece, Rome, and Persia where the colours and workmanship were superb.

The light is kept low to protect the richness of the colours, and the overall effect is breathtaking.

## Vieux Lyon

Its narrow streets may be packed with visitors but the sense of history remains. There are over 300 Renaissance mansions in this cramped quarter. Look in the courtyards to see old stairways, doors and windows, that in some cases haven't changed for a few hundred years. Access is free, but be mindful of the fact that these are people's homes, not tourist attractions.

Signs indicating *traboules* mark the covered alleys that link streets and pass through courtyards, once used by silk weavers to keep their goods dry in wet weather. Others exist in the Croix Rousse district.

These streets gave birth to the marionette character *Guignol,* his wife *Madelon* and Beaujolais-drinking friend *Grafron.* These puppets created by a silk weaver are still seen and celebrated today. The **Musée International de la Marionette,** housed inside the **Musée Historique de Lyon** collects examples of these and other puppets from around the world.

VIEUX LYON FROM RIVER SAÔNE

### Cathédrale St-Jean

An essential part of the old town is the Cathédrale St-Jean, which faces away from the Saône and La Presqu'île. Ornate carvings decorate the door on the west side. Inside are original Gothic stained glass windows and a 14th century astronomical clock. This fascinatingly detailed machine tells the time, day, date and feast day, with moving ornamental figures.

place St Jean
08.00-12.00, 14.00-19.00 Mon-Fri
08.00-12.00 and 14.00-17.00 Sat-Sun, free

## Fourvière

Near the Cathédrale St-Jean entrance is the funicular that leads up to Fourvière. More energetic visitors may prefer to walk, as there are enjoyable views over the rooftops, but some of the streets climb incredibly steeply.

### Notre-Dame de Fourvière
8 place de Fourvière
08.00-19.00 daily, free

At the top of the hill stands the ornate Basilica, built in the late 19th century and visible from all over the city. Even the fanciful exterior does not prepare you for the glorious interior.

Large decorated pillars either side of the nave support the high roof, made up of a series of domes painted in turquoise and gold. The walls have similar turquoise and gold mosaics of grand Biblical scenes, while the entire floor is covered in patterned mosaics. A stone balcony runs beneath the high stained glass windows and above each window is an elaborately decorated arch. A unique and impressive church.

### Musée de la Civilisation Gallo-Romaine
17 rue Cléberg
04 72 38 49 30
10.00-18.00 Tues-Sun, €3.80

### Roman Theatres
6 rue de l'Antiquaille; 04 72 38 81 90
09.00-dusk daily, free

Notre Dame de Fourvière is thought to be located on the site of an ancient Roman Forum in the settlement they named Lugdunum. Not much remains apart from two Roman amphitheatres, today used for concerts. The museum is worth seeing for the dramatically lit statues, models of the ancient settlement and superb mosaics – as good as any in Italy or North Africa.

## La Croix Rousse

The Croix Rousse quarter of Lyon takes its name from a cross made of red stone which once stood on top of the hill to the north of La Presqu'île. It became the centre for Lyon's silk-weaving industry, a poor part of the city where the workers lived. Today it is still a working area, though the silk industry has all but died out. Most people go to see the Maison des Canuts, the Roman remains and the great views over Lyon.

Walk up through the winding streets north of place des Terreaux, or take the metro to the top and walk down. Before you go, pick up a booklet from the Tourist Office to help guide your route down through some of the old passageways leading through courtyards and around houses. These enabled silk workers to get from one street to the next while sheltering from the weather. You need the leaflet as the entrances to the passages are often closed and look like private doorways.

### Maison des Canuts

10-12 rue d'Ivry
04 78 28 62 04
10.00-18.30 Tues-Sat, closed Sun-Mon
free (guided tour in French €5)

Not much remains of the silk-weaving business these days, but here you can learn more about the trade and see examples of modern work. The shop has a workroom at the back where some of the old silk looms are kept. Twice a day at 11.00 and 15.30 a guide gives a talk about the looms and the silk-weaving business.

The shop sells beautifully-coloured examples of modern silk production: ties, scarves, wraps and other items of clothing.

## Centre d'Histoire de la Résistance et de la Déportation

Lyon was the centre for the French Resistance during World War II. It was a dark period in both the city's and the country's history and it is powerfully remembered here – in the former Gestapo headquarters.

Exhibits remind us that some of Lyon's most beautiful places have ugly stories: for example, the execution of five resistance workers, members of the Secret Army, at place Bellecour. The effect of the holocaust on Lyon's Jewish population is graphically described in videos, photos and newspaper cuttings. A visit here is certainly powerful and sombre, but it is also full of uplifting stories of the bravery of French men and women who fought and gave their lives for the cause of freedom.

14 avenue Berthelot
04 72 73 99 06
09.00-17.30 Wed-Sun
closed Mon-Tue and
public holidays
€3.80

MUSÉE LUMIÈRE

## Musée Lumière

25 rue du Premier Film
04 78 78 18 95
www.institut-lumiere.org
11.00-18.30 Tues-Sun, closed Mon
€6

East of the city centre but easily reached on the metro is the home of the Lumière brothers, now a museum with a cinema in the grounds. The entrance to the museum is the gate through which several factory workers walked in 1895 while being filmed by the brothers Auguste and Louis Lumière. This rare film is now generally accepted as the first motion picture.

The achievements of the film-making dynasty are exhibited in what was once the home of the Lumière family. The brothers invented the motion picture camera and many of their old cameras are on display. Selections from the vast archive of motion pictures are continuously screened, including some of the first travel films ever made. The brothers sent cinematographers around the world to the Pyramids, Venice, Tunis, New York and Shanghai, to bring the first moving images of foreign countries back to France. The house itself is worth seeing, and was nicknamed Château Lumière by locals.

Lyon is recognised (even by the French) as a gourmet capital of France. Master of modern cuisine, Paul Bocuse, has his flagship restaurant at Pont de Collonges. He also has five brasseries within the city, including Argenson near the stadium. In all, there are some 25 restaurants in and around Lyon with one or more Michelin stars.

Local food tends to be earthy, with black pudding, tripe, sausage and charcuterie among the regular items on the menu. Another speciality is *quenelles*, a kind of pike dumpling that comes in various guises. Carp and *cuisses de grenouilles* (frogs' legs) are also common. Vegetarians may face a challenge, for even the simple *salade Lyonnaise* will be served with chopped pieces of bacon known as *lardons*.

## Restaurants

See page 287 for price guide.

### Dining tip
Be aware that a *saladier Lyonnais* is a *salade Lyonnais* that has been embellished with delicacies such as sheep's foot, calf's foot or beef muzzle. The amusingly named *tablier du sapeur*, literally the 'fireman's apron', is tripe.

### Near the stadium

**Argenson**
40 allée Pierre de Courbertin
04 72 73 72 73
12.00-14.30 and 19.00-23.00 (Fri-Sat till 24.00)
booking recommended, credit cards accepted
€€€
This road behind the Stade de Gerland seems an unlikely setting for a brasserie owned by star chef Paul Bocuse, but inside it's a smart and lively place. The food may lack the elaboration of his Michelin-starred flagship, but dishes such as lamb cooked with thyme flowers or shrimp risotto show the master's touch. The wine list is good but expensive.

**JOLS**
283 avenue Jean-Jaurès
04 78 72 10 10
12.00-14.00 and 19.30-23.00 Mon-Sat
booking recommended on match days
credit cards accepted
€€
Halfway between the Debourg and Stade de Gerland metro stations is this cheerful fish restaurant, with very modern decor and a popular bar. Start with fresh oysters or fish soup, then try the delicious mussels steamed in a thyme and lemon sauce with spicy *pommes frites*. A simple pot of house wine is available for under ten euros and there is also a good list. The menu offers plenty of meat and pasta choices but it is fish dishes that are the speciality.

### Bouchons
Lyon has a unique kind of eating place known as a *bouchon*. No-one is quite sure where the name comes from, as *bouchon* is the word for a cork in a bottle. Some say this is the source, others claim the word comes from *bousche,* a bottle-stopper made from straw or leaves which would hang outside Lyon's bistros to indicate their business in the days before mass literacy. Or it could originate from *bouchonner*, meaning to rub down a horse, because these were eating places for travellers. Whatever the roots, in a *bouchon* you will find local food served at reasonable prices in a casual atmosphere. Regional wines will be on the menu, and can be bought in a *pichet* or pot. The standard measure for these is 46cl, though you can get them in quarter, half and litre sizes too. Many new restaurants in Lyon simply call themselves *bouchons* when they open, because visitors like to eat in a *bouchon*, but the older ones have great atmospheres and value-for-money food.

DINING, RUE SAINT-JEAN

## Gourmet dining

### Paul Bocuse
40 quai la Plage, au pont de Collonges nord
04 72 42 90 90
www.bocuse.com
12.00-13.30 and 20.00-21.30 daily
booking essential
credit cards accepted
€€€€
If you only have one special meal in Lyon
then it has to be at this three Michelin-starred
flagship restaurant of one of the world's
great chefs. The restaurant is located six
miles from the city centre and is an easy taxi
ride. Begin your meal with the classic black
truffle soup, created in 1975 for the French
President, and end with the chocolate cake
in hommage to Maurice Bernachon. Every
mouthful between will be a well-savoured
memory.

## In the centre of Lyon

### Léon de Lyon
1 rue Pléney (south of place des Terreaux)
04 72 10 11 12
www.leondelyon.com
12.00-14.00 and 19.30-22.00 Tues-Sat
booking essential
credit cards accepted
€€€€
Jean-Paul Lacombe is one of the city's leading
chefs with two Michelin stars. He continues to
set high standards for his versions of the local
speciality, *quenelles*. Jean-Paul excels at roast
meat; his suckling pig and lamb are house
favourites. The restaurant decor is formal,
with gilt-framed paintings on the walls; the
dishes too are works of art.

### Le Bouchon aux Vins
62 rue Mercière (near metro Cordeliers)
04 78 38 47 40
12.00-22.30 daily
booking required on weekends
credit cards accepted
€€€
An ordinary name for an extraordinarily good
place. There are tables on the street and in two
large stone-walled rooms inside. The wine list
is extensive with many sold by the glass. The
cooking is inventive: try cold yellow pepper
soup with anchovy sauce, pork ribs with
honey and ginger or a mouth-watering dessert
of *crème brûlée au poivre de Séchouan*.

**FOOD & DRINK**

### Le Cabaretier
6 rue de la Fronde (off rue Saint-Jean)
04 78 42 38 11
www.bouchon-le-cabaretier-lyon.com
12.00-14.00 Fri-Sun, 19.00-23.00 Mon-Sat
booking recommended
credit cards accepted
€€€

One of the best spots in Vieux Lyon. This quirky place has a decades-old décor from puppets to petrol pumps, with candle-lit tables in the evening. A range of menus appeals to all budgets, and the quality of the food means it's always busy. Especially good are snails in Roquefort, followed by fillet of beef in a pepper sauce or (for two) braised beef cooked in its own juices.

### Le Cyrano
49 rue Mercière (near metro Cordeliers)
04 78 38 13 44
12.00-14.00 and 19.00-23.00 daily
booking not usually necessary
credit cards accepted
€€

Tables are crowded together in the cosy and low-lit dining room of this busy *bouchon*. Converse with your neighbours as you study the menu of Lyonnaise and other regional specialities. *Calamari provençal*, squid cooked in a tomato sauce, has a fresh taste of the sea and the *andouillette* with a mustard sauce has a delicious spicy zing.

### Le Bistrot de Lyon
64 rue Mercière (near Metro Cordeliers)
04 78 38 47 47
12.00-14.30 and 19.00-24.00 daily
19.00-01.00 Fri-Sat, 19.00-23.00 Sun

book on weekends
credit cards accepted
€€

There's a wonderful Belle Epoque style to this bistro, with an ornate ceiling and big mirrors behind a long bar. The bar is very popular and while you shouldn't have to book, there can be a wait on busy evenings. Local specialities include Lyon sausage served on a bed of green lentils with a red Beaujolais sauce, and pike dumplings.

### Le Tire-Bouchon
16 rue du Boeuf (parallel to rue Saint-Jean)
04 78 37 69 95
19.30-late Tues-Sat
booking suggested
credit cards accepted
€€

There are puppets in the window of the bright red frontage at this wonderful place in Vieux Lyon. Be sure to book or arrive early as it's packed with locals. Old magazine covers gaze down from the walls over marble-topped tables. A choice of set menus has French classics like escargot, foie gras, tripe and duck breast in a pepper sauce. The food is as good as the atmosphere.

### Chez Gerard
6 rue des Maronniers (east of place Bellecour)
04 78 42 76 02
12.00-14.30 and 19.00-late daily
book for large groups
credit cards accepted
€€

It can be difficult to choose a restaurant in this pedestrian street lined with eating options, but Chez Gerard offers consistent

quality. There are tables outside and inside in a pink-walled dining room, as well as an additional room upstairs. Waiters disappear down the back stairs and re-appear carrying plates of delicious Lyonnais food including a tasty *boudin noir aux deux pommes*. There are set menus for all budgets, and inexpensive wine. Perfect.

**Le Tablier Bouchon Lyonnais**
10 rue Saint-Jean
04 72 41 96 20
www.letablier-lyon.com
11.30-14.30 and 18.30-24.00 daily
booking not usually necessary
no credit cards
€€
This is a new name on the Lyon restaurant scene in the crowded rue Saint-Jean, so they're trying hard with friendly service. They have bright yellow tables outside and a beautiful stone-vaulted cellar inside. The *salade gourmande* is excellent, a huge plate with tasty *foie gras,* duck breast and chicken giblets. They also have a good variety of *prix-fixe* menus.

**Brasserie Georges**
30 cours de Verdun Perrache
04 72 56 54 54
www.brasseriegeorges.com
08.00-24.00 daily
booking not usually necessary
credit cards accepted
€
A Lyon institution since 1836, this is the archetypal big French brasserie. You won't find inventive cuisine but you will find brisk and friendly service of Lyonnais and other French standards, at reasonable prices. The Art Deco building can seat 650, and the ceiling frescos alone are worth the price of a meal. Stick to staples such as veal stew, Lyonnais sausage or the daily special.

**Chez Martial**
31 rue Saint-Jean
04 78 37 78 30
12.00-24.00 daily
booking not usually necessary
credit cards accepted
€
This little place has tables outside on the popular pedestrian street, while inside are stone walls, huge mirrors and colourful artworks. There's a good range of fixed-price menus: three courses might include an excellent onion soup, steak *au poivre* and the dessert of the day, while a pot of wine is just €9.

# Shopping

Shops are open from 10am-7pm, but some smaller family-run businesses close for lunch. Shops are closed on Sundays.

Two things set Lyon's shopping apart – food and fashion. It's known as a gourmet's paradise, so the excellent food shops and markets are no surprise. Lyon has a large number of top designer stores.

## Fashion

Rue President Edouard Herriott, which runs off place Bellecour, is one of the best designer streets with Max Mara, Dior, Lacoste, Louis Vuitton, Mont Blanc, Cartier and Hermès, as well as some names not widely known outside France, like Chacok and Alain Manoukian. And round the corner at the other end of the street on place des Jacobins is Sonia Rykiel, and a large branch of Printemps.

### Eden Park

6 rue Jean de Tournes (off rue de President Edouard Herriot)
04 78 37 09 96; ww.eden-park.tm.fr
Established in 1987 by French rugby players Franck Mesnel and Eric Blanc who added a pink bow tie to their club kit for the French Championship final match. The chain is known for its quality wearable fashions with a strong rugby theme.

## Markets

### Arts and Crafts

quai Roman Rolland and quai Fulchiron
07.00-13.30 Sunday
On the west bank of the Saône on the edge of Vieux Lyon, dozens of artists and crafts people gather to set up stalls. This is no ordinary craft market, as the standard of workmanship is superb. There are plenty of stalls selling paintings of local landmarks, as you find anywhere, but here also are fine art photographers, sculptors in metal and bronze, toy makers, potters, jewellers and workers in *papier maché*. Buskers entertain, while the bells of Nôtre-Dame ring out from above.

### Books

#### Marché aux Bouquinistes

quai de la Pecherie and quai Saint-Antoine
all day Sat and Sun (near pont de la Feuillée)
Dozens of stalls selling secondhand and antique books on the banks of the Saône.

### Food market

quai Saint-Antoine (east of pont Alphonse Juin)
07.00-12.30 Tues-Sun
Located along the east bank of the Saône where producers from all over the region sell their goods. Even if you aren't able to buy the fresh produce you can find local wines, preserves and other delicacies that will last till you return home. For the browser, and photographer, there are stalls devoted to cheese, to mushrooms, to seafood, and every fruit and vegetable grown in the region.

### Organic Market

place Carnot, immediately in front of gare Perrache
16.00-19.00 Wed, 05.00-13.30 Sun.
An organic fruit and vegetable market.

### Farmers market

boulevard de la Croix Rousse
Saturday mornings
A large general market in the Croix Rousse district.

### Main market

boulevard de la Croix Rousse
08.00-13.30 Tues-Sun
A mix of food and general household goods.

## Food Shops

### Pierre Champion

4 place Bellecour
A fine food shop which specialises in *foie gras* and that other southern speciality, *cassoulet*. He also sells wine, tea, coffee, liqueurs,

**VISA**

ARTS AND CRAFTS MARKET

## Vieux Lyon

At first glance the old quarter seems nothing but souvenir shops and restaurants. Look more closely and you will find some interesting shops, especially near the Cathédrale Saint-Jean.

### Artisans du Monde
14 rue de la Bombardeis
A Fair Trade shop selling crafts from around the world.

### Vincent Breed
16 rue de la Bombardeis
www.cercleverre.com
The glassmaker extraordinaire displays a colourful range of lamps, glassware and 'arts de la table'.

### Diogène
29 rue Saint-Jean
An excellent bookshop with thousands of old volumes on every subject – including rugby.

### Le Bois Debout Gravures
34 rue Saint-Jean
Selling old prints *(gravures anciennes)* with a large stock of nature, history, fashion, travel and other charming items.

## Centre Commercial
Part-Dieu district, opposite gare Part-Dieu.
09.30-20.00 Mon-Sat
One of Europe's largest shopping malls with three floors and a total of 260 shops. Major French chain stores are here including FNAC, (selling CDs, DVDs, games) and Galeries Lafayette. There are several bars, cafés restaurants and some fine food shops.

## Antiques and Galleries

### Boutique Henri Germain
11 rue Auguste Comte, off place Bellecour
04 78 42 69 79
The shop dates back to 1660 and the owner's ancestors are all listed inside, with the names of the kings they served. The store specialises in silk and wallpapers, and is a cross between shop, gallery and museum.

### Cité des Antiquaires
117 boulevard de Stalingrad; 04 72 69 00 00
www.cite-antiquaires.fr
A gallery of more than 120 antique dealers located east of Parc de la Tête d'Or.

mustard, pickles, jams and other tasty treats.

### Voisin
11 place Bellecour
The branch of the famous chain selling chocolates, cakes and pastries.

### Bernachon
42 cours Franklin-Roosevelt
04 78 24 37 98
www.bernachon.com/shopguide
They have been called the best chocolate makers in France, and top chefs pay top prices to have Bernachon chocolate in their dishes. No lover of chocolate can visit Lyon without making a pilgrimage. A house speciality is a *Palais d'Or*, a thin, chocolate wafer sprinkled with real flakes of edible gold leaf. The tasty morsels in their selection box will make you think you've died and ascended to chocolate heaven.

# Golf and other sports

Lyon's citizens may love their food but there are plenty of golf, cycling and other sports to ensure that health and figure are maintained.

## Golf

### Golf de Lyon
Villette d'Anthon, 12 miles east of Lyon
04 78 31 11 33
www.golfclubdelyon.com
08.00-18.00 daily (Sat-Sun till 19.00)
Two wooded 18 hole courses, one flat and one hilly – both have very good holes and challenging golf. Large lakes make for a picturesque and placid setting, and both courses are dotted with bronze animal sculptures. There is a practice ground, putting green and pro shop. The clubhouse has a bar and restaurant, and a terrace overlooking the 18th hole of one of the courses. Advance booking is advisable.

### Golf de Lyon Verger
1350 chemin de l'Allemande
69360 Saint Symphorien d'Ozon
04 78 02 84 20
www.golf-lyonverger.com
Just fifteen minutes south of Lyon's centre is the Golf du Verger, built around the owner's orchard. Exceptional drainage makes it possible to play all year long in an atmosphere of verdant parkland. An enjoyable course, with its greens well protected by shrewdly situated bunkers.

### Golf Club de Mionnay
Le Beau Logis; 01390 Mionnay
04 78 91 84 84
www.golfclubmionnay.com
An attractive course with plenty of water – in fact, you may find yourself sharing the fairway with a family of ducks! There's a bar and restaurant (food at lunchtimes only), but for a real eating experience, the course is handily just around the corner from the Restaurant Alain Chapel (two Michelin stars). Chapel was one of the founding fathers of nouvelle cuisine, but don't let that put you off: the food here stays true to the original ideal of the best and freshest ingredients presented beautifully, and never descends into frippery or minimalism.

## Cycling

Lyon has an excellent bike-rental scheme. Throughout the city are stands of red bikes – insert your credit card in the machine and remove the bike. It couldn't be simpler. The charge is a mere €1 per hour. The scheme has been so successful that it is constantly being expanded, with more bikes and new stands.

If you want to get out of the city you can rent bikes at this Lyon branch of the French chain:

### Holiday Bikes
199 rue Vendome
04 78 60 11 10
www.holiday-bikes.com

## Tennis

### Tennis Club de Lyon
3 boulevard du 11 Novembre
69100 Villeurbanne; 04 78 89 49 68
www.tennisclublyon.com
Villeurbanne is located east of La Presqu'île. There are 16 outdoor courts, 10 covered courts and a gym.

### Lyon Métropole Sports
84 quai Joseph Gillet (Hotel Lyon Métropole)
04 78 29 53 28

### Tennis Club de la Pape,
323 boulevard Marcel Yves-André
04 78 88 76 64

## Swimming

There are several swimming pools throughout the city.

**Piscine Municipale**
349 avenue Jean Jaures; 04 78 72 66 17
chemin André Latarjet; 04 78 74 33 09

**Garibaldi Swimming Pool**
221 rue Garibaldi; 04 78 60 89 66

**Saint-Exupéry Swimming Pool**
11 rue Pétrus Sambardier; 04 78 29 80 66

## Spa and Fitness

**OL Beauté**
9 Rue Grolée; 04 78 92 90 90
09.00-18.30 Tues-Sat, till 21.00 Thurs
To find out what helps make Olympique Lyonnais one of the top teams in France, book a session here at their favourite spa. Run by local health, fashion and fitness guru Christine Margossian, and designed along feng shui lines, the spa is open to men and women. Sample the various treatments and massages Christine has developed.

## Bowling

**Bowling du 8eme**
80 rue Marius Berliet
04 78 01 21 65
www.bowling-du-8eme.com
14.00-02.00 daily (04.00 at weekends)
It has 14 lanes, 13 pool tables, video games and a bar.

## Boule Lyonnaise

A game similar to boules was played by ancient Egyptians with polished stones and by the Romans with coconuts from Africa. The modern form of pétanque was invented as recently as 1907. It is now played by 17 million people per year in France, and the Fédération Française de Pétanque is the fourth largest sporting body in the country.

In Lyon they play a version called sport-boules or *Boule Lyonnaise*, which is much closer in spirit to the original Provençal game: the boules are launched at a run, and must land within 50cm of the target to be valid. It is the most athletic of the boules games, of which the Lyonnais are justly proud. The following are public Boulodrômes where anyone can join.

**Boules la Favorite**
112 rue Pierre Aubry

**Boules du Château**
boulevard de la Duchère

**Boules Jean Zay**
rue Jean Zay

or if you'd prefer the quieter game of pétanque:

**Parc du Vallon**
boulevard de la Duchère; 69009 Lyon

# Lyon is perfectly located for wine lovers, with Mâcon vineyards to the north and the Rhône river to the south.

## Mâcon vineyards

Mâcon has long been a centre of the wine trade, and the gateway to both the Mâconnais and Beaujolais vineyards. The town is 45 miles due north of Lyon along the A6, with a journey time of about 40-50 minutes. There are also frequent trains from Lyon, taking from 30-60 minutes depending on the number of stops.

**Mâcon**
• tour the Chardonnay vineyards
**Rhône cruise**
• a beautiful way to visit the Rhône valley
**Vienne and St-Romain-en-Gal**
• twin towns on the banks of the Rhône

If you're touring around, a stop at the Tourist Office will provide you with details of twelve different wine routes taking in such names as Chardonnay, Ozenay and Pouilly. You can visit vineyards and stock up on supplies. Many vineyards also serve an excellent lunch.

**Mâcon Tourist Office**
1 place St Pierre; 03 85 38 42 06
www.macon-tourism.com
09.30-19.30 Monday-Saturday
09.30-12.30 Sunday and holidays

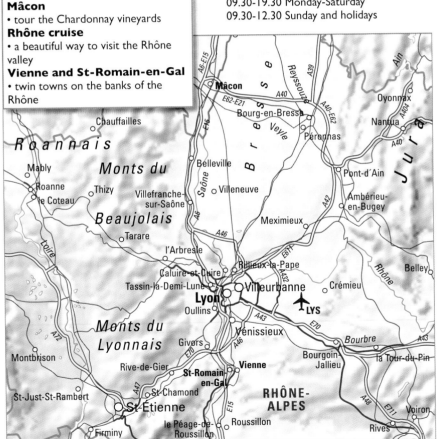

# Rhône river cruise

Situated on the upper Rhône, Lyon is the ideal place from which to embark on a river cruise. If you're short of time you can take a round trip to Vienne to view its Roman theatre, or if you have a longer holiday you can voyage as far as Martigues in the Camargue. On the way you'll pass through nougat country at Montélimar, cruise under the walls of Avignon's papal palace and perhaps stop off to savour Van Gogh's Arles. As an added bonus you'll always be in the heart of the Côtes du Rhône winelands, and never far from a bottle of France's finest.

www.rhonerivercruise.com
www.eurorivercruises.com
www.deilmann.co.uk/pages/rivercruises.html

# Vienne and St-Romain-en-Gal

There are some ugly industrial areas south of Lyon, but there are also the pretty twin towns of Vienne and St-Romain-en-Gal, facing each other across the Rhône.

In Roman times, the twin towns served as the main port for the import and export of wine on the Rhône. Wine production in France during the Roman Empire flourished to such an extent that there was, as there is today, a glut of wine. Romans responded by ordering half the French vineyards (but not the Italian ones, of course) be torn up.

Vienne is pleasant to explore, with Roman ruins scattered throughout the town. There are two Roman theatres, and a temple, as well as smaller ruins. The Cathédrale St-Maurice is vast, and there is a small Beaux-Arts Museum and the Musée de la Draperie. This is fascinating if you have some knowledge about silk weaving in Lyon, as here are some well-preserved ancient working looms.

Across the river is St-Romain-en-Gal and the **Musée Archéologique de St-Romain-en-Gal**, the town's main archaeological site. It is still undergoing excavation, but many beautiful artifacts have already been discovered, including colourful and well-preserved Roman mosaics.

**Getting there**
Vienne is 30 minutes from Lyon by train. By car it's about 20 miles south of Lyon, straight down the A7. The road passes St-Romain-en-Gal, on the far side of the Rhône from Vienne, where the train station is located. It is only a short walk between the two towns.

**Tourist Office**
cours Brillier, near the junction with quai Jean-Jaurès
04 74 53 80 30
www.vienne-tourisme.com
Mon-Sat:
09.00-12.00, 14.00-18.00
Sun:
10.00-12.00, 14.00-17.00

**Musée Archéologique de St-Romain-en-Gal**
10.00-18.00 Tues-Sun
closed Mon; €3.80

SAINT-ÉTIENNE

# Scotland plays two matches in Saint-Étienne, one against Italy, and USA plays Samoa.

**Getting around Saint-Étienne**
Public transport is run by STAS, with an extensive network that goes out to the stadium. At the time of writing a new tram line is being built through the city centre and out to the railway station.
You can buy tickets which allow you access to trams and buses for one hour or one day, or buy a book of ten tickets.
Purchase tickets at tobacconists or at STAS ticket office: place Dorian
04 77 33 31 35
www.stas.tm.fr
Place Dorian is a main bus and tram station, off the southeast corner of place de l'Hôtel de Ville.

**Tourist Office**
16 avenue de la Libération
08 92 70 05 42
09.00-19.00 Mon-Sat
09.00-12.00 Sun

Saint-Étienne has an industrial history, and is renowned in France as a coal-mining city and a manufacturer of arms. It comes as a surprise, then, to find an attractive city centre with pleasant squares surrounded by rolling green hills.

Rugby World Cup 2007 fans will most likely gather in the large attractive central square, place Jean-Jaurès, where there are several lively bars and restaurants. One side of the square backs on to the Hôtel de Ville, or town hall, where giant screens may be placed for showing live matches. All around the square, the local bars and cafés will be invited to set up stalls to sell food and drink.

It is almost 25 years since the last coal pit closed in Saint-Étienne, and what was history has now become heritage as the city tries to understand and celebrate its past. The Musée de la Mine is a powerful display exploring the coal-mining heritage of the area, while the Musée d'Art et d'Industrie is an excellent museum with collections on three of Saint-Étienne's other industries: ribbon-making, cycle production and the manufacture of arms.

The city's cultural side is on display in the Musée d'Art Moderne, which has the best collection of modern art after the Pompidou Centre in Paris.

PLACE DU PEUPLE

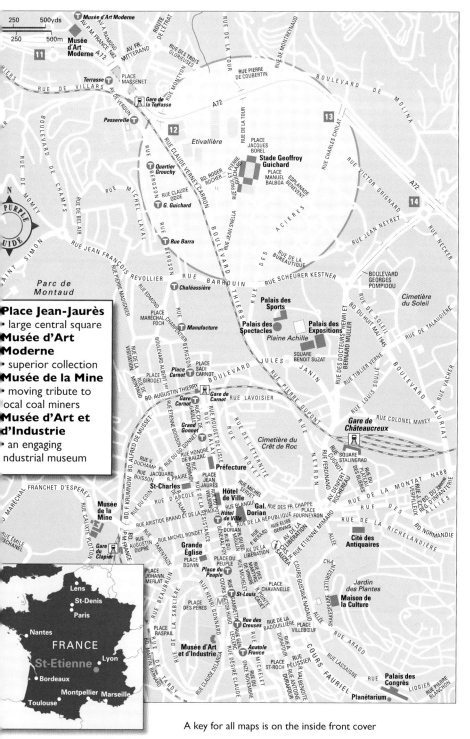

250   500yds
250   500m

**11**

Musée d'Art Moderne
AV. P.M. FRANCE N82

Musée
d'Art
Moderne A72

AV. FR.
MITTERAND

ROUTE
DE L'ETRAT

RUE DES TROIS
GLORIEUSES

RUE DE LA TOUR

RUE DE MONTREYNAUD

AV. P.M. RAIMOND

ROUTE
DE L'ETRAT

RUE PIERRE
DE COUBERTIN

BOULEVARD   DE   MOLINA

Terrasse
PLACE
MASSENET

Gare de
la Terrasse

RUE   DE   VILLARS

AV. DE VERDUN

A72

Passerelle

RUE DE LA TOUR

**12**

Etivallière

PLACE
JACQUES
BOREL

**13**

RUE CHARLES CHOLAT

RUE CLAUDE VERNEY

RUE PAUL ET PIERRE
RUE PUIGCHALK

Stade Geoffroy
Guichard

PLACE
MANUEL
BALBOA

ESPLANADE
BENEVENT

RUE   VICTOR   GRIGNARD

A72

Quartier
Grouchy

BD. ROGER
ROCHER

CARRON

RUE CLAUDE
ODDE

**14**

G. Guichard

ACIÈRES

RUE JEAN NEYRET

RUE   NECKER

Rue Barra

RUE JEAN SNELLA

RUE DE LA
BUREAUTIQUE

RUE   DES

Parc de
Montaud

RUE BARRIOUIN

RUE SCHEÜRER KESTNER

BOULEVARD
GEORGES
POMPIDOU

Cimetière
du Soleil

Chaléassière

RUE   DES

**Place Jean-Jaurès**
• large central square

Palais des
Sports

BD. DU HUIT MAI 1945

RUE   DE   TALAUDIÈRE

**Musée d'Art
Moderne**
• superior collection

Manufacture

Palais des
Spectacles

Plaine Achille

Palais des
Expositions

RUE DES DOCTEURS
BERNARD MULLER

BOULEVARD

**Musée de la Mine**
• moving tribute to
local coal miners

SQUARE
BENOIT SUZAT

RUE TIBLIER VERNE

RUE LOUIS SOULIÉ

RUE VACHER

**Musée d'Art et
d'Industrie**
• an engaging
industrial museum

Place
Carnot

PLACE
SADI
CARNOT

JULES

JANIN

RUE PIERRE DUPONT

Gare de
Carnot   RUE LAVOISIER

Gare de
Châteaucreux   RUE COLONEL MAREY

RUE   LOUIS   SOULIÉ

RUE   VACHER

Gare
Carnot

Grand
Gonnet

Cimetière du
Crêt de Roc

SQUARE
STALINGRAD

RUE
NEYRON

Préfecture

RUE DE L'ÉTERNITÉ

AV. DENFERT
ROCHEREAU

RUE DE LA MONTAT   N488

Musée
de la
Mine

Gare
du
Clapier

St-Charles

PLACE
JEAN
JAURÈS

Hôtel
de Ville

Gal.
Dorian

RUE DES FR. CHAPPE

PLACE
FOURNEYRON

RUE   DE   LA   RICHELANDIÈRE

Hôtel
de Ville

RUE DE LA
RÉPUBLIQUE

Cité des
Antiquaires

BD. NORMANDIE

Grande
Église

PLACE
BOIVIN

Place du
Peuple

COURS GUSTAVE NADAUD

Jardin
des Plantes

Maison de
la Culture

PLACE
CHAVANELLE

St-Louis

Rue des
Creuses

RUE DE LA
BADOUILLÈRE

PLACE
VILLEBŒUF

Musée d'Art
et d'Industrie

Anatole
France

PLACE
ST-ROCH

COURS   FAURIEL

Palais des
Congrès

Planétarium

FRANCE

Lens

St-Denis

Paris

Nantes

St-Etienne   Lyon

Bordeaux

Montpellier   Marseille

Toulouse

## STADE GEOFFROY-GUICHARD

## Getting to the stadium

The easiest way to get to the stadium is on the city's STAS tram network.

**Nearest airport**

The Aéroport de Saint-Étienne-Bouthéon is about 10km from the stadium, and has its own train station linking it with the Gare Saint-Étienne Chateaucreux in the city centre.

**Car**

The stadium is north of the city centre, about 1km off the A47. From Lyon the journey time is about 40-50 minutes. Those travelling by car should use public carparks around the city and walk or take a bus to the stadium.

**Train**

The city's main station is Saint-Étienne Chateaucreux, about 2km from the stadium. Taxis are available, and a new tram link is being built between the station and the town centre, from where it is easy to catch another tram to the stadium.

**Bus**

Take Line 9 north to the stop for the stadium.

**Tram**

Take Line 4 north to the stop for the stadium.

REMEMBER TO PURCHASE YOUR TRANSPORT TICKETS WELL IN ADVANCE OF THE MATCH TO SAVE TIME QUEUING.

| Stade Geoffroy-Guichard capacity 35,650 | | |
| --- | --- | --- |
| Matches | Date | Pool |
| Scotland v Portugal | 9 September, Sun | C |
| Samoa v USA | 26 September, Wed | A |
| Scotland v Italy | 29 September, Sat | C |

## The stadium and around

14 rue Paul-et-Pierre-Guichard

04 77 92 31 70

'This is the Cauldron' reads the sign above the tunnel as you walk out onto the pitch of Saint-Étienne's Geoffroy-Guichard stadium, reminding visitors of its reputation as a fearsome place in which to play. Built in the English fashion, with four separate stands looming over the pitch, it seems to put the fans right into the faces of the players. The stadium was opened in 1931 and named after the businessman who provided the funding, a local man who founded the Casino supermarket empire. This is home of the Saint-Étienne soccer team, known throughout France as *'les verts'* (the greens), a nickname earned in the 1970s when they were regularly league champions, cup winners and successful in Europe. The stadium was improved in time for the 1998 FIFA World Cup, when it hosted several matches. The teams playing here during Rugby World Cup 2007 will be feeling the heat of 'The Cauldron'.

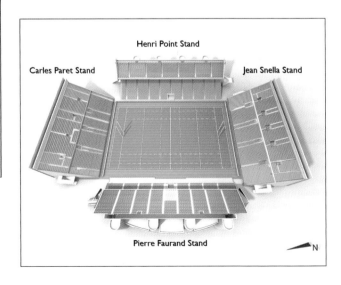

Henri Point Stand

Carles Paret Stand

Jean Snella Stand

Pierre Faurand Stand

N

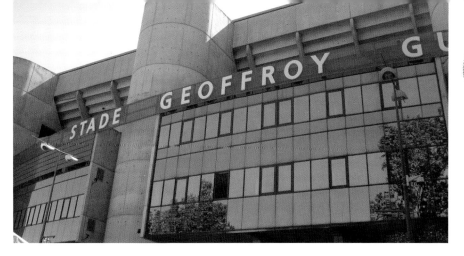

## Bars near the stadium

For restaurants near the stadium see Food & Drink.

### Le Chaudron Vert
23 rue des Trois Glorieuses (just north of A72)
04 77 74 23 18
12.00-15.00 and 19.00-23.00 Mon-Sat
open Sunday for match days
booking essential on match days
most credit cards
€€
Right by the stadium, and named after it, this casual restaurant/bar/hotel is packed on match days when they set up an outside bar and BBQ. Plain food is served on match days: roast veal with green salad and potatoes; other days offer a wider menu.

## Bars in the centre

### Rue des Martyrs de Vingré
Lined with cafés and bars, many of which have screens for sport, the street is always busy, especially off avenue de la Libération.

### Le Saint Patrick
44 rue des Martyrs de Vingré
04 77 25 11 52
There's always a convivial atmosphere in this Irish pub in the centre of town offering a large selection of whisky, beer and darts.

### Little Rock Saloon
21 rue des Martyrs de Vingré
04 77 38 92 15
Extra-large steaks, chicken wings, real hamburgers – they're all here at this country-style American steakhouse, and they have large screens.

### Le Glasgow
place de l'Hotel de Ville
One of the most popular bars in town was named after Saint-Étienne's 1976 European Cup victory against Bayern Munich in Glasgow. But it is French through and through with tables outside on the square and a smarter eating area inside. They serve typical brasserie fare with French and Belgian beers both in the bottle and on draught.

### Le Piccadilly Circus
3 place Neuve
04 77 32 28 75
Known as 'le Pica' by local students, it's a small restaurant and bar with an attractive terrace.

### The Smoking Dog
5 rue Georges Dupré
04 77 47 23 57
A British-themed bar well situated on a pedestrian street and with a large screen.

135

## Place Jean-Jaurès

The heart of Saint-Étienne's central square is a lovely fan-shaped fountain. At the north end is a small, grassy park with an ornate bandstand. The west side of the square is dominated by **Cathédral Saint-Charles**. At first sight the church's grey stone and pillars make the interior seem dark and dingy, but once your eyes adjust to the low light you can admire the beautiful mosaics and stained-glass windows, many depicting the lives of female saints. At the southern end of the square is the **Hôtel de Ville**, with shopping arcades around its base.

The biggest secret of the place Jean-Jaurès lies underneath your feet. An enormous and very smartly-designed car park takes drivers circling down underground, making maximum use of the space available.

Hôtel de Ville's grand facade overlooks **place de l'Hôtel de Ville**, where screens are planned for the duration of Rugby World Cup 2007.

## Jean Jaurès

Throughout France there are streets and squares named after Jean Jaurès. He was born in Castres in 1859 and was one of the country's first social democrats. He graduated in philosophy and became a lecturer at the University of Toulouse.

Jaurès was a passionate supporter of workers' rights. He founded the socialist newspaper *L'Humanité*, and fervently believed in the importance of free education. He was also a confirmed pacifist and, with the First World War looming, did everything within his power to persuade leaders to negotiate a solution to the impending conflict. The day before France became embroiled in the war, Jaurès was assassinated in Paris by a young, mentally unstable French nationalist who resented Jaurès' pacifist views.

Jaurès now rests in the Panthéon in Paris, while his name lives on in almost every French town and city.

## Musée d'Art Moderne

La Terrasse
04 77 79 52 52
10.00-18.00 daily, closed Tues
€4.50 (free on first Sunday of the month)

Saint-Étienne's impressive Modern Art Museum is another of the city's surprises. With 15,000 pieces, it is the biggest collection of modern art after the Pompidou Centre in Paris. Its black-tiled exterior was designed to remind visitors of the city's coal-mining past, but walk through the doors and you are greeted by vast white spaces, intended to inspire a feeling of spirituality and symbolise an outlook to the future.

It may seem unusual to find such a comprehensive modern art collection in a working class city like Saint-Étienne but industry here generated great wealth. Many of the industrialists were patrons of the arts, interested by the way in which both workers and artists used the same materials. Private collections were amassed and were later donated to the city to be housed in this museum.

Today the museum attracts 16,000 visitors annually. Many are local people who visit repeatedly. So vast is the permanent collection that it is rotated every three months, and there are also six temporary exhibitions each year.

As such, it is impossible to predict which artworks will be on display at any given time. What is certain is that the works will be impressively presented, as the large rooms and their vast white walls reinforce the impact of some striking paintings and sculpture.

Galleries are spacious, and the works are displayed so each piece can be individually appreciated. One of the collection's highlights is a very early Pablo Picasso drawing from 1905: *Nu Aux Jambes Croisées*. From more modern times, Andy Warhol is well-represented as the museum owns several of his works, including a self-portrait and a portrait of Elizabeth Taylor. Looking to the future, the museum is also proud of the work it does with children. In addition to the large numbers of annual visitors, over 20,000 children come through the doors every year, with 12 members of staff employed exclusively to work with them.

## Musée d'Art et d'Industrie
### (Art and Industry Museum)

2 place Louis Comte
04 77 49 73 00
10.00-18.00 daily
closed Tues
closed 12.30-13.30 Mon
€4.50

Saint-Étienne was once a much richer town than it is today, the wealth mainly produced through three very different industries: armaments, textiles and bicycles. These provide the three sections of this recently modernised museum, housed in a mid-19th century building originally intended for the sub-prefecture but never used for that purpose.

Still France's main city for the production of ribbons, today the fabric making industry has expanded to include the manufacture of seat belts, labels, medical fabrics and even artificial veins. In the past Saint-Étienne's workers made ribbons for priests' vestments and traditional clothing for other parts of France. For example, a traditional Brittany costume would be adorned by ribbons made here. Today the museum houses the largest collection of ribbons in the world, an astonishing three million samples, some going back over 200 years.

The weapons collection is the second-largest in France after the Musée de l'Armée in Paris. It shows the development of firearms from early cannons to elaborately decorated muskets and rifles that are works of art. There is a double-barrelled gun once owned by Napoleon, and a duck hunting rifle of Louis XIV. Since François I, Saint-Étienne has made weapons for the kings of France. Displays go right up to the present day.

The English may have invented the bicycle in the mid-19th century, but someone brought one to Saint-Étienne and the idea was quickly adopted. The city began building its own bicycles and soon became the biggest cycle production centre in France.

On display are amusing examples of quirky early bicycles, and a 1936 tandem which is said to have been invented when the French introduced the concept of paid vacations. There are bicycles where you change gear manually, or by back-pedalling, right through to modern machines where the rider changes the gears vocally. It's a fascinating collection in a fascinating museum.

## Musée de la Mine
## (Museum of Mining)

3 boulevard F. d'Esperey
04 77 43 83 23
10.00-12.45, 14.00-19.00 daily
closed Tues
guided visits in French 10.30, 15.30
last tour departs 90 mins before closing
€5.60 with guided visit

There were once 200 coal mines in Saint-Étienne alone and another 100 in the surrounding area. One of the biggest was the Couriot Mine, where 2,000 miners would come each day and descend to the coal seams, some 700m underground. The pit closed in 1973. It was re-opened as a museum in 1981, designed to be a tribute to the workers.

And a powerful tribute it is. The buildings above ground have been left more or less as they were, the most impressive being the two vast changing rooms where 900 and 1,100 miners respectively would change before and after their shifts. One of the few alterations occurred when a film company came to shoot a movie here and left behind hundreds of mining outfits

hanging from the ceiling on pulleys, just as they did in reality. It's a dramatic and eerie sight.

Further on are the miners' lamps and helmets, and the tokens labelled with miner's names, so that everyone knew who was down the mine at any one time. Tokens came in three different shapes (round, square and triangular) for the three different shifts which kept the pit working 24 hours a day. The tokens are real, from the last people to work in the mine when it closed for the final time, and the names show the multi-racial nature of the workers: French, German, Italian, North African.

You can don a helmet and ride the cage down to the reconstructed tunnels where miners would spend their working lives. After the Second World War there were almost 25,000 miners in the city: one man in every six worked in the mines. Some of the guides are ex-miners, but in the mines themselves there are now only cardboard cut-outs of the men, the horses, and the children who worked with them. Different sections of the tunnels re-create different periods of mining history. This is one of the very few mining museums in the world where visitors can go into actual mining tunnels. It's impossible not to be moved by the experience. The beauty and strength of the museum is in the simple and honest depiction of life in the mines.

### Guided Visits

While it is possible to visit the buildings above ground whenever the museum is open, the underground section can only be seen on a guided visit. These are conducted at regular times in French, but book ahead because of restrictions on visitor numbers. For guided visits in English and other languages, advance booking is required.

**FOOD & DRINK**

## Restaurants

See page 287 for price guide.

### Near the stadium

**Les Négociants**
115 rue Bergson (near tram stp Rue Barra)
04 77 93 65 28; www.lesnegociants.fr
11.30-14.00 Mon-Fri, 19.30-21.30 Fri
open before matches on Sat and Sun
closed August
booking advised on match days
credit cards accepted
€€

The best restaurant near the stadium is this buzzing old-fashioned place that's been here for 50 years. It serves up fabulous dishes such as rabbit tart in a mustard and pepper sauce at unbelievably cheap prices, and the owner puts on special themed menus when there's an international match on at the stadium, five minutes away. Check the website for these menus and for extended opening hours during Rugby World Cup 2007.

**Casino Cafétéria**
Stade Geoffroy Guichard, rue Paul et Pierre Guichard, 42000 Saint-Étienne
04 77 79 05 07; www.casino-cafeteria.fr
07.30-21.00 daily
phone ahead on match days
most credit cards
€

For a quick bite walk through the huge Saint-Étienne stadium shop and into this self-service cafeteria. It's part of a nationwide chain that was founded and still has its headquarters in Saint-Étienne. You can get simple snacks like sandwiches and burgers, or a cooked dish such as steak frites.

### In the centre of Saint-Étienne

**Restaurant André Barcet**
19 bis cours Victor Hugo (near tram stop St Louis)
04 77 32 43 63; www.restaurantandrebarcet.com
12.00-14.30 daily, closed Tues
19.00-21.30 daily, closed Sun and Tues
booking required
credit cards accepted
€€€€

Just north of place Louis Comte is a classic restaurant featuring one of the city's top chefs. Barcet has been honoured as a *Meilleur Ouvrier de France*, and his menu gourmand includes such mouthwatering dishes as asparagus with foie gras that showcase his talent. The walls are peach-coloured, the tablecloths immaculately white and the service formal. Here the food is the focus, and it deserves to be.

**Corne d'Aurochs**
18 rue Michel-Servet
04 77 32 27 27; www.aurochs.fr.st
12.00-13.45 Tue-Fri and 19.30-22.00 Mon-Sat
booking advised
credit cards accepted
€€€

A few blocks east of the place de l'Hôtel de Ville, this bistro only opened in 1986 but looks as if it's been here since 1886. Kitchen whisks hang from the ceiling, and the bull's head on the wall refers to the meatiness of the menu. *Pieds de cochon* is one speciality, while the *souri d'agneau* cooked with lemon, fennel and olive oil is delicious. The jovial owner pops out of his kitchen regularly to serve dishes or chat to the customers. One of the best places to eat in Saint-Étienne.

## L'Epicurien

13 rue Praire
04 77 41 09 19; www.epicurienrestaurant.com
12.00-14.00 Mon-Fri, 19.00-late Tue-Sat
closed Sun
booking suggested
credit cards accepted
€€€

North-west of place Jean-Jaurès is this stylish grey-walled restaurant. On a warm day try and book a table in the little courtyard out back. Menus range from €13-€65, the last including a glass of wine with each course. Mains include dishes such as a *burger de foie gras* or a 27-spice tajine, and there's a good regional wine list too. Highly recommended.

## El Sombrero

9 cours Victor Hugo (near tram stop St Louis)
04 77 32 91 22
12.00-13.45 and 19.00-22.30 daily
bookings suggested
most credit cards
€€

A few minutes walk south of the place du Peuple is this Mexican extravaganza. Multi-coloured cushions adorn black seating, while Mexican mirrors, masks and paintings line the walls. It's no surprise to learn that it won a prize for its décor. It should win one for its food too, with inventive versions of Mexican dishes such as cactus salad or red pepper with crab meat. Mexican wines and beers are served, and tequila, of course.

## Épicerie

place Massenet (near tram stop Terrasse)
04 77 21 05 87
11.30-15.00 and 18.30-late Tues-Thurs
11:30-late Fri-Sat
booking advised on weekends
credit cards accepted
€€

Off avenue la Libération is this chic *salon de thé* and restaurant, where glass-topped tables and subtle lighting create a modern, minimalist atmosphere. A choice of eleven teas is on offer, along with immaculately-presented dishes such as gazpacho Andalous or tandoori chicken, and desserts like pear soup with red wine. The food tastes as good as it looks and there's a wide range of wines by the glass.

CORNE D'AUROCHS

# Shopping

The first supermarket chain in France, **Casino**, came from Saint-Étienne.

The best shopping in the city is in the small specialist shops. A good street to find is **rue des Martyrs de Vingré**, a few blocks southeast from the Hôtel de Ville, off avenue la Libération. Close by is **rue Pierre Bérard**, lined with bookshops and stationery shops.

### Cornand
rue des Martyrs de Vingre
A fine food shop, selling olives, pastis, mustards, caviar, foie gras and other gourmet foodstuffs.

### J'ai Deux Amours
rue des Martyrs de Vingre
A shop selling the best of local design in arts, crafts and furniture.

### Le Verre Galant

JEAN-JACQUES MALEYSSON

6 rue François Gillet (off rue de la République)
04 77 37 81 79
10.00-19.00 Tues-Sat
lunch served from 12.00-14.00
Owner Jean-Jacques Maleysson has a special interest in Rugby World Cup 2007 coming to Saint-Étienne – and it's not just that he hopes to see his sales soar. Jean-Jacques played rugby for the University of Saint-Étienne, and toured England, Ireland and Scotland. 'I liked them all,' he says, 'and I am so pleased that Scotland is coming to Saint-Étienne.' A photo of Jean-Jacques with his team hangs on the wall of his shop, which has a good stock of local wines along with whiskies and armagnacs, as well as more unusual wines that catch his eye. 'I worked on a vineyard for three years,' he says, 'and then two years ago I opened my shop. I want to introduce people to the wines that I enjoy and to talk about wine with my customers.'
Le Verre Galant (The Gallant Glass) also serves an inexpensive lunch, and Jean-Jacques is applying for a bar licence in time for Rugby World Cup 2007. *Salut!*

### Weiss Chocolates

PAUL DUCASSE

8 rue du Plateau des Glières
04 77 49 41 41; www.weiss.fr
When the England team stay at their training headquarters, Pennyhill Park, they are probably unaware that they're eating chocolates made in Saint-Étienne. Weiss is the leading local chocolate maker and the shop has been here since 1882. In addition to Pennyhill Park, Weiss also supply Raymond Blanc, Fortnum and Mason, and London's Michelin-starred restaurants. They supplied superchef Alain Ducasse when he did the catering for Concorde.
'Saint-Étienne has always had a strong chocolate-making tradition,' says Weiss President, Paul Ducasse (no relation to Alain) 'The first maker came here in 1770, and at one time there were 26 chocolate-makers in the city, but now there are only five or six.

'Our chocolate is 100% produced in Saint-Étienne. We buy the beans and roast them ourselves, and only a few makers in France still do this. Half the beans come from the Ivory Coast, and we buy others from Latin America and Madagascar. All our chocolate bars have at least three different beans. African beans bring a strength to the chocolate, while Latin American beans bring a flavour and a sweetness, so we are blending all these things.'
The results are superb, and you may sample before you buy, or attend one of the special events held regularly; a recent event involved pairing wine with chocolate.

**VISA**

# Golf and other sports

The French sports magazine *L'Équipe* recently voted Saint-Étienne the third best city in France for sport. It was also voted best city in the country for sports for disabled people. With a population of 180,000 people, about 40,000 of these have a membership of at least one sports club. The city has 40 gyms, five swimming pools and 55 football pitches. Below are just a few of the options.

## Golf

**Golf de Saint-Étienne**
62 rue Saint Simon; 3km northwest of centre
04 77 32 14 63; www.golf-st-etienne.com
08.00-20.00 daily in summer
09.00-18.00 daily in winter
An 18-hole course that is open every day to non-members. Green fees start at €17 at certain times of day, otherwise it's €30 during the week and €37 at weekends. There's a large club shop and an excellent restaurant.

## Tennis

**Saint-Étienne Tennis**
130 boulevard Antonio Vivaldi; 04 77 74 69 03
www.club.fft.fr/Saint-Etienne-tennis

**Tennis Club de Saint-Étienne**
30 rue Balay; 04 77 25 90 96

**Tennis Club de l'Iseron**
Chemin des Tourettes, Saint-Victor-sur-Loire
04 77 90 58 06

## Basketball

**Le Basket Club de Saint-Étienne**
Stadium Pierre Maisonnial
24 rue Burdeau; 04 77 32 01 70
About 2km east of the city centre.

## Swimming

**Piscine R. Sommet**
35 bis Blvd Jules Janin; 04 77 43 38 38

**Piscine P. Poty**
38 rue du Dr Poty; 04 77 80 41 23

**Piscine Grouchy**
179 rue Bergson; 04 77 74 37 13

**Piscine de la Marandinière**
Blvd K. Marx; 04 77 25 01 81

## Sailing

There are several options on the Loire at the Port of Saint-Victor-sur-Loire.

**Saint-Victor Watersports Base**
04 77 90 34 92

**French Training School**
04 77 90 44 31
Training courses for people of all ages and and skill levels, including the disabled.

## Sarbacane

Saint-Étienne has a peculiar local sport called Sarbacane. A sarbacane is a blowpipe, and it's used to blow darts through, producing something that is a cross between conventional darts and a hunt from the Amazon jungle!

To learn more about it contact:

**Comité Départemental des Jeux de Sarbacane de la Loire**
Maison Départementale des Sports
4 rue des 3 Meules; 04 77 59 56 81

# The Loire is the longest river in France and it cuts a large gorge through the Massif Central just outside Saint-Étienne.

The Loire may be best-known for the châteaux along its banks as it makes its way to the sea near Nantes, but this 1000km-long river rises here in the Massif Central. Drive west from Saint-Étienne and you are immediately in beautiful rolling countryside. Drive a short 10km from the city centre to reach the stunning little village of Saint-Victor-sur-Loire.

**Saint-Victor-sur-Loire**
- village with dramatic views
**Gorges de la Loire**
- a gorge made by the Loire river
**Lac de Grangent**
- a manmade lake with plenty of boating activities
**Lyon**
- centre of gastronomy

## Saint-Victor-sur-Loire

It is usually so peaceful here that it seems like a completely new world. Walk up to the village church, dating back to the 11th century, and you are presented with truly breathtaking views of the **Loire Gorge** and **Lac de Grangent**. Here you look down on the Loire as it curves through a 360-degree loop around a small, wooded spit of land. Beyond and to the sides are tree-covered hills with hawks circling overhead. White sails glisten on the blue waters and sometimes you can catch sight of an eagle.

## Lac de Grangent

The lake was created by the Grangent Dam built on the river Loire in 1957. The Dam is about 80km from the source of the river Loire, and has created a 23km lake. It's easy to drive around the lake, and pull off at the various viewpoints, but the best way to enjoy it is to get down onto its surface and take a boat ride. The lake is used for all kinds of leisure activities, including fishing, yachting, speedboats and pedalos. A speedboat whizzes you round the lake, taking in the seabirds and fishermen, the hikers and the sunbathers, perhaps stopping to chat with a kayaker or watch an eagle soaring on the thermals. Around the lake you will see islands and a château, an idyllic youth hostel, and the village of Camaldule. In the village is a priory which was built in 1626 by monks who came from Italy and settled here. Take a trip on the lake and you'll know why they didn't want to leave.

**Bateau École C. Raffet**
2 rue des Creuses, 42000 Saint-Étienne
04 77 32 00 84
Rent a speedboat to tour the lake.

## Lyon

There's usually at least one train per hour from Saint-Étienne to either Lyon's Gare de Perrache or Gare Part-Dieu and the journey takes about 45-60 minutes. Choose Perrache if possible, as it's much nearer the main sights. If you are travelling on from Lyon, using the TGV to Paris or Marseille, these depart from Gare Part-Dieu. Lyon should not be missed if you have the time, even for a day visit.

BORDEAUX

CHÂTEAU SMITH HAUT LAFITTE

# Bordeaux will be awash in green when the Irish descend on the city for two opening matches. Canadians challenge Australians in a British colonial play-off.

Beer-drinking rugby fans may find themselves switching to wine in Bordeaux, a prosperous and sophisticated city at the centre of France's best known vineyards. Bordeaux has countless elegant squares of which place de la Bourse is the most striking – large and semi-circular, it was built facing the river in the 18th century for the booming wine trade. Wine merchants settled in the Chartrons district north of the centre, still gentrified though lately taken over by the antiques trade.

At the heart of Bordeaux is the Golden Triangle: three streets forming a triangle around the place des Grands-Hommes and Notre-Dame church. This area oozes prosperity and is filled with smart shops and restaurants as well as stylish residences.

Bordeaux has several small intimate museums located around the cathedral. Of these the Musée d'Aquitaine is by far the best, though the city is best appreciated by just being outside in the streets, enjoying the architecture... then stopping for a glass (or two) of wine.

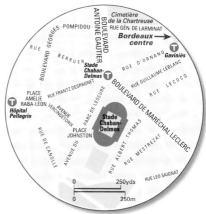

### Getting Around Bordeaux

Bordeaux has a good bus and tram network, but no metro. At the **Tourist Office**, place de la Comédie, you can buy various day passes lasting from one to six days, or from tobacconists you can get a pack of ten tickets, each one valid for an hour's travel. Don't forget to validate your ticket in the machine when you board.

PLACE DE LA BOURSE

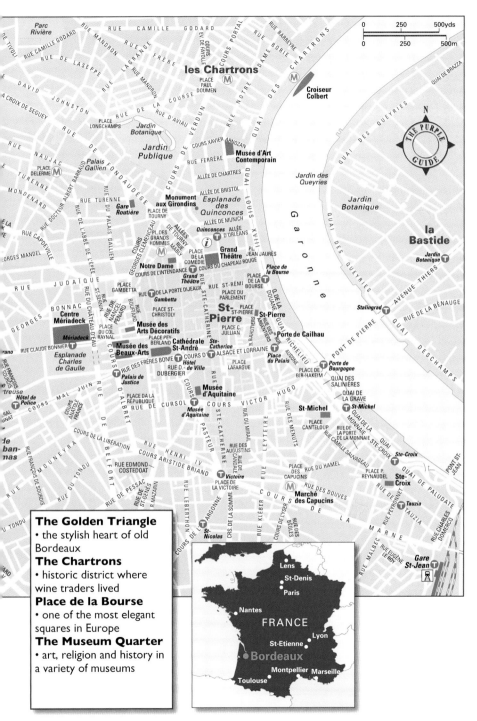

# BORDEAUX

les Chartrons

**The Golden Triangle**
• the stylish heart of old Bordeaux
**The Chartrons**
• historic district where wine traders lived
**Place de la Bourse**
• one of the most elegant squares in Europe
**The Museum Quarter**
• art, religion and history in a variety of museums

## Getting to the stadium

The stadium is about 2.5km southwest of the city centre, best reached by the city's tramway system.

**Nearest airport**
Bordeaux-Mérignac
05 56 34 50 50
About 10km west of the city centre, and the stadium. Shuttle buses run every 45 minutes to both the city centre and to the railway station. If you want to go direct to the stadium, take a taxi.

**Car**
Bordeaux is not the easiest city to drive in so it is better to take the tram. Those travelling by car should use public carparks around the city and walk or take a bus to the stadium.

**Bus**
Lines 9, 12, 26 and 93 all pass near the stadium.

**Train**
Bordeaux's main station, the Gare Saint-Jean de Bordeaux, is about 2km southeast of the city centre. The stadium is about 4km west of the station and there will be a shuttle bus services.

**Tram**
Line A to Stade Chaban-Delmas, direction Bordeaux St-Augustin, two stops before the end of the line. The journey takes 10-15 minutes.

REMEMBER TO
PURCHASE YOUR
TRANSPORT TICKETS
WELL IN ADVANCE OF
THE MATCH TO SAVE
TIME QUEUING.

## Stade Chaban-Delmas  capacity 34,462

| Matches | Date | Pool |
|---|---|---|
| Ireland v Namibia | 9 September, Sun | D |
| Ireland v Georgia | 15 September, Sat | D |
| Canada v Japan | 25 September, Tues | B |
| Australia v Canada | 29 September, Sat | B |

## The stadium and around

place Johnston
05 56 98 49 34

The stadium was new and held only 26,000 people in 1938 when France first hosted the FIFA World Cup. Brazil beat Sweden 2-1 for third place here in Bordeaux. In 1986 capacity was increased to 50,000 but later reduced to 35,000 for the 1998 FIFA World Cup Finals when Bordeaux staged several games. In 2001 the stadium was re-named to honour Jacques Chaban-Delmas (1915-2000) a long-serving Mayor of Bordeaux and a Prime Minister of France.

The Stade is primarily a football venue but it does stage several rugby games a year. France played their first international there in 1957, and various French and European cup games have graced the turf. With two games from Ireland and one from the Australians, the Chaban-Delmas stadium will be home to some of the best rugby the ground has ever seen.

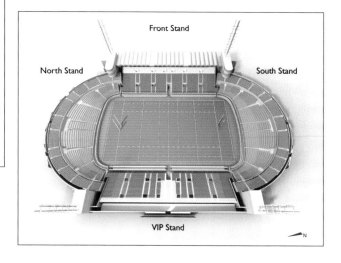

# Sports bars

## In the centre

The place de la Victoire has several bars, cafés and restaurants, and more in the surrounding streets. The area is one of the real nightlife hubs of the city.

**Connemara**
18 cours d'Albret; 05 56 52 82 57
www.connemara-pub.com
A smarter than usual Irish pub near the cathedral with nine screens in its six rooms. They show a range of sports, including rugby league and Irish hurling and also have regular live music – and Ben & Jerry's ice cream!

**Le Cafe des Sports**
5 cours de l'Argonne; 05 56 31 42 24
Bordeaux's premier sports bar is a well-known meeting place for rugby fans, and players themselves often drop in after matches. Two big screens in two bars show all games.

**Molly Malone**
83 quai des Chartrons; 05 57 87 06 72
www.molly-pub.com
On Bordeaux's waterfront is a traditionally-styled Irish pub and restaurant. Service is with a smile, and a giant screen shows rugby when available. There are also regular live music nights.

**Le Golden Apple**
46 rue Borie (Chartrons district); 05 56 70 03 85
www.britpub.net
A more tranquil bar where you can enjoy a game of darts, the Golden Apple describes itself as a 'pub brasserie Britannique'. The blend of Irish and English adds to the charm and offers a wide range of beer and whiskies.

**O'Rowlands**
50 rue de Pessac; 05 56 99 18 76
A little pub and restaurant that prides itself on being a home from home for Irish visitors. The upstairs dining room is the place to go for authentic Irish food and beer.

**The Blarney Stone**
114 cours Victor Hugo; 05 56 31 87 20
Beloved of rugby fans for its giant screen and giant breakfasts, The Blarney Stone is an English-speaking Irish pub which welcomes sports fans. The draught beers and ciders change regularly, and the pies and salads are famously large and delicious.

**Frog et Rosbif**
23 rue Ausone; 05 56 48 55 85
www.frogpubs.com
Bordeaux's only microbrewery pub, the Frog is part of a small national chain.

**Down Under**
104 cours Aristide Briand; 05 56 94 52 48
A welcoming bar, the Down Under serves Aussie draught and bottled beer and is open daily till 2am.

**Musée d'Aquitaine**
20 cours Pasteur
05 56 01 51 00
11.00-18.00 Tue-Sun
free

**Musée des Beaux-Arts**
20 cours d'Albret
05 56 10 20 56
11.00-18.00 Mon-Sun
free

**Musée des Arts Décoratifs**
39 rue Bouffard
05 56 00 72 50
14.00-18.00 Wed-Mon
free

**Cathédrale St-André**
place Pey-Berland
05 56 52 68 10
7.30-11.30, 14.00-18.30
daily in summer
closed Tues in winter
free

**Tour Pey-Berland**
place Pey-Berland
05 56 81 26 25
10.00-18.00 daily
last entrance 17.30
€4

# The Golden Triangle

The eye of Bordeaux's Golden Triangle is the **place des Grands-Hommes**, with a striking iron and glass market hall that was built in 1900. It is very reminiscent of buildings that were going up in Paris at about the same time, and despite some modernisation inside, retains that elegant turn-of-the-century feel. The market is confined to the basement and more modern shops now occupy the upper floors. It's an eye-catching city landmark, visible down the several streets which radiate from here.

The three points of the triangle are: the big and busy **place Gambetta**, the **place de Tourny** and the city's real centre, the **place de la Comédie**. This has been the heart of city life ever since it began its modern development in the 17th and 18th centuries, and even before that, when a Roman temple stood here. Today visitors and students sit on the steps of the 1780 Grand Théâtre, with its columns, statues and colonnades, or in the cafés and restaurants that dot the edges of the large square.

From place de la Comédie, the pedestrianised shopping street cours de l'Intendance runs down to place Gambetta, while the allées de Tourny leads up to the place de Tourny. The streets inside the Triangle make for pleasant walking as there are some first class food shops and a handful of good restaurants.

**Notre-Dame** was built in the late 18th century and is one of very few Baroque churches found in Bordeaux. Notice the impressive wrought-iron work, a decorative

GRAND THÉÂTRE

art that flourished in 18th century Bordeaux and is found throughout the city. Notre-Dame's especially intricate examples can be seen in front of the chapels and the baptismal font. The church also has a fine 18th-century organ – played from time to time at one of the free concerts held here occasionally.

## The Museum Quarter

South of the Golden Triangle is the city's cathedral, at the centre of a clutch of museums. The area can easily be explored in a day, for the museums are compact.

### Musée d'Aquitaine
Our favourite museum tells the story of Bordeaux and the surrounding areas from prehistoric times. One atmospheric display reconstructs an archaeological dig. There are Roman mosaics and coins, medieval mosaics, and a vast stone frame of a 16th-century rose window. An excellent collection, very stylishly displayed.

### Musée des Beaux-Arts
By comparison, this is disappointing for a city the size of Bordeaux. Much of the building is given over to temporary exhibitions, limiting the core collection to a few rooms in one wing. Only a fraction of the 3,000 works are on display at any one time. The collection focuses on European art from the 15th century onwards, and while there are works by such well-known names as Eugene Delacroix, Henri Matisse, Titian and Joshua Reynolds, whether these are on show at any particular time is not certain.

### Musée des Arts Décoratifs
An interesting museum housed in the 1779 mansion of a wealthy Bordeaux aristocrat and merchant. In addition to viewing the extensive collection of fine art objects, you also get the feeling of what it would have been like to live in a prosperous family home. The rooms are filled with fine examples of furniture, statues, clocks, prints, paintings, portraits, ceramics and many other exquisite items.

### Cathédrale St-André
King Louis VII married Eleanor of Aquitaine here in 1137. One wall remains of the original 12th-century church but most of the building dates from the 13th and 14th centuries.

### Tour Pey-Berland
A separate bell tower topped with a statue of Our Lady of Aquitaine covered in gold leaf. It is open to the public and provides excellent views over the city.

TOUR PEY-BERLAND

PLACE DU PARLEMENT

## Place de la Bourse

It is clear as soon as you enter the place de la Bourse that it is the most beautiful spot in the city, and one of the most beautiful squares in France. A semi-circle of harmonious classical buildings, built in the early 18th century, overlook the Garonne river. The central fountain topped by a statue of the Three Graces adds to the visual appeal.

Originally called place Royale, there was once a statue of King Louis XV in place of the fountain. It was demolished during the French Revolution and the square was renamed after the old stock exchange located at the north end. The former customs house dominates the south, with the rather small Grand Pavilion in between.

Place de la Bourse is large and open, giving a wonderful sense of space. Traffic restrictions around the sides of the square make it a peaceful place to be. The best time to visit is early in the morning, when sunlight from across the river bathes the buildings in a soft golden colour, or at night when lights illuminate the square.

## Place du Parlement

Once an old royal marketplace, this square has handsome facades and good restaurants. From here you may wander through the most atmospheric streets of old Bordeaux. Many of the streets in this medieval quarter are named after the silversmiths, ironsmiths and other craftsmen who once worked here.

Rue Parlement St-Pierre leads to the 14th-century church of **St Pierre**. Lovely carvings decorate the arched doorway. The original church was built in Roman times on one of the city's first harbours.

A visit to **Bordeaux Monumental** to peruse the displays on the city's architecture and history will make your stroll all the more interesting. Nearby is **Porte Cailhau**, one of only two remaining medieval city gates, topped by ornate pointed turrets.

**Bordeaux Monumental**
28 rue des Argentiers
05 56 48 04 24
09.30-13.00, 14.00-19.00 Mon-Sat
10.00-13.00, 14.00-18.00 Sun
free

## The Chartrons District

Bordeaux paid for the Golden Triangle with revenues from wine earned in the Chartrons district north of the city centre. Like much of Bordeaux this was originally marshland (one reason the city has no metro system). It was first cleared by the Carthusian monks who settled here in the 14th century and gave the area its name. Wine merchants settled here because it was then outside the city walls, thus avoiding city taxes. Chartrons offered the additional advantage of access to the River Garonne and easy transport. Soon wine families were building themselves suitably impressive mansions, many with cellars stocked with wine barrels.

The Bordeaux wine trade is no longer in the Chartrons district, but many of the mansions remain: some owned privately, others converted into chic hotels and apartments. Antique shops and art galleries line the streets in this pleasant and quiet part of the city.

The vast **esplanade des Quinconces** between Chartrons and the city centre was built in the 19th century on the site of a military fortress, and is yet another claimant to being Europe's largest public square. At one end is the **Girondins monument** with its soaring column, elaborate statues and fountains. The broad esplanade between here and the river is a focus for events.

### Mascarons

Keep your eye out for Bordeaux's unique *mascarons*. There are said to be 3,000 carvings of faces decorating buildings around the city. They depict local characters, prominent citizens, gods and goddesses – a range of characters, sometimes beautiful, sometimes funny, always interesting. The finest examples are at place de la Bourse.

### Bordeaux Wine Festival

early summer, 2008
05 56 00 66 20
www.bordeaux-fete-le-vin.com
Tasting Pass €12, includes 11 tasting tickets on the door, or in advance from the Tourist Office

'Now we can try a Graves. Why not!' The young man pours the third glass of the morning. It's the first morning of the Bordeaux Wine Festival, a feast that turns Bordeaux's esplanade des Quinconces into Bacchus's back garden. It has been held every two years since 1998. Bacchus himself presides over the proceedings in the form of a huge roguish statue bestride a bottle of freely flowing Bordeaux red.

For four days Bordeaux celebrates wine in the best way possible – by drinking it. Various wine regions set up stalls and dispense samples. Best times to go are during the day on Thursday and Friday, when stalls are quieter and producers have more time – and more wine to pour into your tasting glass that comes with a neat little carrying pouch. There's a real air of *bonhomie* about the event.

L'ENTRECOTE

# Restaurants

See page 287 for price guide.

### La Tupina
6 rue Porte de la Monnaie
05 56 91 56 37
www.latupina.com
12.00-14.00 and 19.00-23.00 daily
booking essential
credit cards accepted
€€€€
*Restaurant* magazine recently voted
La Tupina one of the world's 100 Best
Restaurants. It gains the acclaim by serving
authentic southwest cuisine in an unfussy
stone-walled setting, with the meat cooked in
front of the open fire. An especial favourite,
is the duck carpaccio. It's slightly south of the
city centre, close to the Saint-Michel tram.

### Le Petit Commerce
22 rue du Parlement Saint-Pierre
05 56 79 76 58
www.le-petit-commerce.info
09.00-02.00 Mon-Sat, 19.00-23.00 Sun
booking recommended
credit cards accepted
€€€
West of the place de la Bourse is this
unpretentious place, easily passed by and yet
it's one of the best fish restaurants in town.

There are a few tables on the narrow street,
and inside more seating and a bar area. The
décor's kept simple and so too is the food
– fresh fish like turbot, sea bass, sea bream,
red mullet, all perfectly prepared, which is
why locals pack it out every night.

### Bistrot d'Edouard
15 place du Parlement
05 56 81 48 87
12.00-14.30 and 19.30-late, daily
credit cards accepted
booking not usually necessary
€€
This bistro is by far the biggest on this
delightful square, so popular you feel it
could spread out over the entire area and
still sell out every night. It succeeds because
it is efficiently run and the very wide range
of set menus means there's always something
you want to try. The dishes are not formulaic
either, with excellent options such as fillet
of beef with foie gras and a Bordeaux sauce,
and the wine list ranges from cheap pichets
to €55 a bottle.

### Café du Musée
7 rue Ferrère
05 56 91 81 74; www.chezgreg.fr
11.00-18.00 Tue-Sun, closed Mon
booking advised

credit cards accepted

€€

Despite the modest name, this restaurant serves superior food in a popular spot west of the Modern Art Museum. There are two set menus and a choice *à la carte*. The mainly French menu has nods to the Orient with dishes like sushi and salmon satay, and superb desserts: try chocolate mousse with ginger.

## L'Orléans

36 allées d'Orléans

05 56 48 27 11

12.00-16.30 and 19.30-22.30 Mon-Sat

closed Sun

booking not required

credit cards accepted

€€

This brasserie is on the southern side of the esplanade des Quinconces, with pavement tables smartly laid out in maroon and white. Inside there's a bar, mirrors and bright red seats – welcoming brasserie décor. Fresh fish and seafood is a speciality here, such as coquilles Saint-Jacques grilled in parsley, moules or grilled fillets of red mullet. A set lunch or dinner menu is available for €16.

## Peppone

31 cours Georges-Clémenceau

05 56 44 91 05

12.00-14.00 and 19.00-23.00 daily

booking recommended

credit cards accepted

€€

The city's best Italian, that's what everyone locally says about Peppone, northeast of place Gambetta. Queues form before it opens, and there are pavement tables, a small patio inside the doors, and further seating inside. Home-made pastas, a range of about 20 pizzas and a wine cellar where you can go to choose your wine (check the price: the menu makes it appear they all cost the same).

## L'Entrecote

cours du 30-Juillet, entrance at the side (between place de la Comédie and allée de Munich)

05 56 81 76 10

12.00-14.30 and 19.15-22.30 daily

bookings not taken

credit cards accepted

€€

One of a chain of restaurants with a very simple formula: serve steak and chips, with seconds on chips. The only choice is how you want the steak done, and what will you drink? House rosé or house red? The steak is served with a delicious creamy-mustard house sauce, and the crispy chips keep on coming. You do get to choose a dessert, if you have room. The formula is so successful there are often long queues at peak times.

## Chez Jean

1 place du Parlement

05 56 44 44 43

12.00-23.00 daily

booking not required

credit cards accepted

€€

Terrific new arrival on the popular place du Parlement, quickly established as one of the best restaurants in Bordeaux. There are a dozen or so wooden tables on the pavement, with a chance to gaze at the 17th and 18th century buildings that surround the square. Food is simple but creative, from squid in garlic and parsley to sea bream in green tea jelly, and the Café Gourmand dessert plate (coffee plus three miniature desserts) is irresistible.

## Au Bureau

3-5 cours Georges-Clémenceau

05 56 81 49 88; www.au-bureau.fr

09.00-02.00 daily (food served 11.30-00.30)

bookings not necessary

all major credit cards

€

On the corner of place Gambetta, look for the green awnings of this lively pub/brasserie. It has an extensive beer list from all round the world, including beer cocktails and tasting trays. The food is basic brasserie fare – simple but good steaks, tartines, salads and, a speciality, Welsh rarebit. House wine is cheap and the pavement tables are a great place to while away an hour or two.

---

## Lillet

If you want an aperitif but you don't know what, try a Lillet. This local speciality has been hardly known beyond Bordeaux, though it is big in America and its popularity is growing thanks to an appearance in the latest James Bond movie, *Casino Royale*. Lillet appeared in Ian Fleming's first book as an ingredient in 007's favourite cocktail, and the mix of white wine and fruit liqueurs is very refreshing, not unlike a complex dessert wine. There's also a red version, but the white is the original, going back to its creation in 1877. Today over a million glasses are sold every year in the USA, and it is all made in one place, Podensac, a little village about 20 miles southeast of Bordeaux.

# Shopping

Shops are open from 10am-7pm, but some smaller family-run businesses close for lunch. Shops are closed on Sundays.

> The word 'shopping' originates in Bordeaux. It derives from buildings called *échoppes*, where people sold things through their front windows, and which eventually developed into proper shops.

## Fashion

### Haute-couture shopping streets
• place des Grands-Hommes
• cours de l'Intendance to place Gambetta.

### High-Street fashion outlets
• place de la Victoire.
• place de la Comédie
• rue Sainte-Catherine, (runs south from place de la Comédie and said to be the longest pedestrian street in France)

### Eden Park 🏉
12, place Puy Paulin (off rue de la Porte Dijeaux) 05 56 01 45 27; ww.eden-park.tm.fr
Established in 1987 by French rugby players Franck Mesnel and Eric Blanc who added a pink bow tie to their club kit for the French Championship final match. The chain is known for its quality wearable fashions with a strong rugby theme.

## Antiques

The rue Notre-Dame in the Chartrons district is the best for antique shops.

### Village Notre-Dame
rue Notre Dame corner of rue Sicard
05 56 52 66 13
A gallery of 30 different antique sellers located next to the St-Louis church.

## Food

**Market** Grands-Hommes shopping centre place des Grands-Hommes.
**Seafood market** Quai des Chartrons, near Croiseur Colbert battleship; Sunday morning fresh oysters and other seafood.

### Specialist food shops

### Dubernet
corner of rue Mably and rue Michel-Montaigne Specialises in foie gras and other delicious savoury treats.

### Jean d'Aulose
near corner of rue Mably and rue Michel-

L'INTENDANT: GRANDS VINS DE BORDEAUX

Montaigne, near place des Grands-Hommes
A lovely cheese shop.

## Wine

There are plenty of wine-shopping options if you're touring the vineyards, but in the city itself one shop stands out.
**L'Intendant: Grands Vins de Bordeaux**
2 allées de Tourny; 05 56 48 01 29
Not only does it have a huge and impressive range of Bordeaux wines, the shop itself is worth seeing. The wines are displayed along a circular staircase that winds up around several floors and looks quite stunning.

## Cannelés de Bordeaux

Bordeaux has its own special cakes called *cannelés*, first made in the 19th century by nuns at the convent of Saint Eulalie. The sweets have been described as a portable *crème brûlée*, with a caramelised exterior wrapped around a soft vanilla and rum filling. There are many different types, with the outside ranging from soft to hard, and quality ranging from cheap street snacks to gourmet cannelés using rum and vanilla from Tahiti and other exotic locales.

### Baillardran
Grands-Hommes shopping centre;
05 56 79 05 89
One of the best-known cannelés makers has several branches throughout the city. You can see them being made here.

**VISA**

fig. 1

FOR 6 WEEKS, THE WORLD WILL TAKE ON ANOTHER SHAPE.

In 2007, for more than 6 weeks 20 countries from around the world will compete for a chance to reach the finals at the Stade de France and the opportunity to raise the coveted William Webb Ellis trophy. www.edf.fr

EDF, partner of rugby and those who play the game.

iRB

RUGBY
WORLD CUP
2007

eDF

WORLDWIDE PARTNER

# Golf and other sports

## Golf

There are six golf courses in and around Bordeaux, and about fifty in the Aquitaine region altogether.

### The Médoc Golf Pass
www.medocgolfpass.com
This luxury pass entitles you to play at the three following courses:

### Golf du Médoc
chemin de Courmanteau
33290 Le Pian Médoc-Louens
05 56 70 11 90
www.golf-du-medoc.com
Located a few miles north of the city, with two 18-hole courses. Golf du Médoc's primary course (Château) was designed by Bill Coore, one of the world's leading course designers, in a Scottish style: heather, broom and gorse predominate on a difficult but rewarding technical course. The second (Vignes) course is gentler. There are also a practice course and driving range, and an attractive restaurant and bar panoramique in the clubhouse.

### Golf Relais de Margaux
(see address details in Spa section)
The Margaux course is part of the Margaux hotel and spa complex, it is a charming new course on the banks of the Gironde and next to the world-famous vineyards. Carefully designed to catch the unwary, there are numerous water hazards and sand traps dotting the narrow fairways. Combine your golf with spa treatments and wine tasting at the adjacent Relais de Margaux.

### Golf Lacanau Océan
33680 Lacanau; 05 56 03 92 98
www.nouveauxgolfsdefrance.com/
golflacanauocean
Across the peninsula and by the sea, this attractive course has been built over sand dunes and in pine forest. A treat for novice and expert golfers alike.

### Golf Bordeaux-Lac
avenue de Pernon, 33000 Bordeaux
05 56 50 92 72
www.golf-bordeauxlac.com
contact@golf-bordeauxlac.com
Situated 5km north of Bordeaux, Bordeaux-Lac is a flat and wooded course with tricky roughs and difficult to read well-protected greens which require some accuracy.

### Golf Blue Green Bordeaux Pessac
(formerly Golf International de Pessac)
rue de la Princesse, 33600 Pessac
05 57 26 03 33
www.bluegreen.com/pessac
bordeaux.pessac@bluegreen.com
On the western outskirts of Bordeaux, 4km from the city, this is a level course a stone's throw from the Graves vineyards. There are large bunkers and some water hazards around the large top-quality greens. 27 holes provide alternative nine hole layouts. There is a driving range and putting green.

### Golf de Bordeaux-Cameyrac
33450 Saint-Sulpice-et-Cameyrac
05 56 72 96 79
www.golf-bordeaux-cameyrac.com
contact@golf-bordeaux-cameyrac.com
About 15km outside Bordeaux and close to the famous vineyards of St. Émilion and Pomerol, this is a glorious course laid out among mature trees. Fairways run alongside lakes and vineyards in the two courses of 18 and 9 holes. There is a practice course and a putting green.

### Golf Bordelais
Domaine de Kater, Allée Francois Arago
33200 Bordeaux-Caudéran
05 56 28 56 04
www.golf-bordelais.fr
golfbordelais@wanadoo.fr
One of the city's oldest courses, Le Bordelais is tucked away in the northwestern suburbs next to the racetrack. Much attention has been paid to landscaping the course, with sea sand and trees having been brought from around Europe. A little gem (just 18 holes) which is in easy reach of the centre of town.

### Golf de Teynac
Domaine de Teynac, 33750 Beychac-et-Caillau
05 56 72 96 79
www.golf-teynac.com
Close to the St Émilion vineyards and 18km outside Bordeaux, Teynac has the possibility of being a residential course, with three chambres d'hôtes available. The course is a short 18 holes and would suit a beginner or the more relaxed golfer.

## Cycling

Cycling is very popular in Bordeaux, both in and around the city and in order to get out to some of the nearer vineyards. Bikes cost about €6-9 per day to rent, with weekend and week-long rates also available. There are numerous rental places, including

**Vélo Ville de Bordeaux**
69 cours Pasteur; 05 56 33 73 75

**Macadam Sport**
22 quai des Chartrons; 05 56 51 75 51

**Yser Cyclo**
104 cours de l'Yser (off cours de la Marne)
05 56 92 77 18

**Station Vélo Services**
48 cours de l'Yser; 05 57 95 64 21

**Pierre Qui Roule**
32 place Gambetta; 05 57 85 80 87

## Boating

**Force 7**
boulevard du Lac, 33121 Carcans-Maubuisson
05 56 03 47 00
Fifty kilometres northwest of Bordeaux is Lake Carcans, the perfect spot for all kinds of watersports activities.

## River Trips

Several boats offer trips on the Garonne and Dordogne rivers, and out to the Gironde estuary. Walk along the riverfront in the city centre and you will see boats and barges including:

**The Aliénor**; 05 56 51 27 90
**The Burdigala Barge**; 06 07 19 75 86
**The Royal Barge**; 06 07 02 25 30
**The Ville de Bordeaux**; 05 56 52 88 88

## Spa

**Les Sources de Caudalie**
chemin de Smith Haut Lafitte, 33650 Bordeaux
05 57 83 83 83
www.sources-caudalie.com
Just to the south of the city in the heart of wine country, Les Sources de Caudalie is a luxury hotel-restaurant complex containing a unique Vinotherapie Spa. We all know that red wine is an aid to health, but at Caudalie they use it on the outside of the body as well as the inside. A range of hydro-treatments are on offer using mineral-rich spring water mixed with vine and grape extracts, which fight free radicals and boost circulation. Or you could treat yourself to the 'Pulp Friction' massage, where a mixture of grapes and essential oils hydrates and exfoliates your skin.

**Relais de Margaux**
5 route de l'Île Vincent, 33460 Margaux
05 57 88 38 30
www.relais-margaux.fr
If you want to combine spa treatments with golf and deluxe wine tasting then this 4-star luxury resort is the place – only 25 minutes from Bordeaux in the heart of the Margaux region. There's a par-71 golf course and the Harmonia Spa has 17 treatment rooms including four beauty treatment rooms, two whirlpool baths, a hydrotherapy room and a sunbed room as well as a Moorish area with Turkish bath and sauna.

## Horse-Riding

The area around Bordeaux, in the region of La Gironde, is ideal for horse-riding as there's lots of gentle terrain, beautiful scenery and the option to ride on the beaches too.

**Centre Hippique**
Passe du Tottoral, route de l'Amélie,
33780 Soulac-sur-Mer
05 56 09 71 93
About 95km northwest of Bordeaux on the Bay of Biscay, this equestrian centre organises riding tours exploring this beautiful peninsula.

**Les Écuries Dornic**
route de Duras, 33580 Monsegur
05 56 61 68 14
Some 80km or so southeast of Bordeaux, offering American riding and one-day treks. Open all year.

**Centre Équestre**
2 Blasignons, 33190 La Réole
05 56 61 19 85
An hour's drive southeast of the city and right on the Garonne river is the little town of La Réole, with an equestrian centre offering the chance to ride in idyllic countryside.

# When you're used to seeing names like Cognac and St Emilion on bottles, it can be a delightful surprise to see them on road signs and to realise that yes, they really do exist.

In Bordeaux the word château signifies a wine estate, with its own cellar but not necessarily palatial. There are about 10,000 châteaux in the whole Bordeaux region. One of the easiest ways to visit a château is to book a wine tour in Bordeaux through the Tourist Office. Indeed, the advantage of a tour is that some estates will only open for a pre-booked group.

### Pessac-Léognan
• wine region closest to Bordeaux
### Entre deux Mers
• a large wine region east of Bordeaux
### Cognac
• visit the cellars of Remy Martin

Organised tours often visit contrasting châteaux: first a large one followed by a small family affair, or perhaps a new château and then a very old château. Most tours spend the entire day visiting three or four vineyards, with lunch at one of the stops. Many cater for both French and English speakers, and some for other languages – phone ahead.

Tours that visit prestigious châteaux, such as Margaux and St Emilion, tend to be popular so book in advance. Wine-lovers know it's a rare chance to taste exceptional wine.

## Wine tasting etiquette

You may not be accustomed to drinking wine at 10.30 in the morning, but remember that professionals spit out most, if not all, of the wine they taste. They also drink water or nibble bread between glasses to cleanse the palate and soak up the alcohol. No one will raise an eyebrow if you do drain your glass, though be aware that if you visit two châteaux before lunch, and enjoy several glasses at each tasting, you may suffer in the afternoon.

A vineyard tour will explain a great deal about the production of fine wine and will perhaps begin an appreciation of the methods used and the dedication of the vintner. If you're not sure what you're meant to be doing, ask your guide for a quick lesson in tasting etiquette: learn how to identify colour and nose by holding the glass to the light and then swirling it gently round the glass to release the bouquet. The vintner will also be able to recommend the best foods to accompany a particular wine.

## Pessac-Léognan

Pessac-Léognan is perhaps not best known of the Bordeaux regions, but there have been vineyards here since Roman times. It was once part of the Graves appellation, a more familiar name to wine-lovers. This area southwest of the city was created as a separate appellation in 1987. It covers an area of only 1,500 hectares, and has 67 châteaux.

### Château Haut-Bacalan

33600 Pessac; 05 57 89 21 57
09.00-12.00, 14.00-18.00 Monday-Friday
ring first for an English-language guide

One of the oldest vineyards in Bordeaux owes its name to a Monsieur Haut-Bacalan, who bought it from the Marquis de Montesquiou. The Marquis acquired the estate in the 18th century when it was fashionable to purchase land and plant vines. The soil here comes from the Garonne river and is especially gravelly. In fact the vineyard is so close to Bordeaux that it is sometimes referred to as the city vineyard. Grapes here mature earlier due to extra warmth generated by nearby housing, unseen when gazing across eight hectares of vines to distant blue skies.

### Château Luchey-Halde

17 avenue du Maréchal Joffre
33700 Mérignac; 05 56 45 36 15
09.00-12.00, 14.00-18.00 Tuesday-Saturday

Vines established for centuries were torn up when the land was acquired by the army. They were replanted in 1999 when the château became an agricultural school. Operating as a commercial vineyard and a college, the goal here is to produce grapes of excellent quality, the best possible. Grapes are hand-picked and pass through two levels of quality control to weed out inferior fruit, leaving only perfect specimens. A visit here is a chance to learn all about the very latest in wine-making technology.

ENTRE-DEUX-MERS

# Entre-Deux-Mers

*Entre-Deux-Mers* means 'between two seas', and indeed the region of an almost solid mass of vines is clutched between the arms of the Garonne and Dordogne rivers. The brown colour of the Garonne is due to the high presence of clay in subsoil that is very important for the vineyards. The abundance of water creates a permanently high rate of humidity – excellent for growing grapes.

This area is not the best known on the tourist trail, but it is one of the most historic parts of the whole Bordeaux region, with walled towns, churches and abbeys standing tall above a sea of green vines. Within 15 minutes of leaving the city you are driving through rolling countryside, in one of the prettiest parts of Western France, a region that Julius Caesar named *Aquitaine* (country of the waters).

Entre-Deux-Mers châteaux do not include big names like Margaux and

Saint-Émilion, but the vintners are more friendly and have more time for tastings. Here you will discover vineyards both ancient and modern, large and small.

## Château Smith Haut Lafitte

33650 Bordeaux-Martillac (near Seucats)
05 57 83 11 22
open daily but visits must be pre-booked
€7.50

You wouldn't expect one of the best-known names in wine-making to be a Scot, but that is Mr Smith's country of origin. The vineyard was established in 1365, much earlier than Smith's arrival on the scene in the 18th century, and is now owned by former French Olympic skiing champion Daniel Cathiard, a friend and colleague of the legendary Jean-Claude Killy.

Cathiard and his wife Florence have maintained the château's reputation as one of the finest vineyards in Bordeaux, so much so that its wines sell out within hours of their release onto the market. Visiting the château is a pleasant way to purchase a bottle of the sought-after vintages, and the tasting is certainly an incentive to buy.

## Ginestet

19 avenue de Fontenille
33360 Carignan-de-Bordeaux
05 56 68 81 82
contact@ginestet.fr; www.ginestet.fr
visits by appointment only, Mon-Fri

This isn't in fact a vineyard at all as it owns no vines. Ginestet is a *Négociant*, which means it purchases grapes from other producers, and has been doing so since 1897. Ginestet purchases in large volumes to fill its cellars: just one of their two cellars holds between six and ten million bottles. None of the bottles has a label, these are added later according to the needs of Ginestet customers in the global wine markets. The whole system is computer controlled, and the bottling plant produces up to 210,000 bottles every single day. It's wine production on a massive scale, but the tasting proves you can combine quantity with quality.

## Château Montlau

33420 Moulon; 05 57 84 50 71
chateau@chateau-montlau.com
www.chateau-montlau.com
open during working hours, phone ahead

The estate overlooks the Dordogne near the village of Moulon. 'From my back door,' says Armand Schuster de Ballwil, 'I can see vineyards of Saint-Émilion, Pomerol and Château Petrus, the most expensive wine in the world'.

Montlau means the hill of laurels, and there was once a Roman village here. In 830 a wooden tower was built on the hill to control the area, and then in 1150 a stone tower was added. The château's winery dates back to 1472, and the estate's three wines are made in ancient farm buildings in contrast to Ginestet. 'Other vineyards are modernising,' says Armand, 'but I am trying to return the winery to the way it was in the 19th century. Stainless steel doesn't make wine: grapes make wine.'

Armand produces only 150,000 bottles a year, of three different wines, 80% for export. The serenity of the location adds to the taste of the wine. He gazes out over his vines and smiles: 'The grapes enjoy to see the owner every morning!'

CHÂTEAU SMITH HAUT LAFITTE

## Cognac country

Though there's plenty for wine-lovers to discover in the Bordeaux vineyards, a short way north across the River Garonne is a whole other world – with a whole new set of drinks to discover.

### Cognac

It might surprise some people to discover that Cognac is a town, not just a name on a drinks menu. About 120km due north from Bordeaux, it is the home of some of the finest cognac and armagnac makers in the world, mainly because the name, like that of champagne, is protected. Only here can you make cognac, and the town's business directory reads like a Who's Who of the cognac trade: Hennessy, Martell, Courvoisier, Rémy Martin.

The town of Cognac has some attractive medieval buildings and narrow streets in its old centre, and there are naturally plenty of good eating and drinking establishments. Despite the appeal of the cognac houses, most of whom offer tours and tastings, Cognac is a fairly quiet place as most visitors take day trips to one or other of the distilleries and don't stay in town overnight.

### Rémy Martin

20 rue de la Société Vinicole, 16102 Cognac
05 45 35 76 11; www.remy.com
Rémy Martin is one of the biggest and oldest names in Cognac, going back to 1724. It has two locations in the town, each offering a different style of tour. Domaine de Rémy Martin is on the edge of town and offers a tour of the distillery with a tasting at the end. Maison de Rémy Martin, (corporate headquarters) located in the town centre, provides a more intimate experience for smaller groups. The visit here includes two cellars (one for blending and one for ageing) that are so ancient no-one is quite sure of their age.

After touring the cobwebbed cellars (webs are left there for a purpose), visitors congregate in modern offices for an intriguing tasting – matching different cognacs to different foods. A chilled VSOP is paired with salmon blinis served with green olive cream. A warm XO brandy is matched with a chicken brochette that's been marinated with spices and honey. In each case, the food and the cognac complement each other perfectly. As educating experiences go this one is luxuriously mouthwatering.

MAISON DE RÉMY MARTIN

CHÂTEAU DE BEAULON

## Pineau des Charentes

Cognac is a brandy known all round the world, but this region produces another drink whose name is not even known in all parts of France: Pineau des Charentes. Fans of the drink go wild for it, and yet outside the Poitou-Charentes region immediately north of Bordeaux it is scarcely encountered. Made of a simple blend of about 2/3 grape juice to 1/3 cognac, it is a simple recipe that is nevertheless capable of enormous variety. The grapes must be very ripe and the fermenting is stopped by the addition of the cognac. A variety of permutations exist depending upon the types of grapes, the quality of the cognac, the blending, the ageing process, and so on.

## Château de Beaulon

17240 Saint-Dizant-du-Gua; 05 46 49 96 13
www.chateau-de beaulon.com
09.00-12.00, 14.00-18.00 daily in summer
closed weekends in winter
€3.50
One of the best pineau tastings is at

Château de Beaulon, which includes a tour of the lovely gardens. The château is signposted from the village of Lorignac, 50kms southwest of Cognac. The château (which cannot be visited) was built in 1480 and later, in the 17th century was the residence of the Bishops of Bordeaux. The gardens are well worth seeing as they contain about 200 different varieties of trees. At the far end of the garden are a series of streams and pools known as the *Fontaines Bleues*. These pools of water are an incredible colour of blue in the centre, caused by the depth and clarity of the water.

After strolling through the gardens, the tasting at the château allows you to test the depth and clarity of their Pineau des Charentes. The château produces six different types of pineau in both red and white varieties, using Semillon and Sauvignon grapes, aged in oak barrels for at least five years, with some aged for ten years. The result, when chilled, is a superb and unusual aperitif.

# TOULOUSE

# TOULOUSE

## In this fun-loving city, any excuse will do for a celebration – none more so than rugby, a sport embraced with great passion.

Known as the *Ville Rose* (pink city), Toulouse casts a warm glow over its visitors. It may be best known for its aeronautics industry and industrial suburbs, but the historic old town along the banks of the Garonne paints a much prettier picture. With no local stone at their disposal, Toulouse's forefathers became artisan bricklayers, building magnificent churches, townhouses and civic buildings in handsome red brick that turns from fiery orange to soft pink in the setting sun, hence its nickname. After dark, the Plan Lumière lights up the main monuments and the riverbank.

Toulouse is a university city, with one of the largest student populations in the country, who lend it a lively, youthful buzz. Soak up the scene in the many outdoor cafés, or the culture in the impressive art museums. The city dates back to Roman times, and has a decidedly Mediterranean air.

Here the Canal du Midi begins its run to the sea. Both the riverbank and the canal are prime places for strolling and cycling. The riverside is often the focus for Toulouse's multitude of festivals.

**Place du Capitole**
• the heart of Toulouse, for history, festivals and café culture
**Basilica Saint-Sernin**
• the greatest pilgrimage church in the south of France
**Les Jacobins**
• a massive monument to the region's medieval history
**Mansions of the Woad Merchants**
• sumptuous Renaissance townhomes
**Musée des Augustins**
• Romanesque art housed in a medieval monastery
**Cathédrale Saint-Étienne**
• the venerable hub of Toulouse's medieval quarter

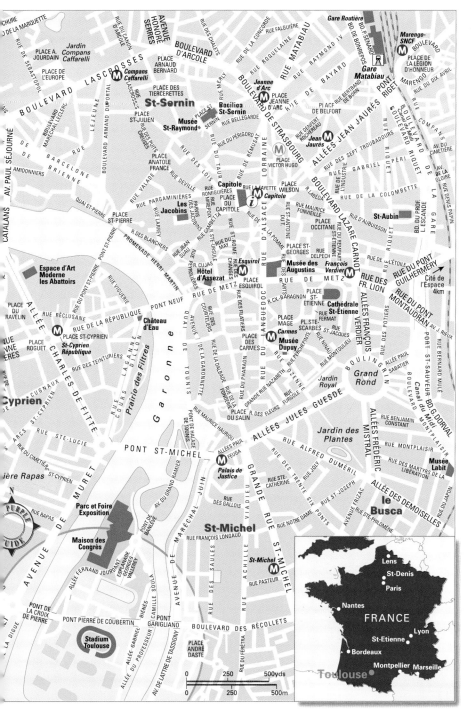

A key for all maps is on the inside front cover

## Getting to the stadium

The stadium is 1.5km south of Pont Neuf, on Île du Ramier, in the river Garonne.

**Nearest airport**
Toulouse-Blagnac
08 25 38 00 00
Located 10km northwest of the city centre, and 14km from the stadium. Shuttle buses travel from the airport into the city centre every 20 minutes. On match days buses will travel to the stadium.

**Car**
The E80 périphérique (ring road) passes across the Île du Ramier, about 1km south of the stadium. Those travelling by car should use public carparks around the city and walk or take a bus to the stadium.

**Train**
The Gare Toulouse-Matabiau is north of the city centre and about 5km north of the stadium. Look for shuttle buses to the centre and the stadium.

**Bus**
Several buses go past the stadium. Take either bus number 1 or 12, and alight at Pont Saint-Michel, or take number 92 to the Daste stop.

REMEMBER TO PURCHASE YOUR TRANSPORT TICKETS WELL IN ADVANCE OF THE MATCH TO SAVE TIME QUEUING.

## Le Stadium  capacity 35,700

| Matches | Date | Pool |
|---|---|---|
| Fiji v Japan | 12 September, Wed | B |
| France v Namibia | 16 September, Sun | D |
| Romania v Portugal | 25 September, Tues | C |
| New Zealand v Romania | 29 September, Sat | C |

## The stadium and around

1 allée Gabriel Biénés
08 92 69 31 15

The rugby heart beats strong in Toulouse. The local rugby club, Stade Toulousain, also known as Toulouse, plays in the French premier league and qualified for the Heineken Cup. The club's home ground is the Ernest-Wallon stadium, located northwest of Toulouse city centre, with a capacity of 20,000. Rugby World Cup 2007 games will be held at Toulouse's football stadium, located on an island south of the city centre, and known simply as, Le Stade, or Le Stadium.

Le Stadium opened as a bull-ring in 1949 but soon became the home of Toulouse FC, as it remains today. The first rugby international was France v Czechoslovakia in 1956. France went on to score memorable victories here over New Zealand in 1977 and again in 1995. Le Stadium was renovated in time for FIFA World Cup 1998.

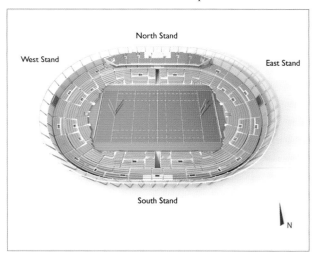

North Stand

West Stand

East Stand

South Stand

N

## Bars and screens

### Rugby bars

**Bar Basque**
7 place Saint-Pierre
05 61 21 55 64
One of many bars on place Saint-Pierre in the heart of Toulouse. Described by a fan as 'not very Basque, but very rugby', the Bar Basque is a Toulousian institution. With bars on two floors and plenty of space, it's a traditional rallying point and welcomes all rugby fans.

**Le Saint-Pierre**
11 place Saint-Pierre
05 61 12 35 73
This bar has nicknamed itself *ballon ovale,* the oval ball, in reference to the traditional shape of a rugby ball. It has a big waterfront terrace that attracts a lively crowd while inside a big screen shows matches. On Saturday nights they stay open until 5am.

**Bar Chez Tonton**
16 place Saint-Pierre
05 61 21 89 54
The rowdiest of Toulouse's rugby venues is occasionally closed down by the police when customers have become too excitable (throwing your friends into the river seems to be the done thing).

**La Couleur de la Culotte**
5 place Saint-Pierre
05 34 44 97 01
'The Colour of Your Underpants' attracts a young student-based clientele with low-priced cocktails and house music, but on match days it's swamped by rugby fans. Décor is unusual, with Empire wallpaper and chaises-longues. They do a good deal on tapas with an apéritif.

TREVOR BRENNAN, DE DANÚ

**De Danú Irish Bar**
9 rue du Pont-Guilhemery (Canal du Midi)
05 61 62 58 79
With Trevor Brennan (former Irish international) on the management team, De Danú has a well-deserved reputation as a primary sports bar in Toulouse. Three giant screens continuously show sport – mainly rugby.

### Other sports bars

**The Frog & Rosbif**
14 rue de l'Industrie
05 6199 2857
One of six pubs and microbreweries around France, brewing their own special varieties of beer and welcoming sports fans. Flags of all nations decorate the ceiling, and big screens show all football and rugby matches.

**Place Wilson** is another good centre for watering holes where many bars, such as Le Wallace, stay open late.

### Screens planned for the centre
Large screens are being planned to be showing Rugby World Cup 2007:
• **place du Capitole**, the main square, where markets and music concerts are often held
• **Prairie des Filtres**, a grassy area located on the west bank of the river Garonne across pont Neuf
• **place Saint-Pierre**, east end of pont Saint-Pierre, known as rugby headquarters

## Place du Capitole

This enormous square covering one hectare in the heart of Toulouse is named for the Capitole, or City Hall, which stretches for 128 metres along the eastern side. It is the place for outdoor concerts and festivals, Wednesday and Saturday morning markets or simply people-watching, best done from the string of pleasant cafés which spill out from the arcades lining the western side.

The old city wall ran along the square in Roman times, but the arcades date from the mid-19th century. Look up at the arcade ceiling to see a more recent addition: a series of modern paintings depicting the history of the city. Note a tribute to rugby in the ceiling above Grand Café Albert.

### Le Capitole
05 61 22 34 12
09.00-19.00 Mon-Fri, 10.00-19.00 Sat-Sun
admission free

The arcades are a great vantage point for admiring the 18th-century Capitole itself, with its elegant facade of pink brick and stone. The eight marble columns are a clue to its name; they represent the eight Capitouls, or consuls, who governed the city in medieval times. The building's right wing houses the Théâtre du Capitole, where opera and ballet performances are staged. The impressive stone portal leads into the foyer; upstairs, the Salle des Illustres and other rooms house beautiful murals of the history of the city. Through the portal's east side, the 16th-century donjon (keep), part of the original Capitole, houses the Tourist Office.

---

### Getting around Toulouse

The city has a single-line metro system, with a second line due to open in 2007, in addition to an extensive bus network. Tickets cover both services and can be bought on the bus, at metro stations, at tobacconists and offices of the transport company, Tisséo (www.tisseo.fr). Single tickets cost €1.30, a day pass €4, or a book of ten tickets costs €11.

**Tourist Office**
Donjon du Capitole, 31080 Toulouse
05 61 11 02 22; www.toulouse-tourisme.com
09.00-19.00 Mon-Sat, 10.30-17.15 Sunday
A city pass (€13) gives discounts on museums, selected shopping, tours and attractions.

---

## Philippe Verger

Rugby-playing Philippe Verger thinks he's got the best job in the world: Director of the Tourist Office in rugby-mad Toulouse. 'But rugby isn't just about the sport in Toulouse,' he says. 'It is about culture, music, food, drink, everything. It is about teaching children the ethics of rugby, the values of the game.'

Next year is an important one for Toulouse, and not only because of Rugby World Cup 2007, it is also the centenary of the Toulouse Rugby Club. Philippe is helping to plan various grand celebrations. There will be competitions for businesses, a contest for bakers to bake the best loaf in the shape of a rugby ball and prizes for the best shop window display, as well as public events to include everyone, including children, and women visitors, who may not be rugby fans but want to enjoy the atmosphere. Philippe plays number 4 or 5 for the local A.S. St Sulpice Rugby Club, 2006 Pyrenees Champions and has also

played at Stade de France® in Paris. He is the ideal man to be planning events. His enthusiasm for the game of rugby shines through, and his passionate belief in the sport is admirable. 'I think it is the only game to teach children the best values, of sportsmanship, of team-playing, of hard work, of courage. All these things help them to develop as citizens, and as people. No other sport does this. We are going to make Toulouse the best place, absolutely the best place to be, during Rugby World Cup 2007.'

## Toulouse street signs

As you stroll along the streets of Toulouse, you will notice the bilingual street signs. The top sign is in French, the bottom sign in Occitan, the traditional language of the south. The name of the language refers to the word 'Oc', which means 'yes'. Occitan is a bit like Spanish and is also spoken in north Spain and in the Italian Alps.

Some of the old signs were colour-coded to help people orient themselves in the days of high illiteracy. Yellow signs indicated streets parallel to the Garonne, white signs were for those perpendicular to the river.

PLACE DU CAPITOLE

# Basilica Saint-Sernin

05 61 21 80 45

September:
08.30-18.15 Mon-Sat, 08.30-19.30 Sun
October:
08.30-11.45, 14.00-17.45 Mon-Sat
08.30-12.30, 14.00-19.30 Sun

The basilica is the largest Romanesque church in the Western world, and also one of the oldest. But it is impressive for its sheer beauty alone. Rising above a series of rounded apses and tiered roofs is a striking, five-tiered, octagonal bell tower, a style typical of Toulouse. The exquisite carvings above the southern entrance are early 12th century. Inside, it is larger and lighter than most churches of its type, with many windows, a huge nave with double side aisles, and an ambulatory. This was one of Europe's greatest pilgrimage churches. The chapel walls and crypt contain reliquaries holding 175 'true' relics of numerous saints, many donated by Charlemagne.

The simple marble altar was consecrated by Pope Urban II in 1096, but the site is much older. The remains of a Roman cemetery and a 5th-century church, supposedly dedicated to St-Sernin, were found here. St-Sernin was the first bishop of Toulouse, when it was still a Roman city. He was martyred in AD 250. During a sacrificial ritual, the Romans were unable to kill a bull and blamed it on the Christian influence. They tied St-Sernin to the bull and it dragged him through the streets to his death. Rue du Taur, which leads to the basilica from place du Capitole, was named for this event. The surrounding area is Toulouse's student quarter.

## Les Jacobins

Parvis des Jacobins
05 61 22 21 92
09.00-19.00 daily
cloister €1.50, exhibitions €2.50

Toulouse's architectural skill with brick is best seen in this remarkable church and monastery complex. It was constructed between 1230 and the early 14th century by the Dominican Order, which was founded in Toulouse, and served as the city's first university. The outside of the church is utterly plain, but the sheer size and mass of it is impressive. That was the intention. At that time the Catholic church was under fire for its materialism, and other sects like the Cathars were calling for a more pure, simple religion. The Church wanted to show its dominance, and so built this imposing church, but without adornment outside.

Inside it's a different story. The huge single nave – built for preaching to the crowds – is unique in the French Gothic style. It is divided by colossal columns which fan out to look like palm trees on the ceiling's ribbed vaulting. Between the stained-glass windows, the bricks are painted to look like stone (stone indicated wealth, while brick was seen as 'poor'). Only the rose window is original. The medieval windows were destroyed when Napoleon installed barracks and stables here. The church houses the tomb of Saint Thomas Aquinas. You can also visit the cloisters, a place of repose and a good spot for viewing the superb bell tower. The old refectory is used for temporary art exhibitions.

## Musée des Augustins

21 rue de Metz
05 61 22 21 82
www.augustins.org
10.00-18.00 Wed-Mon (till 21.00 Wed)
€3 adults, free under age 18

Founded during the Revolution, this is one of the oldest museums in France. It is set in a 14th century Augustinian monastery and holds an unparalleled collection of Romanesque art. If you've ever wanted to get up close to a gargoyle, this is the place – a gargoyle gallery lines the cloisters surrounding the restored botanical garden. The adjoining rooms are filled with impressive medieval church sculpture. **Salle Capitulaire** contains one of the museum's masterpieces, a 15th century *Madonna and Child*, notable for its exquisite carving and expressive pose. Religious paintings are displayed in the large church nave, including works by Perugino and Peter Paul Rubens. Organ recitals take place here on Wednesday evenings on the replica 17th century organ.

The highlight of the museum is the collection of Romanesque capitals, which came from three major churches in Toulouse. It is visually stunning, with the white capitals displayed on top of red columns, in row after row, disappearing to the far end of the huge room. Altogether they have 250 capitals, though not all are on show. The sculptural work is outstanding. Each one is different and tells a story. The most famous capital depicts the beheading of St John the Baptist, from the cathedral cloister of St-Etienne.

Upstairs, the **salon rouge** is covered in 19th century French paintings, including four works by Henri de Toulouse-Lautrec.

GARGOYLE GALLERY, MUSÉE DES AUGUSTINS

## Cathédrale Saint-Étienne

place Saint-Étienne
05 61 52 03 82
08.00-19.00 daily

As the bishop's seat, the cathedral is the most prestigious church in Toulouse, though it gets less attention than its rivals, possibly because its inharmonious architecture makes it harder to fathom. It was built or remodelled in stages from the 11th to the 17th centuries, leaving a mixture of Romanesque and Gothic styles. The interior is oddly out of alignment due to a lack of funds to complete the new church in the 13th century, and its subsequent connection to the old church several hundred years later. Still, there are treasures to be seen, including the beautifully carved walnut choir stalls, the bishop's throne, the marble altar, and the 16th and 17th century tapestries. Their blue colour has survived well and comes from the woad dye which brought Toulouse so much wealth in that era.

In the square in front of the cathedral is the city's oldest fountain. From here, wander through the medieval part of town, with its quiet neighbourhoods and squares such as **place Saintes Scarbes,** formerly the district of the nobility, now full of antique shops and galleries.

Peek into open courtyards to see grand mansions such as **Hôtel d'Ulmo** (1530) on rue Ninau. On the corner of rue Croix Baragnon and rue des Arts is the oldest house in Toulouse, dating from the 14th century.

## Mansions of the Woad Merchants

During the 15th and 16th centuries, much of Toulouse's wealth came from its trade in woad (or pastel in French), a plant which yielded a coveted blue dye. The woad merchants used their riches to build sumptuous town houses. Most remain in private ownership, and can be seen on a guided tour from the Tourist Office. The two listed below are open to the public.

Although **Hôtel de Bernuy**, built 1530-1550, is now a school the inner courtyard is open to the public. You can see its sculpted Gothic doorway, window decoration and splendid internal staircase.

The finest Renaissance mansion is **Hôtel d'Assézat,** built in 1555 for Pierre d'Assézat, a Capitoul. From the courtyard you can admire the ornate stone facade with classical columns, sculpted doorways and a covered gallery. It now houses the Fondation Bemberg, with artworks from the Renaissance to French modern.

DOOR DETAIL, HÔTEL D'ASSEZAT

**Hôtel de Bernuy**
rue Gambetta; 08.00-17.00 Mon-Fri

**Hôtel d'Assézat**
rue de Metz; courtyard free
• **Fondation Bemberg**
10.00-12.30, 13.30-18.00 (till 21.00 Thur) closed Mon; €4.60

FERNAND LÉGER AT LES ABATTOIRS

## Les Abattoirs

76 allées Charles-de-Fitte
05 34 51 10 60
www.lesabattoirs.org
12.00-20.00 Tue-Sun, Apr-Sept
11.00-19.00 Oct-March
€5-€10 depending on the exhibition,
students €3

The city's pride and joy is this superb modern and contemporary art museum, set in a converted slaughterhouse. The handsome red-brick building on the river's left bank dates from 1831, and was a working abattoir until its closure in 1989.

This new incarnation makes a fantastic space for the museum's collection of 2,000 artworks, displayed in rotation or as part of temporary exhibitions. All the major art movements from the mid-20th century to the present are represented, from France and the Mediterranean to America and the Far East.

The enormous space allows for large artworks and installations. A highlight of the museum is Picasso's huge theatre backdrop, entitled *The Stripping of the Minotaur in the Harlequin Suit*, which is on show six months of the year. The exterior and courtyard feature sculptures and mosaics by Fernand Léger. There is a mediathèque and a café.

**FOOD & DRINK**

LA BRASSERIE DU STADE

# Restaurants

See page 287 for price guide.

### Restaurant Michel Sarran
21 boulevard Armand Duportal
05 61 12 32 32
www.michel-sarran.com
12.00-13.45, 20.00-21.45 weekdays
closed weekends and Wed lunch
booking essential
credit cards accepted
€€€€

The undoubted superstar of the Toulouse restaurant scene is Michel Sarran, and his flagship restaurant has two Michelin stars. It's about half a kilometre north of the place Saint-Pierre. The downstairs dining room is modern while the upstairs is more traditional, and the menu combines the two notes. Starters include a farm yoghourt and Perigord truffle tart with port confit (€48), while mains could be a casserole of black pork fillet in thyme, served with apples in vine juice and country bacon.

### La Brasserie du Stade
114 rue des Troënes
05 34 42 24 20
www.stadetoulousain.fr
12.00-15.00 Mon-Fri, 20.00-late Wed-Fri
booking advised
credit cards accepted
€€€

Michel Sarran's Brasserie du Stade is built into the Ernest-Wallon stadium and is run by the same chef whose main city restaurant has two Michelin stars (see above). This large dining room manages to be both stylish and sporty, elegant yet relaxed. Sports photos in dark red frames stand out against the yellow walls, and along one wall is a trophy cabinet that includes a Heineken Cup won by Stade Toulousain.

The cuisine, though, is streets ahead of any other sporting restaurant anywhere. There is a dish of the day at €15, and menus at €21 and €28. Typical dishes include *magret de canard* with a tapenade crust and courgette flowers, or *la nage de poissons et langoustines aux baies roses*. Just don't ask for a player's autograph when he's tucking into food like this. Superb.

### L'Envers du Décor
22 rue des Blanchers
05 61 23 85 33
08.00-02.00 Tuesday-Saturday
booking suggested
credit cards accepted
€€€

Just a hundred metres or so east of place

Saint Pierre is this characterful little place, with wooden beams, low lights, quirky artwork on the walls and fabulous food. There are a few outside tables but it isn't the best view in the city, so eat inside. There are several fixed-price menus and à la carte, with dishes such as scallops in a Creole sauce, or duck *au poivre*. The friendly owner is also rightly proud of his interesting and inexpensive wine list.

**Restaurant du Théâtre**
3 rue Labéda (near place Wilson)
05 34 45 05 45
12.00-14.30, 19.00-22.30 Tuesday-Saturday
booking advised
credit cards
€€€
Part of the building housing the Théâtre National Toulouse Midi-Pyrénées, this lively place has a modern stylish look, with lots of black and chrome and a sleek bar running down one side of the long, thin room. The excellent menu is a mix of traditional and modern, so that foie gras comes with mango chutney, and duck breast is served with Szechuan pepper.

**La Gourmandine**
17 place Victor Hugo
05 61 22 78 84
12.00-14.00, 19.45-23.00 Tuesday-Saturday
booking not usually necessary
credit cards accepted
€€
This extremely popular bar/brasserie sits near the Victor Hugo market, with lots of pavement tables and inside a rustic wooden-beamed look. In the evening drinks come with free tapas, and a sports screen shows matches. Menus include a basic 2-course €13 menu and a 3-course Gourmand option for €25. One taste of dishes like pork with a Colombo sauce or fresh fruit tiramisu and you know why it's constantly busy.

**Restaurant des Abattoirs Chez Carmen**
97 allée Charles de Fitte
05 34 31 94 84
20.00-23.00 Tuesday-Saturday
booking suggested; credit cards
€€
Any restaurant that can claim Frédéric Michalak as one of its customers, not to mention other Toulouse rugby players, has to be worth a look. Directly opposite the entrance to the Abattoirs Modern Art Museum, Chez Carmen used to serve the meat supplied by the abattoir and now caters

## Toulouse Sausage
One of the city's specialities is, of course, the Toulouse sausage. No visit to the city would be complete without sampling it, though you'll often find it used in that great southern French speciality, cassoulet (a baked dish made with white haricot beans, garlic, pork and duck fat). The sausage is usually made from pork, with smoked bacon, wine and garlic. The result is deliciously meaty – one of the world's great sausages!

to art lovers as well as rugby players, who obviously enjoy dishes such as pig's feet and *tête de veau*. It does have a reputation for doing the best meat in the city.

**Los Piquillos**
90 route de Blagnac
05 61 57 00 57
Bar: 18.00-02.00 Tuesday-Saturday
Restaurant: 19.00-23.00 Tuesday-Saturday
booking advised
€€
A few minutes walk from the Ernest-Wallon stadium is a rugby (and bullfighting) themed Basquais restaurant owned by Jean-Marie Cadieu, a Toulouse rugby legend. Decorated in Spanish bodega style, and with a sunny terrasse and garden, the bar is ideal for post-match relaxation with the house sangria and a plate of tapas. If you feel like more food, go to the restaurant and try the house specialities of *sepia a la plancha* (spicy cuttlefish) or *brandade de morue* (salt cod purée).

**Le J'Go**
16 place Victor Hugo
05 61 23 02 03
12.00-14.30, 19.30-23.30 daily
booking advised
credit cards accepted
€€
Right alongside the Victor Hugo market, this bar-restaurant is a must for sports fans. There's a bull-fighting bar on one side of the building with a big screen TV at the back, and a restaurant on the other, with more tables outside. Lots of the Toulouse rugby stars eat here, no doubt enjoying the regional speciality of *porc noir* (black pork), which features in many of the dishes.

FOOD & DRINK

183

RUE SAINT-ROME

# Shopping

Shops are open from 10am-7pm, but some smaller family-run businesses close for lunch. Shops are closed on Sundays.

From its indoor market to its historic shopping streets, Toulouse has something for every taste and budget, including two special rugby shops.

## Shopping Streets

The city's main shopping thoroughfare is rue d'Alsace Lorraine. It's lined with grand 19th-century apartment buildings which now house shops and businesses. Along here you'll find clothing stores and chain store branches, including Galeries Lafayette.

Rue Saint-Rome, running south from place du Capitole, is one of the oldest streets in Toulouse. It was home to the Capitouls from the 13th century onwards. Today it's a lively pedestrian shopping street, lined with clothes shops, but as you browse don't forget to look up and admire its wonderful medieval architecture, which extends along rue des Changes. Between here and the river you'll find funkier shops along rue Cujas selling everything from hats to jazz music.

In the medieval quarter, east of rue du Languedoc, rue Croix-Baragnon, rue Bouquières and rue des Tourneurs are pleasant shopping streets for everything from sweets to home accessories. Many antique dealers can be found around the lovely place Saintes-Scarbes.

### La Faiencerie
11 rue Croix-Baragnon; 05 61 53 12 54
As much art as home décor, this shop sells a wide selection of the region's famous hand-painted, brightly coloured earthenware.

### La Fleurée du Pastel
Hôtel Pierre-Delfau, 20 rue de la Bourse (near Hotel d'Assézat)
05 61 12 05 94
The clothing, accessories and decorative items sold here are all made from authentic *pastel*, or woad, the plant whose blue dye brought Toulouse its wealth in days gone by.

**VISA**

## Victor Hugo Market

place Victor Hugo
06.00–13.00 Tues-Sun
A bustling indoor market forms the hub
of the lively place Victor Hugo. It's full of
shiny stalls brimming with local produce,
from fresh seafood and French cheeses
to sausages, hams and pâtés made from
the local speciality *porc noir* (black pork).
Toulouse's large Spanish population is
catered for by specialist butchers such as
Maison Garcia, and Pierre Oteiza who sells
Basque products.
The streets surrounding the market square
are lined with great restaurants and
gastronomic boutiques, perfect for edible
gifts and souvenirs. For cheeses, try Betty
or Xavier. For foie gras, there's Ducs de
Gascogne and Samarran. And for chocolate,
L'Atelier du Chocolat de Bayonne and
De Neuville. Maison Busquet has a good
selection of regional wines and gourmet
products. There are also a handful of
antiques shops around the square.

## Rugby shops

### Eden Park ⟨⟩⟩

10, rue Croix Baragnon (off rue du Languedoc)
05 61 25 23 20; www.eden-park.tm.fr
Established in 1987 by French rugby players
Franck Mesnel and Eric Blanc who added a
pink bow tie to their club kit for the French
Championship final match. The chain is
known for its quality wearable fashions with
a strong rugby theme.

### Stade Toulousain Rugby

75 rue Alsace Lorraine
(at junction with rue de Remusat)
05 61 21 67 81
This city centre sports shop looks
deceptively small from the outside, being
squeezed between two converging streets.
Inside it's huge, extending back a long way.
There are many choices of men's, women's
and children's clothes as well as the usual
jerseys, hats and other rugby paraphernalia.
Some of the clothes are very stylish indeed,
much better than the average sports shop
collection of baseball caps and team jerseys.

VICTOR HUGO MARKET, BETTY CHEESE SHOP

## The Flower of Toulouse

The pink city whose wealth came from blue dye has another favourite colour: violet.
French soldiers returning from the Napoleonic wars in Italy in the 19th century first
brought the violet to Toulouse. It soon became a great success with florists, perfumers and
confectioners. By the 20th century more than 600,000 bouquets were sent out each year to
Paris, Northern Europe and Canada. But this delicate winter flower was nearly wiped out by
diseases. Luckily, horticulturalists set out to save it and since 1985 it has been cultivated once
again in the area's greenhouses. The violet is so loved by the people of Toulouse that they
celebrate it each year at the end of February with its own festival: the Fête de la Violette.

### Maison de la Violette

Canal du Midi, face au 2 boulevard Bonrepos
(near Gare Matabiau)
05 61 99 01 30

# Golf and other sports

## Golf

There is no shortage of golf clubs in and around Toulouse, and you can get a full list at the Tourist Office. Here are some of the more local options within a fifteen minute drive of the city:

### Golf de Toulouse La Ramée
ferme du Cousturier, 31170 Tournefeuille
05 61 07 09 09
golf.laramee@wanadoo.fr
Having the advantage of being the closest course to central Toulouse, La Ramée welcomes beginners and juvenile players as well as the more advanced.

### Golf de Teoula
71 avenue des Landes, 31830 Plaisance du Touch
05 61 91 98 80
08.30-18.30 daily
www.golftoulouseteoula.com
A few minutes drive out of the city and with magnificent views of the Pyrenees, this is a glorious course surrounded by mature oaks and eucalyptus. There are great practice facilities and a restaurant and bar.

### Golf de Borde Haute
le Domaine Estolosa, Lieu dit Borde Haute, 31280 Dremil Lafage
05 62 18 84 00
www.estolosa.fr r
A friendly course with restaurant and conference centre attached.

### Golf International de Toulouse Seilh
route de Grenade, 31840 Seilh
05 62 13 14 14
www.guidedesgolfs.fr/m.p/toulouseseilh.html
Host venue of the Toulouse International Open, this golfing resort complex is ten minutes from the airport with two 18-hole courses, a three-star hotel, restaurant, outdoor pool and tennis courts. Private lessons, training courses and practice areas.

### Golf de Toulouse Palmola
route d'Albi, 31660 Buzet sur Tarn
05 61 84 20 50
closed Tuesdays
www.golfdepalmola.com
A picturesque and challenging course to the north-east of the city. Also has a restaurant and swimming pool.

### Golf Club de Toulouse
2 chemin de la Planho, 31320 Vieille Toulouse
05 61 73 45 48
golf.toulouse@wanadoo.fr
With splendid views over the river Garonne to the city in the distance, this is a pretty and well-maintained course that welcomes visitors.

### Olympe Club
200 route de Blagnac, 31200 Toulouse
05 61 57 02 86
Ten minutes from the centre of the city, this is an attractive wooded course on the banks of the Garonne. There are practice holes and a restaurant and bar.

GOLF DE TEOULA

## Bike Rental

Cycling is popular in Toulouse and it is supported by the city. You will find a city-operated bike rental facility just outside the Tourist Office. There is also a cycle hire office along the Canal du Midi, at port Saint-Sauveur, and another at the railway station.

Hire charges are €1 for a half-day, €2 for a full day and €3 for a day and overnight. A €260 deposit by cheque or VISA card is required to rent a bike.

The rental offices offer two free maps: One details three recommended cycling routes around the city and the other shows all the cycleways in the city.

One of the most popular trips is the easy ride along the Canal du Midi. If this is your preferred route, rent your bike at port Saint-Sauveur.

### Vélo Station Capitole
place Charles de Gaulle, (opposite Tourist Office)
08.00-19.00 Mon-Fri, 10.00-19.00 Sat-Sun

### Vélo Station Gare Routière
gare Toulouse-Matabiau
08.00-19.00 Mon-Fri, 10.00-19.00 Sat-Sun

### Vélo Station Port Saint-Sauveur
5 port Saint-Sauveur
10.30-13.00 and 14.00-18.30 Tues-Sat

## Swimming Pools

### Piscine Ancely
allée des Causses, 31300 Toulouse
05 61 49 92 91

### Piscine Bellevue
86 chemin de la Salade Ponsan, 31400 Toulouse
05 61 52 93 53

### Piscine Jacques Chapou
rue Saunière, 31200 Toulouse
05 61 21 93 87

### Piscine Municipale du Parc des Sports
allées Georges Vallerey, 31400 Toulouse
05 61 22 30 14

### Piscine de Pech David
chemin des Côtes de Pech David, 31400 Toulouse
05 61 55 12 89 05

## Karting

### MP Kart Outdoor
21 rue Juan Manuel Fangio, 31600 Muret
05 34 46 08 08
With a half-mile circuit boasting such sophistications as chicanes and gravel traps, this karting venue should please the most demanding enthusiast. About fifteen minutes drive from central Toulouse.

### MP Kart Indoor
6 rue Garcia Lorca, 31200 Toulouse
05 61 47 14 14
A great indoor karting circuit complete with a bridge and a tunnel.

## Boat hire (Canal du Midi)

For more on the Canal du Midi see overleaf (Beyond Toulouse), and Beyond Montpellier.

### France Passion Plaisance
03 85 53 76 70
www.france-passion-plaisance.fr
Two to twelve-berth boats to cruise along the Canal du Midi, in and around the Toulouse area. Prices from €300 per weekend.

### Locaboat
ecluse de Négra, 31450 Montesquieu-Lauragais
05 61 81 36 40
www.locaboat.com/gb
30 km to the southeast of Toulouse at Négra, Locaboat will rent you a whole range of motor cruisers from two to twelve-berth. Prices start from around €800 per week.

**BEYOND TOULOUSE**

# Situated halfway between the Atlantic and the Mediterranean, Toulouse is surrounded by pretty rolling countryside and historic towns. It's a great area for sightseeing, from Cathar castles to a boat trip along the Canal du Midi.

## Canal du Midi

The Canal du Midi begins in Toulouse and runs for 240km, reaching the Mediterranean at Marseillan, near Sète. In Toulouse it connects to the Garonne river and its side canal, which runs west to the Atlantic. The linking of these two great seas, discussed since Roman times, was finally realised in the 17th century through the determination of one man: Pierre-Paul Riquet.

Riquet, the son of a count, was born in Bezier in 1609. His lucrative job as

controller of Languedoc's salt tax made him a wealthy man. When he retired at age 58, he turned to his long-held dream of building the Canal du Midi. Riquet saw the economic and strategic advantages of a waterway which bypassed the long journey around Spain and persuaded King Louis XIV to support the project. He overcame the main obstacle – a steady water supply – by harnessing the springs and streams of the Black Mountain into a huge reservoir and channelling it to fill the canal.

**Canal du Midi**
• tranquil waterway for cycling and boating
**Carcassonne**
• fortified hilltop medieval city

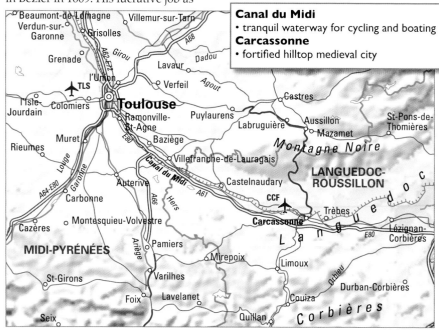

Construction began in 1667 and took 14 years to complete. Riquet spent his entire fortune on building the canal. Sadly, he died six months before it opened in 1681. For over 200 years the canal was a great commercial success. Although it declined with the coming of the railroads, it remains an engineering marvel.

Today the Canal du Midi is used solely by pleasure boats. Its tranquil banks are lined with plane trees, some 300 years old, while the old towpaths are used for cycling and walking paths. Half of the 63 locks are still manually operated, and the oval lock basins, stone bridges and canal tunnels add to its beauty. Home to a variety of birds, fish and wildlife, the canal was designated a UNESCO World Heritage Site in 1996.

A 90-minute ride on the *Bateau Solal* from Carcassonne, with a guided commentary, takes you through two locks and is a good introduction to the canal. For other options, from catered cruises to houseboat rentals, ask at the Tourist Offices or see **www.midicanal.fr**

### Bateau Solal

Carcassonne harbour
(opposite train station)
06 07 74 04 57
daily departures at:
10.00, 14.00, 16.00 and
18.00
€8 adults, €6 children

## Carcassonne

The old citadel is one of the most dramatic sights in the south of France. Set on a hill high above the river Aude, it is surrounded by medieval walls with an army of 52 watch towers and turrets, topped by distinctive conical roofs. The fortress is unusual for its double ring of stone walls three kilometres deep. The vacant ground between the two sets of walls is known as the *lices*.

Le Cité, as it was first called, was settled in 600 BC and is now a UNESCO World Heritage Site. The inner walls date from the Gallo-Roman period and the exterior walls are medieval. The massive outer ramparts that surround the entire perimeter of the hill were begun in 1226; fortifications continued throughout the 13th century. The present fairy-tale style was the work of Viollet-le-Duc, who restored the walled city in the 19th century, adding such fanciful features

### Getting there

There are frequent trains daily from Toulouse to Carcassonne. Journey time is 45 minutes to 1 hour. Carcassonne also has an airport 15 minutes west of the city centre, and there is hourly shuttle service into town.

### Tourist Office

28 rue de Verdun, Ville Basse (main office)
04 68 10 24 30; www.carcassonne-tourisme.com
09.00-18.00 daily, open all year

There are two branches:
porte Narbonnaise in Cité, open year-round
port du Canal, open April-October

as pointed roofs and arrow slits in the medieval towers.

Entrance is through two gates: **porte Narbonnaise** in the east, near the car park, and the more strenuous, but atmospheric **porte d'Aude** on the west. The area inside the walls is mostly given over to touristic shops and restaurants, particularly around the two main squares, place St Jean and place Marcou.

## Restaurants in Carcassonne

See page 287 for price guide.

**Les Fontaines du Soleil**
33 rue du Plo; 04 88 47 87 06
12.00-14.00, 19.00-late Mon-Sat
booking advised
credit cards accepted
€€€
One of the best places in the restaurant-packed streets of the medieval old city, the Fontaines is run by chef Michel Bousquet and his wife. Bousquet has worked in some top restaurants and now weaves his magic here in his own place. It's very simple with wooden floors and tables tucked into several small rooms, but the food is top quality. Bousquet does one of the best cassoulets that you'll taste, and his speciality dessert of *soufflé glacé avec creme de cassis* is mouthwateringly wonderful.

**La Trivalou**
69 rue Trivalle; 04 68 71 23 11
12.00-14.30 Wed-Mon, 19.00-late Wed-Sun
booking not usually necessary
credit cards accepted
€€

Just a short walk northeast of the tourist crowds in the old town, with many restaurants clamouring for custom, is this authentic and simple eating place. Half a dozen outside tables are sheltered from the occasional passing car by potted palms, and inside is a local bar with a few more tables. It's delightfully unpretentious and the menu is heartily regional with some inventive flourishes: tripe, beef, pork in a cucumber sauce, duck with honey. Excellent.

CARCASSONNE

## Château Comtal

09.30-18.30 April-September
09.30-17.00 October-March
€6.10 for 40-minute guided tour
A feudal castle built by the Trencavels, the 12th century Viscounts of Carcassonne. A guided tour gives access to the towers and walks along the inner ramparts. Views are spectacular. During busy times it's best to book ahead at the Tourist Office.

## Bastide Saint Louis

Also called *Ville Basse*, or lower town. It was laid out in 1260 in a checkerboard pattern around place Carnot, connected to Le Cité by the lovely Pont Vieux (old bridge), which spans the river Aude.

From here are fine views of the citadel and the pretty rue Trivalle. The lovely Canal du Midi runs along the northern end of this quarter. Boat trips run from the loch basin opposite the train station.

## The Cathars

A religious sect who believed in dualism (the struggle between the forces of good and evil), they flourished in Italy, Spain, northern France and particularly in Languedoc during the 12th and 13th centuries. Their view of the material world as ruled by evil clashed with the increasing materialism and corruption of the Catholic Church, who branded them heretics. In 1209 Pope Innocent III mounted a vicious military campaign (the Albigensian Crusade) to wipe out the Cathars.

Roger Raymond Trencavel, Viscount of Carcassonne, defended the Cathars but was forced to surrender after a 15-day siege led by Simon de Montfort. The brutal campaign continued throughout the region, right up to the walls of Toulouse. By 1230, the Cathars were largely destroyed and their lands seized for the French crown.

# MONTPELLIER

STATUE OF ZEUS, PLACE DU NOMBRE D'OR, ANTIGONE

# Montpellier is going all out to celebrate Rugby World Cup 2007, hosting South Africa, USA Australia, Samoa and Fiji.

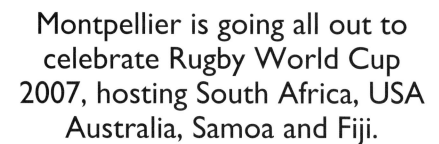

In a recent poll, Montpellier was voted the city where most French people would like to live. Much of the centre is traffic-free with open spaces, pedestrian streets and lively squares. The large place de la Comédie has the most central tramstop and is also the location of the Tourist Office.

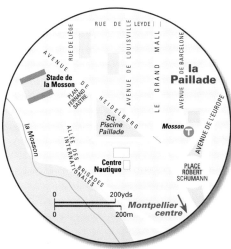

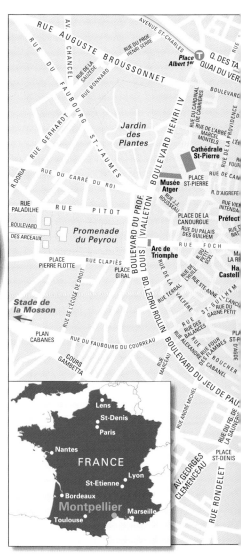

Montpellier's brightly painted trams are part of the city's charm and a main form of transport together with the bicycle. For many locals cycling is the preferred mode of travel.

The city has an international student population, many of whom come to study at the acclaimed medical school founded in the 12th century. The mix of cultures gives a lively cosmopolitan buzz to the city and contributes to its positive and friendly atmosphere.

Montpellier was at the height of its economic power in the medieval period, and today it is once again on the ascendant. The historic and the modern contrast beautifully here; from mansions in the old town to the ultra-contemporary angles of Antigone.

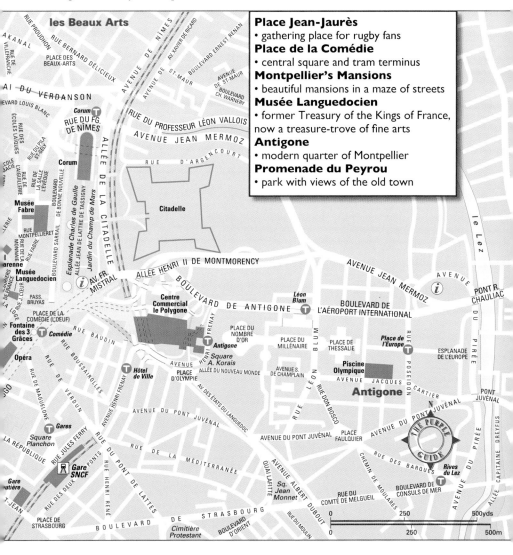

**Place Jean-Jaurès**
• gathering place for rugby fans
**Place de la Comédie**
• central square and tram terminus
**Montpellier's Mansions**
• beautiful mansions in a maze of streets
**Musée Languedocien**
• former Treasury of the Kings of France, now a treasure-trove of fine arts
**Antigone**
• modern quarter of Montpellier
**Promenade du Peyrou**
• park with views of the old town

## Getting to the stadium

**Nearest airport**
Montpellier Méditerranée
04 67 20 85 00
About 7km southeast of the city centre. Regular shuttle buses link the airport with the city, where you can catch a tram to the stadium.

**Car**
The stadium is on the west side of the city. Exit the main A9 road at number 31 and park in public carparks around the city. Then walk or take a bus to the stadium.

**Train**
Montpellier's main station, the Gare St-Roch, is in the city centre, a few minutes' walk from place de la Comédie tram terminal.

**Bus**
Lines 14, 15 and 25 go to La Mosson stadium.

**Tram**
Take Line A, direction of La Mosson; it is the final stop on the line.

## Getting around Montpellier

Purchase a City Pass at the Tourist Office.
day €12, two day €18 three day €22. Includes public transport, free or reduced entry to attractions, a free tour.

**Tourist Office**
place de la Comédie
04 67 60 60 60
09.00-19.30 Mon-Fri
09.30-18.00 Sat, 10.00-13.00, 14.00-17.00 Sun

REMEMBER TO
PURCHASE YOUR
TRANSPORT TICKETS
WELL IN ADVANCE OF
THE MATCH TO SAVE
TIME QUEUING.

### Stade La Mosson  capacity 33,650

| Matches | Date | Pool |
|---|---|---|
| USA v Tonga | 12 September, Wed | A |
| Samoa v Tonga | 16 September, Sun | A |
| Australia v Fiji | 23 September, Sun | B |
| South Africa v USA | 30 September, Sun | A |

## The stadium and around

avenue de Heidelberg
04 67 15 46 00

Stade La Mosson is located 6km due west of the city centre. It takes its name from the river Mosson, which runs through Montpellier's suburbs. The stadium has grown in parallel with the growth of the city itself.

In the early 1970's the ground only held 3,000 spectators, seated on wooden stands. As Montpellier Paillade Sporting Club rose through the ranks from non-league to league football, the stadium grew to a capacity of 17,000 by 1977. In 1990, the team won the French Cup, and by 1998 the newly-built Stade la Mosson, with its expanded capacity of 35,500, hosted several FIFA World Cup matches. The stadium was damaged by flooding in 2002, when the Mosson burst its banks, and is being renovated in time for Rugby World Cup 2007.

Australia's national team will have their training base camp in Montpellier's new Yves du Manoir Stadium, built specially for the Wallabies with a capacity of 12,000.

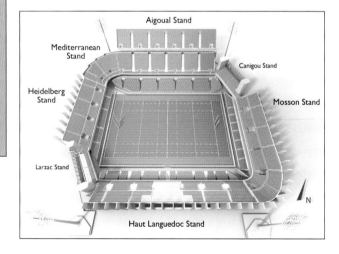

## Bars and screens

### Place Jean-Jaurès

and the surrounding pedestrianised streets have many bars and restaurants that are sure to be packed with fans during Rugby World Cup 2007.

### Planned large screens

• place Jean-Jaurès
• place de la Comédie
• place Zeus in Antigone

PLACE JEAN-JAURÈS

## Sports bars

### Temple's Bar
5 place Jean Jaurès
04 67 60 46 79
Located right on place Jean-Jaurès, this English pub gives a warm welcome to rugby fans of all nations. They have a giant screen showing all matches.

### Fitzpatrick's Irish Pub
5 place Saint Côme
04 67 60 58 30
www.fitzpatricksirishpub.com
A much-loved and authentic Irish pub, with a great atmosphere especially on rugby days. Screened sports and live music evenings are the usual thing – they'll be showing 'every kick of Rugby World Cup 2007.' The barmen pride themselves on having the cellar equipment which provides the perfect Irish pint.

### Le Corto
12 rue Candolle
04 67 66 35 67
One of the oldest pubs in the city, this cool, dark, medieval bar sees itself as the social centre of rugby in Montpellier. The large and characterful *patron* known as 'L'Ours' (the Bear) is said to drink more than his customers. The local honey wine, *hydromel*, is a speciality.

### Ayers Rock
108 rue de Rhodes
04 67 65 54 76
Sister bar to Ayers Rock in Lyon, and sharing its exuberance and love of rugby, this Australian-themed bar with cocktail-juggling waiters and big screens attracts a young and lively crowd.

### O' Carolan's
5 rue Petit-Scel; carré Saint Anne
04 67 60 98 18
Tucked away on a pretty little square in the heart of the old town, this is another Irish pub with friendly staff, a great atmosphere, quiz nights and match screenings.

### The Greyhound
13 place de la Comedie
A British pub serving a wide range of beer on tap.

### Mac Coy Saloon
285 rue Hélène Boucher
ZAC Fréjorgues Ouest
34130 Mauguio (near the airport)
04 67 20 25 57
For homesick US fans, the Mac Coy Saloon stands proudly in a shopping plaza near the airport. Western-themed, with staff dressed as cowboys and native Americans, the Mac Coy makes no concessions to authenticity or good taste. But if you can eat a 2 kilo steak in under an hour they'll waive your bill (the record is said to be 35 minutes).

## Nightlife

### The Rockstore
20 rue Verdun
04 67 06 80 00
18:00-04:00 Mon-Sat
www.rockstore.fr
This is a nightclub and music venue, featuring a variety of live bands.

## Place de la Comédie

To walk into place de la Comédie, Montpellier's main square, is to be reminded how city life ought to be. It's a vast, open plaza surrounded by busy cafés and bars, alive with the sound of talented buskers, and a meeting point for local people and visitors. Built in the middle of the 19th century, the beautiful buildings provide an elegant backdrop for modern city life.

The broad, pedestrian **rue de la Loge** leads from the west side of the square to **place Jean-Jaurès** in the city centre. A jumble of narrow streets run off to either side, lined with medieval mansions, shops, churches and some eye-catching trompe-l'oeil murals. Pleasant restaurants and cafes seem to fill every corner and square. In Montpellier ancient and modern live together in easy harmony.

At the south end of place de la Comédie is the old 1888 opera house, and the lovely *Fontaine des Trois Graces*. The Three Graces statue has an interesting history. Originally just a statue, city fathers were forced to surround it with water to stop drunken university students climbing up to kiss the maidens. Look closely around the fountain and you will see a red line on the ground. This ovoid shape marks the boundary of the original city square, looking from above like an egg, a symbol of the city.

### Corum

The modern opera house and convention centre is north of place de la Comédie, through the leafy **esplanade Charles de Gaulle**. Climb up to the terrace above the building for good views over the rooftops of the old town.

## Musée Languedocien

7 rue Jacques Coeur; 04 67 52 93 03
14.30-17.30 Mon-Sat
15.00-18.00 Mon-Sat, 15 June-15 Sept
€6 adults, €3 students

The nondescript exterior gives no clue to the treasures within this beautifully restored 15th century mansion. Inside is a fine collection of Languedoc art, archaeology and history from prehistoric times to the 19th century.

On the **ground floor**, the temporary exhibitions room contains the mansion's original 1445 ornate wood ceiling, with polychrome blue and red painted patterns. Adjoining rooms display Romanesque sculptures from regional churches beneath another beautiful coffered ceiling.

In the 17th century, the mansion was purchased by the treasurers of France, entrusted by the king to collect taxes and manage royal estates. The neoclassical inner courtyard is their legacy: two levels of Doric and Corinthian columns are topped by striking carvings of the sun, the royal motif of Louis XIV.

A monumental spiral staircase leads to the **first floor** and fine collections of decorative art, medieval religious objects, 16th-18th century furniture, tapestries and pottery. Be sure to see the rare celestial sphere by Italian cosmographer Vincenzo Coronelli. The ostentatious salons were once the private apartments of the Lunaret family who bought the house in 1816.

The **second floor** contains collections of Gallo-Roman, Greek, Etruscan and Egyptian antiquities, in addition to a room of prehistoric exhibits. Don't miss the unusual collection of mule bridal plaques from the Cevennes. A truly wonderful museum.

## Montpellier's Mansions

book a guided tour at the Tourist Office

The private mansions in the old town are a reminder of Montpellier's prosperity in medieval times. Behind massive entrance gates are handsome interior courtyards, carved stone staircases and architectural details. Most of the buildings are closed to the public except on these guided tours.

The tour also visits a medieval *mikve*, or Jewish ritual bath. This atmospheric 13th century bath was discovered in the cellar of a mansion and is one of the best preserved in Europe.

### Hôtel des Trésoriers de la Bourse

4 rue des Tresoriers de la Bourse (off rue Saint Guilhem)
usually open to the public and often hosts art exhibitions in the courtyard.

HÔTEL DES TRÉSORIERS DE LA BOURSE

## Musée Fabré

39 boulevard Bonne Nouvelle
04 67 14 83 00
phone for opening times

The recently renovated museum spreads across three buildings along the esplanade Charles de Gaulle. It displays some 800 works of primarily European art from the 16th-20th centuries. Famous artists include Gustave Courbet, Eugène Delacroix, Henri Matisse and Robert Delaunay. There are many works by Pierre Soulages. Collections of decorative arts, drawings and engravings are also on display in addition to temporary exhibitions.

## Promenade du Peyrou

A large park on the west of town with fountains, terraced gardens, statues and views over Montpellier's old town.

### Arc de Triomphe

Built at the end of the 17th century, the Arc de Triomphe looms at the end of rue Foch on the site of one of the old city gates. It marks the entrance to promenade du Peyrou, which was built to showcase the massive equestrian bronze of Louis XIV.

King Louis expressed a desire for a royal square to be built in his honour, but in a quiet show of independence, Montpellier city authorities waited until the King died and then built his monument outside the city walls.

Today the airy promenade is a relaxing spot for a Sunday stroll. It leads to the **Château d'Eau**, an octagonal pavilion at the end of an aqueduct that brought water to the city in the 18th century.

Nearby is the 13th century Faculty of Medicine, the oldest medical school in the western world, housed in a medieval monastery that adjoins the **Cathedral of Saint-Pierre**. The cathedral is often closed but you can't miss its most striking feature – a canopy porch whose lofty pillars are topped by conical roofs. You can visit the inside on a guided city tour, which also provides the only opportunity to climb to the top of the Arc de Triomphe for a grand view over Montpellier. Book at the Tourist Office.

ARC DE TRIOMPHE

## Antigone

You wouldn't normally expect a housing estate to be a visitor attraction, but Montpellier's modern Antigone district is a happy exception.

Conceived as low-income housing with a difference, Antigone is integrated with recreation and civic spaces, restaurants and other facilities. It is located east of the city centre and easily accessed through the Polygone shopping centre, or via the tram.

Designed in a neo-classical style by the Catalan architect Ricardo Bofill in the 1980s, Antigone consists of low-rise residential blocks and office buildings made of white stone. Many of these have allusions to Greek and Roman mythology with a glass-clad Olympic swimming pool and the central library.

A broad esplanade stretches through the centre, connecting a series of lovely squares and fountains. In the west, at **place du Nombre d'Or**, is a statue of Zeus in the centre of a delightful fountain where the water spouts in a sequence of playful leaps rising to a soaring geyser. In the centre, the **place de Thessalie**, boasts a striking circular fountain supported by statues of three young men.

At the eastern end the **esplanade de l'Europe** contains a statue of Nike and overlooks the River Lez.

HÔTEL DU RÉGION, ANTIGONE

# FOOD & DRINK

# Restaurants

See page 287 for price guide.

### Le Jardin des Sens
11 avenue St-Lazare (off av. de Nîmes, north of the city centre); 04 99 58 38 38
www.jardindessens.com
12.00-14.00 Thurs-Sat, 19.30-22.00 Tues-Sat
booking essential
credit cards accepted
€€€€

The Pourcel brothers are the star chefs in this part of France, and this is their flagship restaurant with three Michelin stars, north of the Corum at the hotel of the same name. They raise local Languedoc cooking to gourmet heaven with dishes such as fillet of pigeon stuffed with pistachios, or white truffle tarts with foie gras carpaccio.

### L'Ancien Courrier
3 rue de l'Ancien Courrier (off rue Saint Guilhem)
04 67 60 98 46
12.00-15.00 and 18.30-22.30 Mon-Sat
booking suggested
most major credit cards
€€€

This delightful little place has a handful of tables in the courtyard of an old Montpellier mansion, with more tables inside. There are menus at €16, €23 and €30, plus a la carte and an extensive list of wines from €16 to €1,580. The cooking is tasty and inventive, with even the cheaper menus offering such dishes as tomato stuffed with tapenade and fillet of daurade with pine nuts and sesame.

### Comptoir de l'Arc
place de la Canourgue
04 67 60 30 79
07.00-24.00 Mon-Sat, 10.00-24.00 Sun
booking advised weekends
credit cards accepted
€€€

Locals really rate this place on the corner of a traffic-free square just northeast of the Arc de Triomphe. There are tables outside by the trees and roses, and the creative (à la carte only) menu includes such delicious dishes as tuna marinated in avocado, pasta with ginger, and frogs' legs served with three sauces.

### Restaurant Cerdan
8 rue Collot, near place Jean-Jaurès
04 67 60 86 96
12.00-14.00 Mon-Fri and 19.00-late Mon-Sat
booking not usually necessary
most credit cards
€€€

Housed in a 12th century building, with a high stone-vaulted ceiling, the dining room has a cellar-like ambience. They serve an unusual mix of specialities from Normandy and Algeria – specifically from the town of Oranie, where the owner's family originated. There are set menus at various prices from €13.50 to €34.50 with a very good range of choices, including salmon fillet in a mustard sauce and *trou normand*.

RESTAURANT CERDAN

### Welcomedia
Opéra Comédie, place de la Comédie
04 67 02 82 65
www.welcomedia.fr
07.00-01.00 Mon-Sat
booking advised
credit cards accepted
€€

This very popular spot on place de la Comédie is located in the old opera house. It has an outdoor terrace bar/café, and a smart bar inside with a more formal restaurant, so there's plenty of choice. Try the tapas, with a glass or two from the wide regional wine list.

### Bistro d'Alco
4 rue Bonnier d'Alco (just north of the Préfecture); 04 67 63 12 89
12.00-14.00 Tues-Sat and 19.30-22.30 Mon-Sat
booking suggested
most credit cards
€€

On a quiet corner behind the place du Marché aux Fleurs is this terrific bistro with just eight tables on a raised terrace. The wine list is printed on a giant bottle, and the day's dishes are written on a blackboard.

Choosing is always difficult – the sign of a good menu. Options include octopus in parsley, duck breast in honey or aubergine caviar with smoked salmon. The owner is both efficient and friendly. The set menu is a bargain – two courses for €13 or three courses for €16. Highly recommended.

### Le Café Riche
8 place de la Comédie
04 67 54 71 44
11.00-23.00 daily
booking not usually necessary
major credit cards
€€

This brasserie on the main square is just about the most popular in town, for people-watching, rendezvous and enjoying a drink or a meal ranging from a light salad to grilled beef. Lots of wines by the glass, sports screens when there's a match on, and free wifi access. It's called the Café Riche but look for the big 1893 written across the awnings.

### Café des Arts
3 rue Saint Guilhem
04 67 60 81 87
12.00-24.00 daily
booking not usually necessary
most credit cards
€

Lively café-restaurant right by the market on a little square full of bars and restaurants. The speciality here is pizza, for about €10-13,

## Quiet Corners

One of the real joys of Montpellier is that large parts of it are pedestrian zones. There are many traffic-free squares hidden away where you might find one or two restaurants or cafés. The atmosphere on a warm evening is wonderful, so arm yourself with a good map from the Tourist Office (it is very easy to get totally lost in these back streets) and wander around till you see a place that takes your fancy.

on either a tomato or a crème fraîche base. Both are excellent. The house wine is €9 a litre, but buy a bottle – you get what you pay for.

### Bleu Thé
6 rue de la Croix d'Or (off rue de la Loge)
04 67 60 41 81
11.00-19.00 Mon-Sat
bookings not usually necessary
most credit cards
€

There is a current fashion in France for tea rooms and this is a lovely little place. It is in a very quiet pedestrian street just south off the main rue de la Loge. They serve coffee, tea, breakfast, brunch, salad, hot and cold dishes. Inside is a pastry counter with tempting displays.

COMPTOIR DE L'ARC

ESPRIT DE RUGBY

# Shopping

Shops are open from 10am-7pm, but some smaller family-run businesses close for lunch. Shops are closed on Sundays.

## Rugby shops

### Esprit de Rugby
19 rue des Étuves; 04 67 60 52 30
A small rugby shop located in one of the city centre's main shopping streets. It only has two rooms but manages to pack in many interesting items. There are amusing miniature shirts for babies as well as the usual adult jerseys, track suits and t-shirts, and rugby balls, some of them signed by local heroes.

### Eden Park
16 rue Foch
04 67 02 76 66; ww.eden-park.tm.fr
Established in 1987 by French rugby players Franck Mesnel and Eric Blanc who added a pink bow tie to their club kit for the French Championship final match. The chain is known for its quality wearable fashions with a strong rugby theme.

## General shops

### Le Polygone
09.30-19.30 Mon-Sat
This multi-storey shopping centre has branches of the Galeries Lafayette department store, FNAC, C&A, INNO, Zara and other major chains, plus a host of shops selling clothing, shoes, cosmetics, books,

sports gear and other goods. It is located off the northeast corner of place de la Comédie, on the west side of the Antigone district.

### Rue de l'Ancien Courrier
This cobbled street runs through the heart of the old quarter. Its old mansions now house a variety of boutiques and designer shops, selling men's and women's fashions, shoes, baby clothes and other gifts.

## Food and drink shops

Montpellier has many shops selling delectable local treats, such as *les croquants de Montpellier* (almond biscuits) and *les grisettes de Montpellier* (small round sweets flavoured with honey and liquorice). Rue St-Guilhem has several shops specialising in tea, wine, chocolate and other foodstuffs. Others to look out for include:

### Pinto
14 rue de l'Argenterie (off rue de la Loge)
04 67 60 57 65
Gérard Pinto has advised Michelin-starred chefs on their menus, and his gastronomic shop is one of the places to find the local specialities. Try *délice des Trois Grâces*, a rich dark chocolate with the taste of spicy French gingerbread, made with 65% cocoa. Foie gras, truffles, olives, jams, spices, and speciality oils and vinegars are among the inventory.

### Comtesse du Barry
18 rue de l'Argenterie (see above)
04 67 66 20 20
Next door to Pinto, this gourmet chain shop sells French gastronomic products.

## Flower market

### The Flowering Stadium
06.30-13.00 Tuesday
On Tuesday mornings, the car park at Mosson stadium is turned into a giant flower market. Shops and nurseries come from all over the region to set up stall in the biggest flower market for miles around. You can also buy seedlings for fruit and vegetables.

## Postcards

### Images de Demain/Hollywood
10 rue de la Vieille; 04 67 66 23 45
Rue de la Vieille is a short, narrow passage in the old quarter lined with thousands of picture postcards. On display is a fabulous range of cards, including movie stars, rock musicians, novelty cards and some featuring stunning photography. You won't want to post them.

*VISA*

# Golf and other sports

Montpellier has two international golf courses just 15 minutes outside the city centre. Many more await in the wider region of Languedoc Roussillon. You can get a Golf Pass that includes five green fees for a single player, which is valid for 21 consecutive days and can be used on 15 courses. Information and booking is available at the Tourist Office.

## Golf

### Golf de Montpellier-Massane
Baillargues (A9 exit 28 – Vendargues)
04 67 87 87 87
Located in Baillargues on the east side of the city, this course is easy to reach. The 27-hole golf course was designed by California architect Ronald Fream. Also on the grounds are a clubhouse, tennis courts, swimming pool, balneotherapy centre, hotel, gastronomic restaurant and brasserie.

### Golf de Fontcaude
Juvignac (A9, Montpellier west exit, towards Lodève-Millau)
Domaine de Fontcaude – route de Lodève
04 67 45 90 10
This championship course is north of Montpellier, in a beautiful setting with a real Mediterranean feel. The golf course has 27 holes, with a clubhouse, swimming pool, hotel and restaurant. There are plans for tennis courts, sauna, and other facilities.

## Cycling

Montpellier has 150km of cycle paths. You can cycle round the city centre and environs, into the countryside, or on back roads all the way to the beach. The sea is only 10 kilometres away. The bus and tramway company TaM also operates inexpensive bike rental at TaM Vélo, with a convenient city centre office near the train station. You can pick up maps and itineraries which include routes to the Odysseum, Mosson, the Zoo de Lunaret or the Domaine de Grammont. Bike rental costs €1.50 per hour, €3 half day and €6 for a day. Off road, electric bike and tandem rentals are also available.

### TaM Vélo
27 rue Maguelone; 04 67 22 87 82
www.tam-way.com
09.00-19.00 daily

## Canoeing

Saint-Bauzille-de-Putois is a centre for canoeing and kayaking and is located 40km north of Montpellier on the River Hérault. Several companies offer equipment rentals and courses of varying lengths.

### Canoë le Moulin
chemin de Sauzèdes, Saint-Bauzille-de-Putois
04 67 73 30 73
www.canoe-france.com
open daily Mar-Oct

### Canoë du Montana
opposite Tourist Office; Saint-Bauzille-de-Putois
04 67 73 36 76
www.canoe-cevennes.com
open daily Apr-Oct

### Canoë le Pont Suspendu
chemin de Sauzèdes, Saint-Bauzille-de-Putois
04 67 73 11 11
www.canoe34.com
open daily Mar-Oct

## Swimming

### Piscine Olympique d'Antigone
195 avenue Jacques-Cartier
04 67 15 63 00
Glass covered Olympic swimming pool in the modern Antigone district.

## Ice skating

In the heart of the Odysseum entertainment complex, Vegapolis is Montpellier's impressive sport and leisure ice-skating rink. The 3000 square metres of ice is divided into an Olympic-sized main rink and a games arena on another level. There are giant screens, light shows, music and entertainment. You can skate all year round, and skate hire is included in the admission price.

### Vegapolis
04 99 52 26 00
www.vegapolis.net
open daily, hours vary; €6.90 adults, €5.90 children

# There's fun to be had: cruise the Canal du Midi at Béziers, stay in a vineyard owned by a rugby player, or go jousting in Sète.

## Cruise to Toulouse

The **Canal du Midi** meets the Garonne river and a side canal at Toulouse, thereby connecting the Atlantic with the Mediterranean. A colossal feat of engineering by Béziers' own Pierre-Paul Riquet, the canal was opened in the 1680s. Set in gorgeous countryside, most of the length of the canal is lined with enormous shady plane trees, and is now a UNESCO World Heritage Site.

Join the canal outside Béziers at the Fonséranes locks, a staircase of eight steps which serves the biggest change in altitude on the canal's length. The choices of boat hire are endless:

Hourly:
• a tiny self driven electric boat
Daily:
• a larger motor cruiser
• a tourist boat through the set of locks to the Malpas Tunnel, the first ever built to accommodate a canal
Weekly:
• berths on converted barges or purpose-built craft will take you to Carcassonne (6 days), the most popular and picturesque part of the route, or as far as Toulouse (2 weeks)
• a solar-powered barge which will get you there even on cloudy days

www.francealacarte.com/soleil_doc.htm,
www.bargesinfrance.com
www.franceafloat.com

**Canal du Midi**
• empties into the sea here
**Béziers**
• medieval rugby-mad city
**Chateau l'Hospitalet**
• Gérard Bertrand's vineyard
**Sète**
• jousting by the seaside

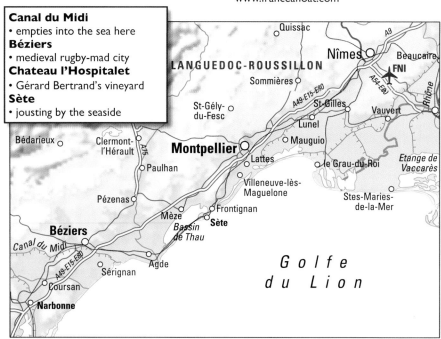

# Béziers

The medieval city of Béziers is mad about rugby. The local team, AS Béziers Hérault, was founded in 1911. They were a major force in premier league French rugby throughout the 1970s and 1980s but have now been relegated to Pro D2.

Béziers was pillaged in 1209 during the Albigensian Crusades and the entire population massacred, Cathar and Catholic alike ('Kill them all, God will know his own,' was the order given at the time). The town was given a new lease of life in the 1660s, when the Canal du Midi was built and trade boomed. Today, tourists are the only cargo on the canal.

Dominating the Béziers skyline, is the impressive **Cathedral**. It took two centuries to rebuild the original structure destroyed in the 1209 siege. Don't be put off by the forbidding exterior: inside it is graceful, light and airy, with a beautiful vaulted cloister.

**Musée des Beaux Arts**
Hotel Fabregat, place de la Révolution, 34500 Béziers; 04 67 28 38 78

09.00-12.00; 14.00-18.00 daily
closed Sun and Mon morning
The museum houses one of the best collections in the region with an excellent display of Greek vases and paintings by Hans Holbein, Giorgio de Chirico and Raoul Dufy.

**Le Fairway**
50 avenue St Saëns, 34500 Beziers
04 67 76 39 52
Not a rugby bar per se but Béziers' most popular sports bar with all the big matches screened, and popular with rugby fans, local and international alike. You can eat here too.

**Château l'Hospitalet**
D168 route de Narbonne Plage
(south of Béziers near Narbonne)
11100 Narbonne; 04 68 45 36 00
09.00-20.00 daily July-Sept
09.30-12.30, 14.00-19.00 Oct-June
www.gerard-bertrand.com
This vineyard is one of four owned by ex-rugby star, Gérard Bertrand. After his father's sudden death in 1987, Gérard, only 22, had to abandon his international rugby career to take charge of the family winery in Corbières. Gérard is a natural vintner, he made his first wine at the age of ten and has an in-depth knowledge of the Languedoc terroir. The Hospitalet estate covers 800 hectares overlooking the Mediterranean and includes a hotel and two restaurants. In addition to the winery, there is an art gallery, a crafts village and local wine for sale.

BÉZIERS CASTLE

CANAL ROYAL, SÈTE

# Sète

The coastal town of Sète is 35 km from Montpellier. Its attractive old neighbourhoods are criss-crossed by a series of canals, making it 'the Little Venice of the Languedoc'. Sète is an important fishing port, located between the Mediterranean Sea and the Thau Lagoon with its prized oyster beds. The Vieux Port, in the heart of the city, leads into the Canal Royal, the main waterway. With the fresh fish market so close at hand, there's no better place than the city's restaurants to try local specialities like *bourride* (monkfish in aioli sauce) or *la tielle* (octopus and tomato pie), as well as oysters and shellfish.

Take a stroll along the pretty Canal Royal, lined with colourful buildings, restaurants and cafés and crossed by several bridges; look for the statue of the water jouster near Pont de la Civette. Or just sit on the grandstand beside the quay and watch the pleasure boats pass by. You can hire your own boat or take a one-hour cruise along the coast or the lagoons. The rocky outcrop of Mont St-Clair, 175m high, rises to the west of the city centre. A viewing tower at the top affords a wonderful panorama over the town, lagoon and coastline.

**Tourist Office**
60 Grand'Rue Mario Roustan
04 67 74 71 71
www.ot-sete.fr
09.30-18.00 Mon-Fri,
09.30-12.30, 14.00-18.00 Sat-Sun

The writer and artist Paul Valéry was from Sète, as was singer Georges Brassens, and there are museums dedicated to them. Nearly 450 painters and sculptors have made their home in Sète, including Pierre Soulages.

Sandy beaches stretch for 12 kilometres west to Cap d'Agde. The first can be reached in about a half-hour's walk along the promenade that begins at the Vieux Port. The long, wide promenade is great for cycling, skating and strolling, with walkways leading down to the beaches on the corniche.

There are several trains a day to Sète from Montpellier. As you approach Frontignan, the previous stop, the lagoons come into view. Between here and Sète you may see flocks of flamingos feeding in the shallow waters.

## Water Jousting

'*Les Joutes*' is a medieval style joust that takes place on the water, rather than on horseback. There are two teams manning long wooden boats, brightly painted in their team colours of red or blue. The jousters are local fishermen dressed in nautical white. One stands atop the jousting platform, which extends from the stern some three metres above the water. Others sit below on the platform ladder for balance. Ten oarsmen row the rival boats towards each other, directed by a helmsman, while a drummer and oboe player sit in the bow playing the traditional jousting song.

Jousters hold a lance and a shield. As the boats pass on the left, they try to knock each other into the water. Often, a jouster will be thrown into the air by a direct hit. Last man standing is the winner. A brass band pumps up the crowd with songs and trumpet salutes to the victors after exciting passes.

Water jousting was recorded in Lyon in the 12th century, but it dates back to Rome and ancient Egypt. The Festival of Saint-Louis has been held annually on Canal Royal on 25th August since 1666. Sète has six jousting societies and a jousting school. Smaller jousting tournaments are held in other towns including the village of Pointe Courte.

BEYOND MONTPELLIER

209

MARSEILLE

# Marseille's Vélodrome stadium will host four Rugby World Cup 2007 games and two quarterfinals.

Marseille has a reputation for being a rugged and cosmopolitan port, sultry and sweaty in the Southern sun. Some of the tales are true – Marseille is hot, especially in the summer, and it is a multicultural port city, with plenty of rough edges. But Marseille is also full of pleasant surprises, like fantastic food and a lively nightlife.

The city is built around the horseshoe shaped harbour, Vieux Port. Two fortresses stand guard at the entrance to the harbour: Fort St-Jean on the north side and Fort St Nicholas on the south. High on a hill overlooking Vieux Port is Nôtre-Dame de la Garde, symbol of Marseille. On the north side is the hilly Panier district, the oldest part of the city. A little passenger ferry, the *César*, chugs its way back and forth between the north and south sides of the harbour, manoeuvering between the many luxury yachts.

In the bend of the horseshoe is the lively restaurant street, quai des Belges. Here you can catch a little train that goes up to Nôtre Dame or go shopping along La Canebière, Marseille's main street. Musée Cantini is located in the streets behind quai des Belges.

The cobbled streets of Le Panier are a pleasure to stroll in during the day but be aware that the heart of old Marseille can be dangerous after dark. A general rule of thumb is that areas north of Vieux Port and La Canebière are less safe for tourists than the areas south of the harbour.

The fish market in Vieux Port provides fresh ingredients for the city's speciality: *bouillabaisse*. Made with saffron, herbs, garlic and a minimum of three kinds of seafood, *bouillabaisse* is as individual and spicy as Marseille itself.

Be sure to visit Chateau d'If, the prison fortress described in *The Count of Monte Cristo*. Take the ferry for the views it offers of Marseille: the long harbour, backed by mountains, is a beautiful sight that belies the city's gritty reputation. Further south is a district called Le Corniche where you will find surprisingly good beaches.

VIEUX PORT: FISH MARKET

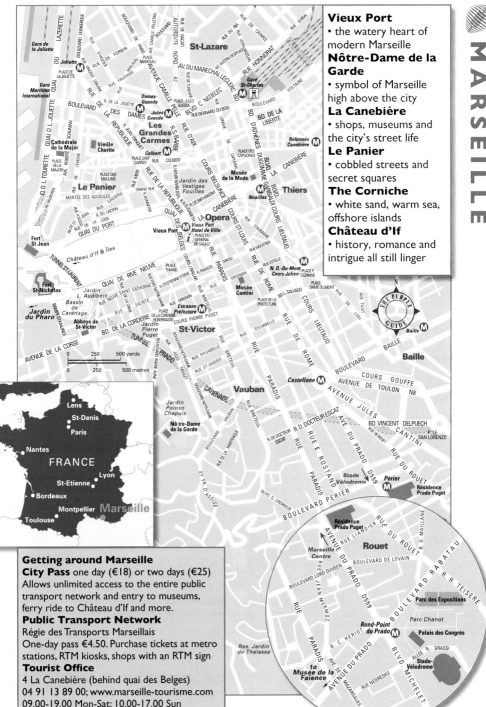

## Vieux Port
• the watery heart of modern Marseille

## Nôtre-Dame de la Garde
• symbol of Marseille high above the city

## La Canebière
• shops, museums and the city's street life

## Le Panier
• cobbled streets and secret squares

## The Corniche
• white sand, warm sea, offshore islands

## Château d'If
• history, romance and intrigue all still linger

**MARSEILLE**

THE PURPLE GUIDE

### Getting around Marseille
**City Pass** one day (€18) or two days (€25) Allows unlimited access to the entire public transport network and entry to museums, ferry ride to Château d'If and more.

### Public Transport Network
Régie des Transports Marseillais
One-day pass €4.50. Purchase tickets at metro stations, RTM kiosks, shops with an RTM sign

### Tourist Office
4 La Canebière (behind quai des Belges)
04 91 13 89 00; www.marseille-tourisme.com
09.00-19.00 Mon-Sat; 10.00-17.00 Sun

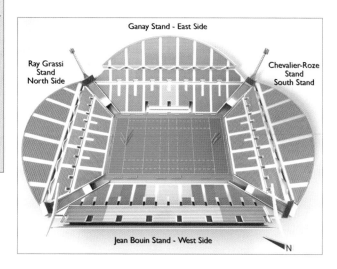

## Getting to the stadium

The Stade Vélodrome is 3km southeast of Vieux Port, straight along the avenue de Prado.

**Nearest airport**

Aéroport de Marseille-Provence is about 25kms northwest of the city centre. There is no metro into the city, but a regular shuttle bus takes you to Gare St Charles, where there is a metro station.

**Car**

Autoroute A50 comes right into Marseille, ending only a couple of kilometres north of the stadium. The Vélodrome has no available parking. Drivers would do better to go to the stadium on foot or by metro.

**Bus**

Bus 83 to Rond Point du Prado

**Train**

The gare SNCF St-Charles is slightly northeast of the city centre and has a Metro station from where you can reach the Vélodrome.

**Metro**

Take Line 2 to the Rond Point du Prado station for the Chevalier-Roze (south) and Jean Bouin (west) stands and to Ste Marguerite Dromel station for the Ganay (east) and Ray Grassi (north) stands. Both stations are very close to the stadium.

REMEMBER TO PURCHASE YOUR TRANSPORT TICKETS WELL IN ADVANCE OF THE MATCH TO SAVE TIME QUEUING.

## Stade Vélodrome  capacity 60,031

| Matches | Date | Pool |
| --- | --- | --- |
| New Zealand v Italy | 8 September, Sat | C |
| Italy v Romania | 12 September, Wed | C |
| Argentina v Namibia | 22 September, Sat | D |
| France v Georgia | 30 September, Sun | D |
| Quarter Final 1 W pool B v RU pool A | 6 October, Sat | |
| Quarter Final 3 W pool A v RU pool B | 7 October, Sun | |

# The stadium and around

3 boulevard Michelet
04 91 76 56 09

The Vélodrome is one of the most famous and feared stadiums in France. It has a reputation for being rough and tough, a place where passions run high, and where home teams, local or national, seldom lose. It is the home of football club Olympique Marseille, known locally as l'OM, the only French club to win the Champions League.

Built in 1937, the original Vélodrome was renowned for the loud roar that the crowd could muster, which was assisted by amplification caused by the stadium design. This effect was lost when the ground was enlarged for the FIFA World Cup 1998, and its capacity increased to the present 60,000.

## Bars near the stadium

The Vélodrome is located in a busy and pleasant part of the city that is full of good eating places; see Food and Drink for listings.

### O'Brady's Irish Pub
378 avenue de Mazargues;13008 Marseille
04 91 71 53 71
A Marseille institution and beloved of rugby fans, O'Brady's is the popular brainchild of local caterer Jean-Luc Bardy. Opened in 1996, the bar reached the semi-finals in a 'Best Sports Bar in France' competition. Jean-Luc sources authentic Irish ingredients for his dishes and there is a real peat fire burning in the hearth on chillier days.

## Bars in the centre

Quai de Rive Neuve in Vieux Port will really be buzzing on match days and is going to be one of *the* places to hang out during the tournament.

### Bar de la Marine
15 quai de Rive Neuve
04 91 54 95 42
07.00-02.00 daily
Part of the charm of this place, which features in Marcel Pagnol's plays and films about Marseille, is its rather scruffy bohemian atmosphere. Inside is an old zinc bar and at the back are tables under stone arches. Most people sit outside at the tables looking out at the buzz of the port.

### Shamrock
15-17 quai de Rive Neuve
04 91 33 11 01
11.00-02.00 Sun-Thurs, 11.00-17.00 Fri-Sat
This typical Irish bar, right on the Vieux Port, has a low-lit interior and beer posters on the walls. They serve Irish, Australian, Dutch and Belgian beers – just about everything except French beer, in fact. The sports screens will be upgraded for Rugby World Cup 2007.

### Le Pelle-Mêle
8 place aux Huiles
04 91 54 85 26
17.00-02.00 daily
If you're in the mood for a smarter bar, this little jazz place on a small canal off Vieux Port is a good choice. They have tables indoors and out, live music at least two nights a week, and they serve *La Cagoule*, a local brew with a nutty flavour.

### OM Café
25 quai des Belges
04 91 33 80 33
08.00-24.00 daily
all major credit cards
The Olympique Marseille sports bar is decked out in the official team colours of blue and white. It's a lively place with a terrace area and a bar with indoor restaurant seating. The walls are plastered with front covers of old sports magazines like L'Équipe, and there are TV screens as well as rugby balls, soccer balls and baseball caps all over the place. Food is basic, mostly steak and salads, simple but reliable.

## Vieux Port

You might wonder what the attraction is when you first arrive at the Vieux Port and witness the noisy traffic, tourists, souvenir sellers and the thousands of boats tied up in the harbour. Allow a day or two to adjust and you'll realise that it is all part of the charm – the buzz of Marseille.

This was once a tiny harbour where ancient Greek and Roman traders bartered olive oil for fish and seafood. The morning fish market on the quai des Belges is a modern reminder of those origins, with fishermen from along the coast coming to display their daily catch.

The entrance to the harbour is guarded by two fortresses: on the north side is the 12th century **Fort St-Jean**, open only for exhibitions. On the south is the **Fort St-Nicolas**, built by Louis XIV, today a military post.

Stroll along the waterfront, stopping at the many bars, restaurants and cafés. If the sight of all those boats makes you want to take to the water yourself, there are several excursions from quai des Belges and quai du Port. You can also cross the harbour on the little ferry **César** for less than one euro.

VIEW OF VIEUX PORT FROM JARDIN DU PHARO

### Jardin du Pharo

07.00-22.00 daily (closes 21.00 in winter)
For the best view of the port, walk along the southern side and up to the gardens around the Palais du Pharo, which was built by Napoleon III for his wife, the Empress Eugénie. You can't visit the palace as it is now a conference centre, but the gardens are a very popular spot with the locals, especially when the sun goes down and casts a warm glow over the busy port down below. From here, Marseille is transformed into a stunning beauty.

CÉSAR FERRY

### Marcel Pagnol (1895-1974)

Vieux Port was the setting for Marcel Pagnol's 1930s trilogy, *Marius*, *Fanny* and *César*. Featured in the films were card games under the arches of the Bar de la Marine, and the cross-harbour ferry that today bears the name of one of the characters.

Pagnol grew up in Provence and wrote affectionately about the lives, hopes and fears of its people. He was raised in St Loup and studied at the University of Aix-en-Provence. He first went into teaching before turning to writing plays. Pagnol later directed films from his own plays.

In the 1980s, two internationally popular films *Jean de Florette* and *Manon des Sources* were adapted by Claude Berri from Pagnol's original story. Pagnol had first written and directed it in 1952 as a single film, *Manon des Sources*, starring his wife Jacqueline.

## Nôtre-Dame-de-la-Garde

rue Fort du Sanctuaire
04 91 13 40 80
07.00-19.00 daily

From almost every point in the city you can see the large golden statue of the Madonna and Child gazing down from atop the narrow bell tower, looking protectively over Marseille. The striking, Byzantine-style basilica has become the city's symbol, visible from the Vieux Port and the Vélodrome alike.

The basilica crowns a steep hill south of the harbour, which you can reach on foot, by bus or on one of the little tourist trains that leave from the Vieux Port. Whichever way you get there, the journey is worth it, as the city views are, like the walk up, breathtaking. The basilica was built in the late 19th century and is surprisingly small inside, with beautiful mosaic floors, red and white striped marble pillars, ornate arches and walls covered in paintings, especially of ships, given in thanks for safe journeys.

## Abbaye de Saint-Victor

3 rue de l'Abbaye
04 96 11 22 60
09.00-19.00 daily
free; crypt €2 (or €1 with a city pass)

Marseille's oldest church overlooks the south side of the port. The present building dates mainly from the 14th century, but an early church built here in the 5th century was the city's first basilica. Today, the interior decoration is kept simple and the atmosphere is all the more beautiful for its simplicity. The gentle sound of chanting and the smell of incense fills the air, providing the perfect retreat from the bustle in the harbour. Be sure to visit the crypt, an ancient burial place with tombs dating back to the 2nd, 3rd and 4th centuries. An otherworldly atmosphere pervades.

## La Canebière

The main boulevard of Marseille travels due east from Vieux Port, and is always busy and chaotic. It is perhaps even more so at the moment owing to construction of a new city tramway system, due to open sometime in 2007.

It's hard to believe it was modelled on the Champs-Élysées in Paris, as the two streets could hardly be more different, each reflecting the character of its own city. La Canebière is noisy, traffic-filled and looks rather shabby – but that's Marseille.

### Musée d'Histoire de Marseille
(Museum of the History of Marseille)

Centre Bourse, 1 square Belsunce
04 91 90 42 22
12.00-19.00 Monday-Saturday
€2

One of the city's better collections is built into the basement of Centre Bourse because major finds were made here when the centre's foundations were being dug. The finds were preserved by incorporating the museum into the structure.

The star exhibit is the amazing *Bateau du Lacydon,* a 2nd century sailing ship. This Roman commercial boat sailed the Mediterranean and often made stops in Marseille, which was then called Massilia. After many long years of service the boat was abandoned in an ancient corner of the old port. Seventeen centuries later the ship resurfaced during construction work.

The museum has plenty of interesting exhibits on the city's history, including ceramics, skeletons, mosaics, handicrafts and model ships. There is an archaeological garden right outside.

### Museé de la Mode

(see the Shopping section)

## Musée Cantini

19 rue Grignan
04 91 54 77 75
11.00-18.00 Tues-Sun (summer)
10.00-17.00 Tues-Sun (winter)
occasionally closed between exhibitions
€3

The Cantini contains the best art collection in the centre of Marseille. It is housed in a 17th-century mansion just off the rue Paradis shopping street in an old part of the city. The museum displays works dating from the late 19th century, with especially fine collections of Surrealist and Fauvist art. Fauvism was a brief movement that followed the post-Impressionists and one of its most significant figures was Henri Matisse. His work naturally features here, along with works from Pablo Picasso, Max Ernst, Joan Miró, Alberto Giacometti, Raoul Dufy and Francis Bacon.

### Musée de la Faïence

157 avenue de Montredon
04 91 72 43 47
11.00-18.00 Tues-Sun (summer)
10.00-17.00 Tues-Sun (winter)
€2

The museum is housed in the Château Pastré located in the attractive park of Campagne-Pastré in the suburb of Montredon. To reach it continue along the promenade beyond the main city beach, Plage du Prado.

Château Pastré was built in 1862 and the interior and is decorated in the particular kind of Mediterranean ceramic work known as faïence. Although the process was probably invented in the Middle East in the ninth century, the craft flourished in Marseille. This museum has several floors with some of the finest examples of faïence ceramic art. There are even a couple of works by Picasso among the modern exhibits.

## Cathédrale de la Major

place de la Major
04 91 90 53 57
10.00-12.00,14.00-17.30 Tues-Sun
free

On the north side of the Vieux Port, round the quai du Port, is a large multi-domed, neo-Byzantine building. It was completed in 1893, and seems even larger when compared to the intimacy of Saint-Victor. The delicacy of the Cathédrale's mosaic floors contrasts with the massive pillars and the amazing domes. Stand underneath them and look up, for the full effect. Propped up next to the Cathédral are the rather forlorn remains of a much older church, mainly dating back to the 11th century but with some Roman elements as well.

## Le Panier

The steep, meandering streets climb up the north side of Vieux Port. It was the first part of Marseille to be settled when Greek traders arrived here some 2,500 years ago. You can sense the history as you wander through the cobbled streets and find quiet little squares. At the highest point is place des Moulins, where 15 windmills once stood. There are restaurants and interesting craft shops tucked away in nooks and crannies. If you're worried about getting lost you can follow *Le File Rouge* (the red line), a tourist trail which guides you round the most historic parts of Marseille. Ask at the Tourist Office for details.

### Musée d'Archéologie Méditerranéenne Musée des Arts Africains, Océaniens et Amérindiens
2 rue de la Charité; 04 91 14 58 80
11.00-18.00 Tues-Sun; €2

Hospice de la Vieille Charité, a 17th century former charity workhouse, is now used as the base for various art exhibitions and concerts, with a bookshop, café and two small but enjoyable museums.

## La Corniche

The proper name is La Corniche Président-Kennedy but it is known simply as La Corniche.

If you come expecting a tough port, it can be astonishing to discover this long stretch of waterfront, leading south out of the city and running for 5 km, backed by a breezy promenade and posh villas.

The Corniche is easily accessible from the city by bus or metro, and is lined with beaches, restaurants, watersports facilities and pretty little harbours like the one at Vallon des Auffes. This fishing village is tucked away below the main road, near the war memorial, but it's worth finding your way down. The picturesque inlet, lined with small boats, crackerbox houses and a couple of good restaurants, seems a hundred miles away from the image of Marseille.

Further on is the chic suburb of Malmousque, feeling more like a separate little town, with its narrow streets, rustic harbour and seafood restaurants.

04 91 59 02 30
May-September
09.30-18.30 daily
October-April
09.30-17.30 Tues-Sun
€5

**Getting There**
Ferries depart from
Vieux Port
at either quai du Port or
quai des Belges.

Summer:
09.00-18.45 daily
hourly departure
Winter:
09.00-17.45 Tues-Sun
variable departure
last ferry coincides with
the closing of Château d'If

€10 return Château d'If
€15 return Îles de Friuol

# Château d'If

The offshore island on which the evocative Château d'If stands is an example of early literary tourism. It owes much of its fame to a novel, *The Count of Monte Cristo* by Alexandre Dumas, and to a prisoner who never existed, Edmond Dantès. It takes only 15-20 minutes to reach the island today by boat from Marseille, but in the days when the Château was a prison, most people never made the return journey. The fictional Dantès was a notable exception, escaping after five years in the prison cells.

Seeing those cells is still a surprisingly haunting experience, even though it has become a popular day trip from Marseille's Vieux Port and the boats are often crowded. Many people prefer to skip the Château and stay on the boat to visit the other small islands offshore, which have more appeal for sunbathers as there is nothing to do on the tiny island of If other than to see the castle, walk around the outside, and catch the return ferry.

The short visit is well worth making, to see and hear the stories that lurk behind these prison walls. As well as featuring in *The Count of Monte Cristo*, the Château is also possibly one of the prisons in which *The Man in the Iron Mask* (another Dumas novel) was held, but this has never been confirmed.

The Château was originally built as a fortress in the early 16th century by King François I, but because of its location and sturdy walls it very quickly became a prison – and a most effective one. Some of the cells today are kept as basic as they once were, while those on the upper floors are quite spacious. Wealthy prisoners could pay for an upgrade to a larger cell with windows and a fireplace. Today some of these cells show historical videos about the Château and clips from some of the films inspired by the Dumas books.

The Sicilian lizard is also a prisoner of If, brought to the island in 1883 on a ship from Italy. The lizard escaped ashore and has since flourished on the sparse island. There is a short trail around the Château with information about local wildlife.

'He was now confined in the Chateau d'If, that impregnable fortress...'

*The Count of Monte Cristo*
Alexandre Dumas

## Restaurants

See page 287 for price guide.

BE AWARE THAT RESTAURANTS NEAR
THE STADIUM WILL BE BOOKED WELL IN
ADVANCE OF MATCHES.

### Near the stadium

#### La Villa
113 rue Jean Mermoz
04 91 71 21 11
12.00-14.30 and 20.00-23.00 Mon-Sat
before and after games at the Vélodrome
booking advised
credit cards accepted
€€€
This classy Italian restaurant has a lovely
shaded terrace as well as an elegant indoor
dining room. The bright green and white
awnings give it a cheerful smart-casual look,
and the menu includes nine types of pizza as
well as specials such as gambas risotto (€24)
and escalope Milannaise (€17.50).

#### Brasserie du Stade
26 boulevard Michelet
04 91 22 03 45
06.00-19.00 Mon-Fri
open weekends on match days, or for group
reservations in the evening (minimum 50 people)
booking required
most credit cards
€€
It will be difficult to book a table during
Rugby World Cup 2007 match days as the
brasserie has been booked by the Biarritz
Rugby Club. That said, this is a genuine
rugby bar with old photos of the Vélodrome
on the walls with other memorabilia. There's
a smarter dining area at the back with
several big-screen TVs and a wood-fired
oven – pizza is a speciality, as are various
kinds of tartare.

#### La Terrasse de St Giniez
22 avenue de Mazargues, 13008 Marseille
04 91 77 89 91
12.00-15.00 daily
closed evenings
booking not usually necessary
most credit cards
€€
A very casual terrace restaurant, set back
from one of the main roads. It specialises in
authentic dishes from southern France. The
menu of the day costs €12-14 and there is
a regular menu that includes tasty options

LA VILLA

like duck breast grilled in honey. With house wine at only €7.50 for 100cl, it's definitely worth a visit for a good but inexpensive lunch.

### Le Vin Sobre
56 rue Négresko,
04 91 32 68 64
www.levinsobre.com
Bistro:
12.00-14.30 Mon-Sat
Shop:
10.00-14.30, 16.30-20.00 Tues-Sat
10.00-13.00 Sun, 10.00-14.30 Mon
booking advised
most credit cards
€€
This terrific little place is both a bistro and a wine shop, so the walls are lined with bottles. Choose your wine from the shop shelves (at shop prices) or sample one of the numerous wines available by the glass. There is a set menu each day at about €20, and an à la carte with such offerings as duck foie gras or *charcuterie*.

### Le Bistrot du Paradis
18 avenue de Mazargues
04 91 77 25 39
07.00-23.00 Mon-Fri, 08.00-23.00 Sat-Sun
bookings not taken
no credit cards
€
It's called a bistrot but it's more of a local bar. Food is only served at lunch and on match days when it's packed and they do a set menu for €20. The décor is blue and white, the colours of Olympique Marseille. There are several sports screens and an open-to-the-sky seating area at the back. This whole street is a good one for bars and cafés within a short walk of the stadium.

### Phoenix d'Or
4 boulevard Michelet
04 91 71 76 27
12.00-15.00 and 19.00-late Tues-Sun
booking recommended
most credit cards
€
If you've ever wanted to try frogs' legs in soy sauce, this is the place. The Golden Phoenix is a smart and charming little Chinese place, with only 10-12 tables. There are fixed menus at €9 and €12.50, and the à la carte includes well-prepared standard dishes like chicken with pineapple and chicken with ginger.

## In the city

### Restaurant Miramar
12 quai du Port
04 91 91 10 40
www.bouillabaisse.com
12.00-14.00 and 19.00-22.00 Tues-Sat
closed Sunday-Monday
booking required
credit cards accepted
€€€€
The Miramar is one of *the* places to eat in Marseille, and has become renowned as the home of bouillabaisse as its website address indicates. There is an outdoor terrace right on Vieux Port, and an elegant indoor dining room. The service is formal, with immaculately-dressed waiters attending to your every need. Chef Christian Buffa has inspired a wide range of regional and mainly seafood dishes, but their *tour de force* is bouillabaisse. Having it here is a theatrical experience – the price is similar to a night at the opera, but worth every penny.

## *Bouillabaisse*

A two-course meal beginning with soup, which is made from fish stock and served with croutons and *rouille* (similar to spicy mayonnaise). While you are sipping the soup, a waiter will prepare fish and seafood at your table, which will then be served on a separate plate. Mussels, prawns, crabs and freshly-caught fish are usually included. An authentic *bouillabaisse* will have three types of fish depending on the season.

Ingredients can include saffron and herbs (basil, fennel, thyme) plus garlic, onion, wine, leeks, and orange peel. It is a memorable experience to have a good one – so indulge at least once!

LA PLANETE

## Café de la Paix
42 rue St Saëns, off quai de Rive Neuve
04 91 55 70 36
12.00-14.30 and 19.00-23.30 daily
booking not usually necessary
credit cards
€€

A large bright terrace runs round two sides of this building in a traffic-free street one block back from the waterfront. There are large glass windows all around the terrace, bright yellow tablecloths and set Provençal menus at €15, plus a more expensive *à la carte*. Fresh fish is their speciality, including *daurade provençal*, the inevitable bouillabaisse and salmon in a lemon sauce.

## Chez Etienne
43 rue de Lorette; 04 91 73 31 55
12.00-14.30 and 19.30-23.30 Mon-Sat
booking advised
no credit cards
€€

Marseille rugby players eat here, as does Michael Caine when he's in town, and there are photos on the wall to prove it. Chez Etienne is a very warm and homely Italian place in the Panier district, with a genial Sicilian owner who makes everyone welcome. The house special is lamb's foot with tripe and spices, but you can have a pizza from the wood-fired oven, seafood spaghetti and a handful of other wonderful dishes.

## Chez Madie
138 quai du Port; 04 91 90 40 87
12.00-14.00 and 19.30-22.30 Mon-Sat
booking not usually necessary
most credit cards
€€

A lovely place that is well worth the walk to the far end of the quai du Port. It is popular with the locals who come here to escape the bustle of the city. Look for the bright red and white table settings along the pavement. The cooking is superb, with dishes such as red mullet tart with tapenade, and duck breast with figs.

## La Planete
45 quai des Belges
04 91 33 14 82
11.30-15.00 and 18.00-late, daily
booking not usually necessary
some credit cards
€

Despite its modern name this friendly, family-run place was opened in 1927. There are tables both outside on this busy corner of the Vieux Port, and inside where there's also a huge fish tank. Fish is the speciality, with four different types of bouillabaisse on the menu, all served properly at your table, with the waiter preparing the fish and shellfish while you are eating the soup. An excellent, inexpensive option.

## Donatello
17 place aux Huiles
04 91 54 06 07
12.00-14.30 and 19.00-23.00 daily
bookings not necessary
most major credit cards
€€

Lively Italian restaurant, always busy and good value, housed in a former warehouse dating from a time when this *place* was a canal. You can watch pizzas being cooked in the wood-fired oven. These are the best bet on the menu, and the house wine is cheap and hearty.

# Shopping

Shops are open from 10am-7pm, but some smaller family-run businesses close for lunch. Shops are closed on Sundays.

Whether you want French fashion or Provençal souvenirs, Marseille is a great shopping city. The main shopping quarter lies just behind the port off La Canebière. To the south, you'll find designer shops along rue Paradis and its side streets. Chic boutiques and European chains occupy the restored grand buildings of the parallel, pedestrianised rue St-Ferreol. To the north of the boulevard is Centre Bourse, a large indoor mall with a branch of the department store chain Galeries Lafayette.

Good local shops and markets sell food, drink, olive oil, soap or colourful Provençal ceramics. There are also terrific local specialities such as *santons* and local biscuits known as *navettes*.

## Local produce

### La Maison du Pastis
108 quai du Port
04 91 90 86 77
If you think you have tasted *pastis* (the regional aperitif that originated in Marseille) because you have had one of the big-name brands in a café or bar, think again. Here, in a shop that's unique in France (according to the owner), you can taste the products of several dozen local producers, some of whom can take several months to mature their pastis. Certain varieties contain up to 14 different ingredients, including coriander, cardamom, anise and two kinds of liquorice. You can also try absinthe and other local products such as tapenade, olives, mustard of pastis, pastis terrine and an exclusive pastis OM (the Olympique Marseille brand).

### Place aux Huiles
2 place Daviel, just north of quai du Port
04 91 90 05 55
This delightful shop next to the Hotel-Dieu specialises in Mediterranean produce, mostly of the edible and drinkable variety. They have a wide selection of olive oils, some of which you can taste, as well as tapenade, mustard, vinegar, honey, cider, local beer, olives and anchovies. In addition there is a special Marseille soap, as well as cosmetics and olive wood carvings.

## Navettes

Navettes have been made in Marseille at the Four des Navettes bakery since the 18th century, and are as popular today as they ever were. The recipe is, of course, the proverbial closely-guarded secret, but they rely on a particular kind of flour, kneaded in an old kneading trough which has slowly-turning blades, and then baked in the original 1781 perfectly round oven, based on a Roman design. The result is a hard and dry but extremely tasty biscuit, that's a popular gift locally and also makes a good souvenir.

**Four des Navettes**
136 rue Sainte
04 91 33 32 12
www.fourdesnavettes.com
07.00-20.00 daily, 09.00-15.00 Sunday

## Santons

The idea of having small indoor cribs at Christmas began in Marseille. Churches were closed during the French Revolution and there were no outdoor cribs for the Christmas season. Deprived of their traditions, people secretly made their own indoor cribs.

In 1798, Jean-Louis Lagnel began making miniature clay figures at his workshop at 13 rue de Refuge in the Panier district. Inspired by local characters, he produced peasants and fishermen in addition to the usual nativity figures. And so the Marseille tradition of the *santon* was born.

Santons are still made today, and there's been a Santon Fair in Marseille ever since 1803 when people began selling the figures on the streets in the build-up to Christmas. Today the city still has a few dozen santon makers, though André Robbe (see box) is the only one who still makes them in the traditional manner.

Other santon makers include:

**Atelier Arterra**
15 rue du Petit-Puits
04 91 91 03 31
www.santons-arterra.com

**Santons Marcel Carbonel**
47 rue Neuve Sainte-Catherine
04 91 54 26 58
www.santonsmarcelcarbonel.com

## The Santon Maker

André Robbe holds a tiny painted figure in his hands, and introduces him as Bartelemé. Monsieur Robbe is the only one of the city's santon makers to use the original method, which is to make a mould of the body of the little model, and add the arms on later. Today all other santons are made in complete moulds. It may be a tiny difference to the outsider, but to Monsieur Robbe it is a question of keeping the tradition alive.

'This is Bartelemé,' he says, 'and his nickname is Pistachio. Every one of the santons has a history, and I create them to reflect the history of that time, using authentic fabric for their clothing. Bartelemé is always happy, very generous by nature, always dreaming. Every time he goes to visit the crib he carries with him everything he owns. When he heard the angels he dressed very quickly and forgot a few garments. On the way to the crib he

## Markets

### Fish Market
quai des Belges, Vieux Port
08.00-13.00 daily
Centuries-old traditional market, where fishermen from the little villages along the Corniche bring their catch to sell each morning. It isn't very large but it has a great atmosphere, with much banter and many fascinating sea creatures.

### Provençal Market
quai des Belges, Vieux Port
08.00-17.00 Sundays
On Sundays, alongside the fish market, local artisans set up their stalls with colourful displays of good quality items.

**VISA**

PROVENÇAL MARKET

chased after some young girls. When he approached the baby his trousers fell down.

'In Provence to have good pistachios you need one male tree to 40 female trees. If you call an older man a *pistachier* it's a compliment because it means he has many lady friends. For a young boy it's not such a good term. It's the same character as the Greek god Pan, which is why his tunic is green. The santons, you see, are like pillars of our society.'

### Le Cabanon des Accoules
24 montée des Accoules
04 91 90 49 66
M. Robbe plans to move his workshop soon, to new premises nearby.

## Fashion

### Museé de la Mode
11, la Canebière; 04 96 17 06 00
10.00-17.00 daily, closed Mon, €3
In the heart of the main shopping district this is a museum of fashion rather than a sales outlet, but why not combine retail therapy with some style inspiration? Housed in Marseille's superb Espace Mode Méditerranée (Mediterranean Fashion Space), the museum reviews French fashion trends over the past 70 years. Designs by Chanel, Yves Saint Laurent and Christian Lacroix are among the thousands of items of clothing and accessories on display.

### Eden Park
13-15 rue Paradis
04 96 11 28 11; ww.eden-park.tm.fr
Established in 1987 by French rugby players Franck Mesnel and Eric Blanc who added a pink bow tie to their club kit for the French Championship final match. The chain is known for its quality wearable fashions with a strong rugby theme.

## Soap

### La Compagnie de Provence
1 rue Caisserie; 04 91 56 20 94
Marseille has a long tradition of soap-making, and still has a few factories producing the real thing with the trademark Savon de Marseille stamp on it. It's made with 72% vegetable oil. You can buy it here at this swish and modern soap and cosmetic specialist, along with perfumes, liquid soaps, lavender soaps and other treats that make great gifts for wives and girlfriends.

## Ceramics

### Serge Moutarlier
7 rue du Petit-Puits, near Vieille Charité
04 91 90 68 32
www.sergemoutarlier.com
Many artisans have shops in rue du Petit-Puits and the adjacent place des Pistoles in Le Panier. Serge Moutarlier creates wonderful novelty teapots, ceramics, plates, cups and more, all in bright Provençal colours: deep blues, greens, yellows.

### La Sardine d'Argile
5 rue du Petit-Puits; 04 91 90 30 72
On the same street at 'The Clay Sardine', Jean-Marc Saman practices the art of faïence, using traditional methods, colours and motifs such as the eponymous fish.

**VISA**

229

# Golf and other sports

With its reputation as a gritty port and big city, people often don't realise that Marseille has beaches and promenades, like other cities on the Mediterranean. Several miles of beach stretch to the south of town, beginning just around the corner from the Vieux Port and easily reached by bus or even on foot, though it's a long walk. All along the Corniche you can indulge in watersports including sailing, powerboating, windsurfing and diving, and it's a popular place to go jogging too.

## Golf

### Golf d'Aix Marseille
Domaine de Riquetti, 13290 Les Milles
04 42 24 20 41
www.golfaixmarseille.com
About twenty minutes to the north of the city, just south of Aix, this course is set in a welcoming parkland of mature trees and well-kept fairways. With clubhouse and bar, driving range and putting green.

### Golf de Marseille La Salette
65 impasse des Vaudrans, La Valentine
13011 Marseille
04 91 27 12 16
www.opengolfclub.com
Just ten minutes from the Vieux Port, La Salette is a hilly course set among pinewoods, with breathtaking views to the mountains inland. There's a restaurant in the clubhouse, and practice holes to sharpen your game.

### Golf d'Allauch
Domaine de Fontvieille, route des Quatre Saisons, 13190 Allauch
0033 4 91 07 28 22
www.golfallauch.com
Ten minutes to the north-east of the city near the hill town of Allauch, this course is only nine holes, but there is a swimming pool and adjoining restaurant and tennis court. Advance booking advisable.

### Golf de Marseille la Salette
65 impasse des Vaudrans, La Valentine,
13011 Marseille
04 91 27 12 16
www.opengolfclub.com

This 18-hole course is in a spectacular location in the hills of Provence on the outskirts of the city.

## Pétanque

*Pétanque* is the southern French spin-off of the popular game of *boules*. It is said to have been invented in 1907 in La Ciotat, about 30km south of Marseille. It is now the most popular sport in Marseille (and indeed in France). The name comes from the Provençal words *ped tanc*, 'stuck feet' or 'feet together' on the ground. The alternative and older version is *jeu provençal*, a more physically demanding game played on a much larger pitch, where the balls are delivered at a run. The Fédération Internationale de Pétanque et Jeu Provençal was founded in 1958 in Marseille and has about 600,000 members in 52 countries.

In 2007, the French are celebrating the centenary of the invention of pétanque with an assortment of events, including the holding of 24-hour pétanque-fétes.

### Boulodrome Pierre Peres
87 promenade de la Plage, 13007 Marseille
This is Marseille's main pétanque field and you can often catch a few matches, especially at weekends. There is also the annual international pétanque championship, held each June at the Parc Borély, 4km south of the Vieux Port, on the coast.

## Horseracing

### Hippodrome de Borely
16 avenue de Bonneveine, 13008 Marseille
04 91 32 70 70
www.hippodrome-borely.com
entrance €5
Horse-racing over the flat, and trotting, are both very popular in Marseille. The season runs from September through to July, so there's sure to be something happening during the Rugby World Cup 2007. Races are usually held on Wednesdays and weekends – the racecourse is in the Parc Borély, 4km south of Vieux Port along the coastal road.

## Boat hire and watersports

### Soleil Rouge Yachting
216 quai du Port
0033 4 91 90 60 67
www.soleilrougeyachting.com
At Soleil Rouge's two locations in the Vieux Port or Port Corbières you can hire a wide range of boats, from sailing catamarans to motor cabincruisers. They'll provide you with a skipper for a short time to help familiarize yourself with your craft's characteristics (if you wish you can keep him on for €200 per day plus food); give you navigational advice and weather bulletins; and then you're on your own. There's also a Corsica office in Ajaccio so one-way trips are a possibility. You can hire by the half-day, the day or the week, and all boats have VHF radio and GPS, a shower, a fridge and a motorized dinghy as standard.

Also:
http://www.midi-nautisme.com
http://www.bookayacht.com

### Jet 13
Port de la Pointe Rouge
plage du Prado/Pointe Rouge
0033 4 91 72 59 90
www.jet13.fr
Here you can rent jet-skis, sea-scooters and powerboats. Prices start from €45.

## Scuba

Marseille is also one of the Mediterranean's great diving centres: there are numerous local islands, reefs and historic wrecks to be explored and the city is well provided with diving centres who can rent equipment and give advice. Occasional but regular finds of sunken treasure or items of

ST RAPHAËL

archaeological importance are made in the region, so you may be lucky.
www.airdive-provence.com
www.le-chant-des-sirenes.com
www.massilia-plongee.com

### Diamond Diving
Broughton Manor, Newport Road
Milton Keynes, MK10 9AA
0044 (0)1908 234 030
info@diamonddiving.net
www.diamonddiving.net
This is an English company based in the south of France that organises diving and accommodation packages in five towns along the Côte D'Azur. Their offering is perhaps most relevant for rugby fans attending games at Marseille as it is a short train journey along the coast to their locations. Group prices and bespoke itineraries available on request. Alex Diamond, Director, is a PADI Instructor and fully qualified in the French system (Brevet D'Etat) and will lead all trips in 2007. He can be contacted on alex@diamonddiving.net or 0033 15 30 52 23.

# Provence is the third-largest region in France, stretching from east of the Rhône river to the Italian border.

Its diverse landscapes include the Alpes-Maritime, which form its northern and eastern borders, and the famous Côte d'Azur along the Mediterranean, with the towns of St-Tropez, Cannes, Cap d'Antibes and Nice. Vincent Van Gogh, Paul Cézanne and Pablo Picasso are just a few of the great artists who found inspiration here. Although it would take considerable time to explore this huge region, many of its highlights can easily be reached from Marseille. These include impressive Roman amphitheatres at Arles and Orange, the medieval bridge and papal palace at Avignon, the vineyards of Châteauneuf du Pape, the wildlife-rich marshlands of the Camargue, and some of the country's best markets at Arles and the elegant city of Aix-en-Provence.

Just along the coast at the delightful resort of Cassis, you can embark on a relaxing cruise of **Les Calanques**, magnificent fjord-like gorges ideal for birdwatching and/or fishing.

**Aix-en-Provence**
• an elegant city with good restaurants, once the home of Paul Cézanne
**Arles**
• Van Gogh painted some of his most famous works here

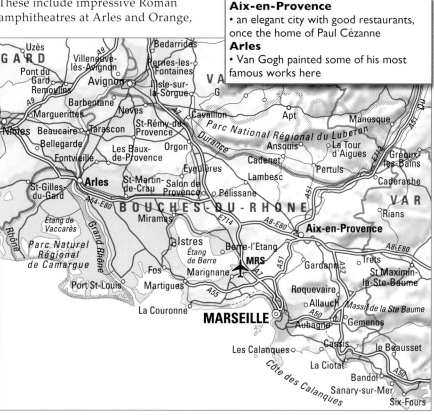

## Aix-en-Provence

It's only 25 km north of Marseille, but Aix-en-Provence seems a world away from the earthy port city. Here the atmosphere is one of genteel prosperity, with handsome mansions, leafy squares and around 40 public fountains which are a much-loved feature of the city. Aix was founded by Romans attracted by its hot springs and was the capital of Provence from the late 12th century until the Revolution. Long known as a centre of art and learning, its well-heeled residents are joined by thousands of students who come to study arts and humanities at its prestigious university. The writer Emile Zola and the painter Paul Cézanne were born in Aix and lived here in the 19th century.

### Cours Mirabeau

The most beautiful street in this beautiful city is its central boulevard, cours Mirabeau, lined on both sides with towering plane trees. It begins at the Rotunda with its monumental fountain representing Justice, Agriculture and Fine Arts, the town's main activities. Three smaller fountains stand along the centre. The oldest, the Nine Canons Fountain, dates from 1691. The middle Hot Water Fountain, known as the 'mossy fountain', is fed by a hot spring. King René's Fountain, at the eastern end by place Forbin, has a statue of the king holding a bunch of grapes, symbolising the Muscat vines he brought to Provence. The boulevard is further graced by elegant 17th and 18th century mansions with wrought-iron balconies, and pleasant cafés where you can survey the passing scene.

The best time to visit Aix is on a Tuesday, Thursday or Saturday morning when a large clothing market runs the length of the boulevard. This is not your run-of-the-mill bargain goods market.

COURS MIRABEAU

You'll find quality dresses, trendy sportswear, Provencal fabrics, lingerie, smart handbags and leather goods. The market continues into the streets of the old town, to the north of cours Mirabeau. There is an antiques and flea market beside the Palais de Justice in place de Verdun, a huge food market centred around place des Prêcheurs, and a colourful flower market in front of the town hall in place de l'Hôtel de Ville. Go early – by 1pm it's all wrapped up and street cleaners are sweeping the streets back to their usual pristine state.

You'll find many upmarket shops along the narrow, semi-pedestrian streets of the old town. Forum des Cardeurs, centre of the medieval Jewish quarter, is now filled with bright cafes and restaurants.

### Cathédrale Saint-Sauveur

07.30-12.00 and 14.00-18.00 daily

This major landmark displays a mix of styles from the 5th to 17th centuries. Noteworthy features include the carved walnut doors at the west entrance, Romanesque cloisters, and the lovely octagonal baptistery to the right of the entrance, which dates from the 4th and 5th centuries and incorporates columns from an earlier Roman temple.

### Musée des Tapisseries

28 place des Martyrs de la Résistance
04 42 23 09 91
10.00-18.00 Wed-Mon; €2.50

Next door to the Cathédrale is the former Archbishop's Palace. On the first floor, the ornate state apartments are now home to the Musée des Tapisseries, the Tapestry Museum. Among the splendid works, woven in the 17th and 18th centuries, are nine huge panels illustrating the life of Don Quixote. There is also a display of costumes from the annual music festival held here in July.

### Musée Granet

place Saint-Jean de Malte
04 42 52 88 32
11.00-18.00 Wed-Mon

To the south of cours Mirabeau is the Mazarin quarter, once the home of the aristocracy. At its heart is the place des Quatre Dauphins, with its lovely dolphin fountain. Nearby is Musée Granet, Aix's main art and archaeology museum, housed in the former priory of the Knights of Malta. Cézanne studied here when the building was used as an art school. It displays eight of his works, along with French paintings from the 16th to 20th centuries, works from the Dutch, Flemish and Italian schools, sculpture, graphic arts and archaeology exhibits from a nearby 2nd century BC Celto-Ligurian settlement. The museum reopens in 2007 after a major renovation, with a new collection of modern works, including pieces by Picasso, Piet Mondrian and Paul Klee. Adjoining the museum is the church of Saint Jean of Malta, a fortified Gothic church built in the late 12th century which served as the priory chapel.

## Les Thermes Sextius

55 cours Sextius; 04 42 23 81 82
www.thermes-sextius.com
This thermal spa complex stands on the site of the old Roman baths in the old town.

**Getting to Aix-en-Provence**
The train station is 8km outside of town, with a shuttle service to the central bus station with departures every 30 minutes.
If you are travelling from Marseille, taking the coach is the best option. Departures occur every 5-10 minutes and the journey takes around 30 minutes, depending on traffic. Buses arrive and leave from avenue de l'Europe, which is about a 5-minute walk from cours Mirabeau. Tickets cost €4.40 and you can purchase them on the bus.
**Tourist Office**
2 place du Général de Gaulle; 04 42 161 161
www.aixprovencetourism.com
08.30-19.00 Mon-Sat, 10.00-13.00,14.00-18.00
Sun and holidays (longer hours in high season)

## Paul Cézanne

The Impressionist painter Paul Cézanne was born in Aix on 19 January 1839. At school he became friends with the writer Emile Zola, who encouraged him to pursue his dream of becoming an artist. Cézanne enrolled in law school to please his father, but studied painting at the same time. After failing the exam to enter the Ecole des Beaux Arts in Paris, he returned to Aix in 1861 to work in his father's bank. Eventually his father gave him a small allowance to support his painting career, and he returned to Paris where he met Monet, Renoir and Pissaro, as well as his future wife Hortense Fiquet.

Cézanne displayed his works in several Impressionist exhibitions during the 1870s, but increasingly spent more and more time in Aix. He returned to Provence permanently in 1886, where he often painted the Montagne Sainte-Victoire and surrounding landscape. In 1899 he rented a flat in Aix in rue Boulegon. Two years later he built his studio at chemin des Lauves, north of the old town, where he painted some of his most famous works. In 1906 he caught pneumonia while out painting in a rainstorm, and died in Aix on 23 October.

The Atelier Paul Cézanne, his studio, has been left as it was at the time of the artist's death and is open to visitors. It's a 10-minute walk or short bus ride from the old town. The Tourist Office has information on tours and other Cézanne sights that can be visited from Aix-en-Provence.

**Atelier Paul Cézanne**
9 avenue Paul Cézanne
04 42 21 06 53
www.atelier-cezanne.com
10.00-19.00 daily €5.50

LES DEUX GARÇONS

# Restaurants

See page 287 for price guide.

### Le Clos de la Violette
10 ave de la Violette; 04 42 23 30 71
12.00-14.00, 20.00-23.00 Tues-Sat
booking required
credit cards accepted
€€€€
A Michelin-starred restaurant set in an elegant Provençal villa with intimate dining rooms. The signature dish is braised sea wolf with crispy fried shallots and spicy sausages. For dessert, try the hazelnut and vanilla cream sauce over layers of sugar cookies and white chocolate.

### Le Passage
10 rue Villars; 04 42 37 09 00
12.00-14.30, 19.15-24.00 daily
booking advised
credit cards accepted
€€€
Owner Reine Sammut has transformed a 19th century candy factory into a large centre of gastronomy featuring a bistro, tapas bar, restaurant, tea room and cooking school. The service is friendly and dishes are well-prepared from market-fresh ingredients.

### Les Deux Garçons
53 cours Mirabeau; 04 42 26 00 51
07.00-02.00 daily
booking not required
credit cards accepted
€€
Founded in 1792, this is the oldest and most famous café on the cours Mirabeau. It's popular with visitors, and was a favourite haunt of Cézanne and Zola. From the outdoor tables you can watch the passers-by on the boulevard and around place Forbin. Inside there is faded belle époque décor. The brasserie-style dishes are good, but a tad expensive for standard fare.

### Antoine Côte Cour
19 cours Mirabeau; 04 42 93 12 51
12.00-14.30, 19.30-24.00 daily
closed Sunday and Monday lunch
booking advised at weekends
credit cards accepted
€€
A friendly Italian style trattoria with a relaxed ambience and home-made food. Fish and pasta are menu staples and the house wine is a tasty Côte-du-Rhône.

### Le Basilic Gourmand
6 rue du Griffon; 04 42 96 08 58
lunch and dinner Tues-Sat
booking not required
€
The set lunch menu is good value at this pleasant restaurant, tucked away on a side street off rue Paul Bert. Traditional Provençal dishes are served in a dining room painted in warm Mediterranean colours and decorated with old posters and memorabilia. There is also a terrace for outdoor dining and live music on occasion.

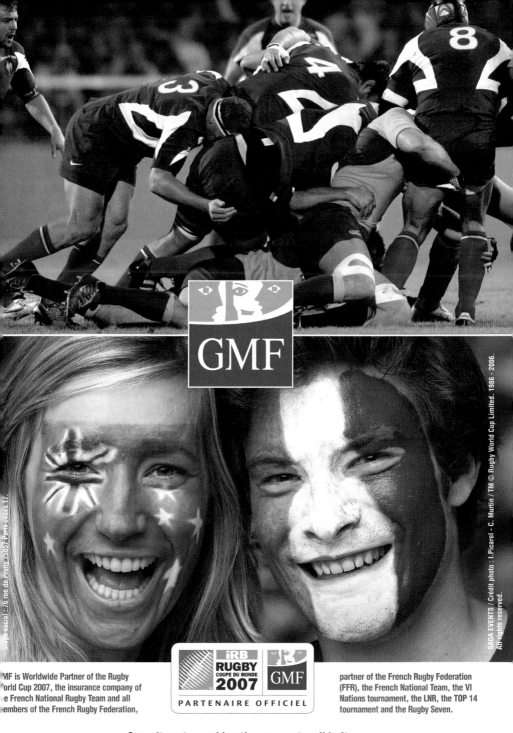

GMF

iRB **RUGBY**
**COUPE DU MONDE**
**2007** GMF

PARTENAIRE OFFICIEL

MF is Worldwide Partner of the Rugby orld Cup 2007, the insurance company of e French National Rugby Team and all embers of the French Rugby Federation,

partner of the French Rugby Federation (FFR), the French National Team, the VI Nations tournament, the LNR, the TOP 14 tournament and the Rugby Seven.

**Commitment, consideration, respect, solidarity.**
**All core values shared by the game of rugby and its partner for over 20 years, GMF.**

**www.assurement-rugby.com**

237

# Arles

Located on the banks of the Rhône at the mouth of the immense delta, Arles was an important Roman colony and became the capital of Gaul. For centuries it was a major port to rival Marseille well into the 1900s, when it was eclipsed by the advent of railroads. Arles would have languished as a depressed industrial town, but for the arrival of one devastatingly poor artist in 1888.

Vincent Van Gogh only spent one year in Arles, but during that time he painted some of his most famous pictures, and famously shared his house with Gauguin. His old stomping grounds are unrecognisable today, but along with the city's superb Roman remains, the Van Gogh legacy continues to draw visitors.

## Arles Market

The best time to visit Arles is on a Saturday morning, when a large market stretches along three boulevards: des Lices, Georges Clemenceau and Emile Combes. This is a real Provençal market, one of the the best. Along with stalls selling soap, bright Provençal textiles, lavender, herbs and colourful pottery, you can have your computer repaired, buy a harness for your horse, get your horoscope read or have your hair done in a mobile hairdresser van. There's also a small flea market. But the

main attraction is food – huge peppers and tomatoes, round courgettes, mounds of onions and strings of garlic, scented honey, tapenades, sprawling spice stalls, olives, cheese, fish, meat and sausages. Musicians stroll through the market like medieval minstrels, stopping to play beside café tables. Arrive early as the traders start packing up around noon.

**Getting there**
The train station is about a 10-minute walk north of the town centre. There are frequent daily trains from Marseille with a journey time of 45 minutes.
**Tourist Office**
boulevard des Lices
04 90 18 41 20
www.arlestourisme.com
09.00-18.45 daily in summer
09.00-16.45 Mon-Sat in winter

## Roman Arles

There are many Roman remains to see. The southeast corner of the city centre is a quiet place to stroll and here you can see parts of the old Roman walls along Montée Vauban and the porte de la Redoute. Near the river are the ruins of the giant Roman baths, the Thermes de Constantin. Columns from a Roman temple are set into a corner of the Hôtel Nord Pinus in the place du Forum. The Théâtre Antique hosts an annual festival of theatre and dance in July.

### Les Arènes
admission €5.50

This impressive Roman amphitheatre dominates the town centre. Built at the end of the 1st century, the arena once had three storeys, and could seat 20,000 people who came to see the gladiator contests and games. In the Middle Ages the arena was made into a

CATHÉDRALE SAINT-TROPHIME

fortress, with two hundred homes and two churches. These were removed in the 19th century, but three of the four watchtowers remain. Today the arena is used for bullfights.

### Cathédrale Saint-Trophime
place de la Republique
cloisters €3.50

The present cathedral was built in the late 11th century. Its portal and facade boast some of the finest Romanesque stone carving in Provence, with striking portrayals of saints, angels and scenes from the Last Judgement.

Inside, there are Aubusson tapestries in the nave and 4th century sarcophagi; one depicting the crossing of the Red Sea is used as a chapel altar. There is more expressive stone carving in the lovely cloisters.

**Opening hours and Monuments Pass**
Opening hours for Arles monuments:
09.00-19.00 daily, September
09.00-12.00, 14.00-18.00 daily, October
If you're planning to visit several attractions, buy a pass at the Tourist Office for €13.50 which covers all the city's monuments and most museums.

## Musée Réattu

rue du Grand Prieuré
04 90 49 38 34
10.00-12.30 and 14.00-19.00 May-Sept
10.00-12.30 and 14.00-17.30 October
€4

Most people visit this riverside museum for the whimsical series of drawings donated by Picasso, in which he explores such themes as the harlequin and the musketeers. There is also a portrait of his mother, and photographs of Picasso in Arles by leading photographers. The eclectic offerings elsewhere in this mansion include 18th century paintings by the museum's founding resident, Jacques Réattu, together with contemporary photography and sculpture, some of which decorate the balconies and courtyard beneath the gothic gargoyles.

## Restaurants

See page 287 for price guide.

### Chassagnette
4 route du Sambuc;
(on D36, 13km south of Arles)
04 90 97 26 96
lunch and dinner daily, closed Tues and Wed lunch
booking recommended
credit cards accepted
€€€€
This Michelin-starred restaurant specialises in the cuisine of the Camargue. The menu is devised according to what is growing in their organic garden. Be sure to begin your meal with tapas made from fresh vegetables and grilled sardines. There is a pleasant outdoor terrace beside the large garden.

### La Gueule du Loup
39 rue des Arènes
04 90 96 96 69
12.00-14.30, 19.00-21.30 daily, closed Sun, Mon
booking required
Visa and Mastercard only
€€€
A small and cosy restaurant located near the Roman arena serving gourmet French cuisine. It was named after the founder who, according to legend, resembled a wolf as he grew into old age. Try the monkfish in

saffron sauce or, for the more adventurous, the fillet of bull braised in red wine. The set menu at €25 is a bargain considering the quality of the dishes and the caring service.

### Le Jardin de Manon
14 avenue Alyscamps
04 90 93 38 68
lunch and dinner daily, closed Tues eve and Wed
booking recommended on weekends
credit cards accepted
€€
A simple, comfortable restaurant serving regional cuisine in a shaded, peaceful garden. The menu changes daily according to what is fresh at the local Provençal markets and some of the dishes can be quite elaborate. The desserts are fabulous so be sure to save room.

### Chez Gigi
49 rue des Arènes
04 90 96 68 59
12.00-14.30, 19.30-24.00 Tues-Sun
booking required for lunch
credit cards accepted
€€
Gigi Boucher came all the way from Quebec, Canada to establish this casual and popular neighbourhood restaurant located close to the arena. Relaxed and affordable, the menu includes both Provençal and Mexican dishes.

## Van Gogh in Arles

Vincent Van Gogh came to Arles from Paris in February 1888. He rented the 'Yellow House' – the subject of one of his most famous paintings – on place Lamartine. Later his artist friend Paul Gauguin joined him. Van Gogh was inspired by the Provence light and countryside and painted some of his most famous works, including *Van Gogh's Chair* and *The Sunflowers*. But he suffered from increasing bouts of madness, which led to a traumatic night in December in which he cut off his ear after a quarrel with Gauguin. He was treated at the Hôtel Dieu hospital, but his condition deteriorated after the departure of Gauguin. In the spring of 1889, Van Gogh left Arles and was admitted to the asylum at St-Rémy-de-Provence.

Sadly, there are no paintings by Van Gogh here in the city that so inspired him. The Fondation Vincent Van Gogh has a collection of works painted in tribute to the great artist, including works by Francis Bacon, Roy Lichtenstein and David Hockney. The Hôtel Dieu is now the Espace Van Gogh, with a bookshop and salon de thé. The lovely flower-filled courtyard has been recreated from Van Gogh's painting.

Van Gogh's yellow house no longer exists – it was bombed in World War II (you pass the site on your way to the train station) – but you can still have a drink at the cafe he made famous in his painting *Le Café la Nuit*. The bright yellow awnings stand out on the place du Forum, a small square filled with cafés. The outside wall of the building is painted in a wash of Van Gogh colours: yellows, greens, golds. Drinks and light meals are served inside or on the large terrace, where it's amusing to watch the groups of tourists passing through and snapping photographs. Be sure to go inside to see the old zinc bar and curving wooden staircase up to the first floor, where you can imagine Van Gogh downing a few glasses of absinthe at one of the balcony tables.

### Café la Nuit
11 place du Forum; 04 90 96 44 56
09.00-24.00 daily, till 02.00 July-Aug

### Espace Van Gogh
rue Dulau; 07.30-19.00 daily
free admission

### Fondation Vincent Van Gogh
26 rond point des Arènes; 04 90 49 94 04
10.00-19.00 daily, June-Sept
09.30-12.00, 14.00-17.30 Tues-Sun, October
€7

CAFÉ LA NUIT

CARDIFF

# With a smart bay area and lively city centre, Cardiff has undergone a transformation from its industrial past.

Cardiff has been smartened up considerably in recent years, without losing any of its distinctive character. The Millennium Centre is a proud new addition to the Cardiff Bay skyline.

The lively mix of restaurants and bars in Cardiff Bay is unrecognisable from the drinking dens that existed here in the days when the harbour was full of ships being loaded with coal mined inland. These ships delivered their precious cargo throughout the world, and sailors from all nations would call into Cardiff creating a rough-and-tumble area around the harbour. Many of the sailors liked the city and its people so much they stayed, resulting in today's vibrant mix of cultures.

The Millennium Stadium is located in the city centre. Near to the stadium is the gothic Cardiff Castle adjoining Bute Park. Those who enjoy Impressionist art should be sure to visit the National Museum where there are several Monet paintings.

Victorian and Edwardian shopping arcades make Cardiff a pleasant place to shop regardless of the weather. The Café Quarter is located just south of these covered arcades.

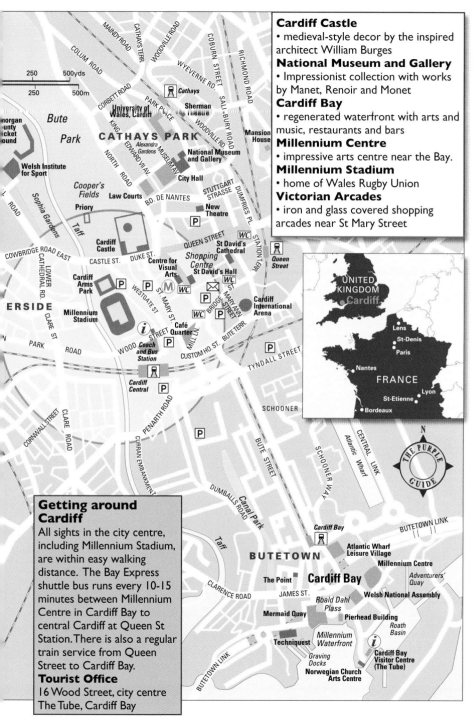

**Cardiff Castle**
- medieval-style decor by the inspired architect William Burges

**National Museum and Gallery**
- Impressionist collection with works by Manet, Renoir and Monet

**Cardiff Bay**
- regenerated waterfront with arts and music, restaurants and bars

**Millennium Centre**
- impressive arts centre near the Bay.

**Millennium Stadium**
- home of Wales Rugby Union

**Victorian Arcades**
- iron and glass covered shopping arcades near St Mary Street

**Getting around Cardiff**

All sights in the city centre, including Millennium Stadium, are within easy walking distance. The Bay Express shuttle bus runs every 10-15 minutes between Millennium Centre in Cardiff Bay to central Cardiff at Queen St Station. There is also a regular train service from Queen Street to Cardiff Bay.

**Tourist Office**
16 Wood Street, city centre
The Tube, Cardiff Bay

## Getting to the stadium

**Nearest airport**
Cardiff International
01446 711777
www.cwlfly.com
Located 10 miles south-west of the city centre. There is a rail link with Cardiff Central station, as well as regular bus services into the city. Trains are the best option on match days, when traffic is heavy.

**Car**
Directions are clearly given from the M4, with different access routes depending on your tickets. Be aware that the city centre will be restricted to traffic on match days.

**Bus**
Cardiff's Central Bus Station is a short walk from the ground.

**Train**
Cardiff has two train stations, Cardiff Central and Cardiff Queen Street. Both are only a five minute walk from the stadium.

**Metro**
Cardiff has no metro system.

REMEMBER TO
PURCHASE YOUR
TRANSPORT TICKETS
WELL IN ADVANCE OF
THE MATCH TO SAVE
TIME QUEUING.

## Millennium Stadium capacity 74,500

| Matches | Date | Pool |
|---|---|---|
| Wales v Australia | 15 September, Sat | B |
| Canada v Fiji | 16 September, Sun | B |
| Wales v Japan | 20 September, Thur | B |
| Quarter Final 2 W pool C v RU pool D | 6 October, Sat | |

## The stadium and around

Westgate Street
029 2082 2228
www.millenniumstadium.co.uk

The Victorian engineer Isambard Kingdom Brunel diverted Cardiff's River Taff to enable him to bring the railway to the city. The drained area was used for sport, and was the location of the original Wales national rugby stadium. Named after a nearby hotel where players would change before matches, Cardiff Arms Park was the soul of Welsh rugby and plans to replace it horrified many fans.

Millennium Stadium took three years to build, and cost £150 million. When it opened for Rugby World Cup 1999, it proved itself a worthy successor and is now the home of both the rugby and football national sides, with rock concerts staged out of season. The stadium's soaring shiplike structure can be seen from all over the city, and inside on match days the atmosphere is unbeatable.

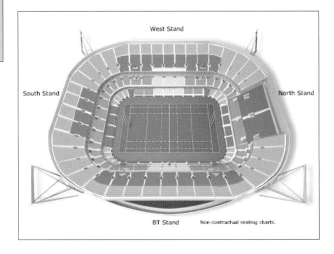

## Stadium tours

Sports fan or not, a tour behind the scenes at the Millennium Stadium is a must. Visit the dressing rooms and walk out onto the pitch, then see the royal box and get the view from the top of the stands. The stadium has the biggest closing roof in the world, and a removable pitch to accommodate rock concerts and other large events.

029 2082 2228
10.00-17.00 Monday-Saturday
10.00-16.00 Sundays and Bank Holidays
no tours on event and match days
booking essential
pay on arrival (Gate 3) £5.50

## Bars near the stadium

Cardiff's Millennium Stadium is all the more enjoyable for being located in the centre, right in the heart of the city, just as rugby is right in the heart of the Welsh people.

### Old Arcade
Church Street
029 2021 7999
11.00-23.00 Mon-Thurs, 11.00-24.00 Fri-Sat
12.00-22.30 Sun
A famous old Cardiff rugby pub that dates back to 1844 and is decorated with all kinds of sporting memorabilia. Visit on a non-match day to really see the decor, which includes an old-fashioned mahogany bar, and a rear lounge bar complete with its original mirror. A great old place.

### Queens Vaults
29 Westgate Street
029 2022 7966
11.00-23.00 Mon-Sat, 12.00-22.30 Sun
Queen Victoria over the entrance looks away disapprovingly, as well she might given the noise during a match. Located a few yards from stadium Gate 4, it does a roaring trade with special prices on pub food and beer several days a week.

### The Goat Major
33 High Street
029 2033 7161
11.00-23.00 Mon-Sat, 12.00-22.30 Sun
Lovely old and unspoilt pub, with a black and white timbered frontage, dark wood panelling and comfy leather sofas. Welsh dishes are on the food menu and every Wednesday they have a lively Welsh Night.

### The City Arms
10 Quay Street
029 2022 5258
11.00-23.00 Mon-Wed, 11.00-24.00 Thurs
11.00-02.00 Fri-Sat, 12.00-22.30 Sun
Opposite stadium Gate 2, is this black and white pub with the bright red dragon above the door. On match days it's more crowded here than it is inside the stadium. There are two big screens to watch the sports action if you didn't get a ticket.

### La Tantra
31 Westgate Street
029 2039 9400
10.00-23.00 Mon-Wed, 10.00-02.00 Thurs-Sat
closed Sun
This hip Turkish themed bar located near Gate 4 is a pleasant change from the old-fashioned Cardiff pubs. Downstairs, Club Tantra is popular with local celebs, including rugby players and Charlotte Church.

QUEENS VAULTS

**Bute Park**
- Cardiff Castle
- Sophia Gardens
- Standing Stones
- Glamorgan Cricket Club
- Welsh Institute of Sport
- Riding School

## Bute Park

Bute Park is an oasis of green in the centre of Cardiff. The River Taff flows through the park and Cardiff Castle stands guard over the south east corner. Sophia Gardens make a pleasant stroll and there are a few small standing stones. The Glamorgan County Cricket Club, the Welsh Institute of Sport and a riding school are within the park's grounds. Any music you hear is likely being played by students from the music and drama college in the park.

Cardiff Castle cannot be accessed from Bute Park. The entrance is a five minute walk along the high street.

Castle Street, Cardiff
CF10 3RB
029 2087 8100
www.cardiffcastle.com
09.30-18.00 Mar-Oct
09.30-17.00 Nov-Feb
open daily
last admission one hour before closing
£6.95 guided tour
£3.50 grounds only

## Cardiff Castle

We highly recommend the 50-minute guided tour to the castle. The tour is the only access to the sumptuously decorated rooms created by architect William Burges for the Bute family.

In the 18th century, Cardiff Castle became the private residence of the Bute family from the Scottish Isle of Bute. It was the 3rd Marquess of Bute, John Patrick Crichton-Stuart (1847-1900) who commissioned Burges to decorate the interiors. The two men shared a passion for medievalism. Together they transformed the castle interior and Burges produced rooms of incredible detail and luxury. It was the first residence in Wales, and only the third in Britain, to have electricity.

Born in London into an engineering family, Burges worked on the restoration of Westminster Abbey in the 1840s and later produced a prize-winning design for Lille Cathedral which was never used.

Burges' first important commission was St Finbarr's Cathedral in Cork. He was then invited to Cardiff to begin work on the castle. Burges' neo-gothic designs for Cardiff Castle never lost sight of the fact that it was a family home.

A man with a sense of humour, Burges never took himself too seriously. He once said that '*mankind has been very much the same in every age, and ... our ancestors joked and laughed as much as we do.*'

Cardiff Castle was Burges' finest achievement – it is a pity he did not live to see it completed.

Each room has its own theme. In the clock tower, the signs of the zodiac decorating the ceiling represent time, while the Norse gods adorning the stained glass window symbolise the days of the week. The Arab room has a ceiling made of cedar wood and gold leaf. Burges died before this room was completed.

The Butes owned vast areas of land in South Wales, and benefited from the increased demand for coal during the Industrial Revolution. Coal mined in South Wales was shipped down the River Taff to Cardiff Bay, resulting in the development of the huge docks of Cardiff and great wealth for the Butes. The family had a yacht, *The Ladybird*, permanently moored in Marseille harbour which they used only occasionally.

Cardiff Castle's keep and ramparts date back 2,000 years to the arrival of the Romans who first built defences here. They were followed by the Normans in the 11th and 12th centuries who built first a wooden and then later the stone fortress still existing today.

# National Museum and Gallery

Cathays Park, Cardiff
CF10 3NP
029 2039 7951
www.nmgw.ac.uk
10.00-17.00 Tue-Sun
closed Mon
free

Cardiff's art gallery has the best collection of Impressionist paintings in Britain. The museum is undergoing renovation until at least 2008, and rooms 1-10 are closed till then, but the Impressionists and post-Impressionists are still on display.

This superior collection of paintings was amassed by two Welsh spinster sisters, Gwendoline (1882-1951) and Margaret Davies (1884-1963), who inherited a large coal fortune from their grandfather.

In **room 12** are sculptures by Edgar Degas and a copy of Auguste Rodin's *The Kiss*. Claude Monet is well represented with three *Waterlilies,* one of the *Rouen Cathedral* works and three Venice paintings. These were bought by the Davies sisters at a Paris exhibition in 1912 and were the sisters' first Impressionist purchase. Alongside Monet are works by Edouard Manet and Pierre-Auguste Renoir. One of the gems in the room is Renoir's *La Parisienne*, first shown at the 1874 exhibition which gave Impressionism its name.

In other areas of the gallery are works by Jacob Epstein, Barbara Hepworth, Henri Matisse, Maurice Utrillo, Max Ernst, LS Lowry and of course a fine display of works by Welsh artists, right through to the present day.

In the same building is the National Museum, with geology, archaeology and natural history exhibits; it is also exceptionally good, but the art collection should be your first port of call.

MONET: *SAN GIORGIO MAGGIORE BY TWILIGHT*

ALWAYS GO FURTHER... FOR MORE COMMITMENT

In the front row of the rugby world for over 10 years, notably alongside the Stade Toulousain, Peugeot has developed its commitment to the game from support at amateur level to sponsorship of professional federations and teams worldwide. A major prop of the Rugby World Cup 2003, Peugeot is set to ram the advantage home in 2007!

**PEUGEOT, OFFICIAL PARTNER OF THE RUGBY WORLD CUP 2007**

**Parking tip**
If driving to Cardiff Bay, the large carpark behind Techniquest is the best value in the area and close to most sights.
Park here and take the bus or train into the city centre, where the large carparks are more expensive.

Bute Place, Cardiff
CF10 5AL
08700 402000
www.wmc.org.uk
open daily from morning till late-night
times vary with performances
guided tours £5

## Cardiff Bay

The area around Cardiff Bay makes a good day (or more) out from the city centre, or it is possible to base oneself here and travel into the city centre on the bus and rail services. These two parts of Cardiff are only minutes apart on public transport, but just a bit too far for most people to walk. Down at the Bay there are bars and restaurants that bustle at night on Mermaid Quay.

Here you will find the Millennium Centre, the science museum Techniquest, a sculpture trail, the Norwegian Church and a branch of the tourist information office housed in the quirky Tube building.

### Wales Millennium Centre

You don't have to see a production here to enjoy a visit to Cardiff's premier arts centre. The outstanding design is best appreciated by taking a guided tour through the public and the backstage parts of the Centre. The visually stunning David Gordon Theatre seats 1,900 and is known for its wonderful acoustics.

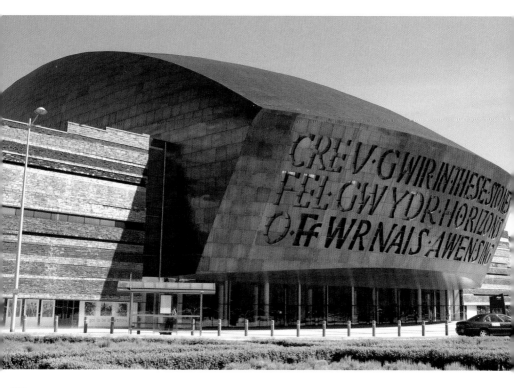

Operas, musicals, ballet, pop and classical concerts are all performed in addition to studio productions. Free concerts are held in the public areas daily.

The facade of sweeping golden-copper is inscribed with two short poems, one in Welsh and one in English. Inside, the lettering acts as windows for bars and restaurants located on different levels. Welsh materials – slate, steel, wood and glass – have all been used imaginatively to great effect. It's a building every Welsh person can be proud of, and a good afternoon out for visitors.

**Tourist Office:**
**The Tube**
Harbour Drive
029 2046 3833
April-October
09.30-18.00 Mon-Fri
10.30-18.00 Sat-Sun
10.30-17.00 Holidays
November-March
closed 17.00 daily

### Norwegian Church

The delightfully incongruous Norwegian Church on the waterfront is quintessentially Cardiff. It sums up the multi-cultural nature of the city together with its sense of history. Built in December 1869 as a mission for Norwegian sailors, it was used by them to pick up their mail, read Norwegian newspapers, and socialise over a cup of coffee with a plate of waffles. The building was threatened with demolition till the Norwegian Church Preservation Trust was established. In 1987 it was moved from its previous location elsewhere in the bay to its new home. The church houses an art gallery with temporary exhibitions, and a good café.

Harbour Drive, Cardiff
CF10 4PA
029 2045 4899
09.00-17.00 daily
free

### Sculpture Trail

The waterfront is livened up with a series of sculptures ranging from the dramatic to the whimsical. *Wife on the Ocean Wave* shows a cheerful family sailing away in an old tin bath. Pick up a leaflet at the information centre in the Tube, next to the Norwegian Church, so you don't miss any of the sculptures.

# Restaurants

Cardiff's multi-cultural nature is reflected in the restaurants, from Norwegian to Latin American, and every country in between. The Café Quarter and the Mermaid Quay are lively at night.

See page 288 for price guide.

## Near the stadium

### Topo Gigio
12 Church Street
029 2034 5903
www.vendittogroup.co.uk/topogigio.htm
12.00-15.00, 17.30-23.00 Sun-Thurs
12.00-24.00 Fri-Sat
book on match days
credit cards accepted
££
With a lively authentic Italian atmosphere, Topo Gigio is a popular spot with players and other celebrities whose photos and magazine cuttings line the walls. There is additional seating at the back and upstairs, where there is a view into the active kitchen. The menu offers delicious home-made pizzas and fresh pastas, and also a selection of fresh fish. The food is excellent, and so is the buzz.

### Champers
61 St Mary Street
029 2037 3363
12.00-14.30 and 19.00-24.00 daily
book on match days
credit cards accepted
££
This incongruously-named Spanish tapas bar is located south-east of the Stadium near the edge of Cardiff's Café Quarter. The dark interior could be found anywhere in Spain, with a long bar filling one side of the room and a good tapas menu including *chorizo picante fritos*, *patatas bravas* and *jamon serrano*. Sample a variety of tapas accompanied by a good Spanish wine or have a full meal from the main menu. In typical Spanish tradition, Champers fills up later in the evening.

### Las Iguanas
8a Mill Lane
029 2022 6373
www.iguanas.co.uk
12.00-23.00 Mon-Thurs, 12.00-23.30 Fri-Sat
12.00-22.30 Sun
book on match days
credit cards accepted
££
In the heart of the Café Quarter is this incredibly colourful and popular Latin American bar/restaurant. The menu includes Brazilian lime chicken (Pele's favourite)

TOPO GIGIO

alongside more familiar Mexican dishes such as *chimichangas* and *fajitas*. Deadly cocktails too, using Cachaça spirit all the way from Rio.

## Cardiff

### Salt
Stuart Square, Mermaid Quay
029 2049 4375
11.00-24.00 Sun-Thurs, 11.00-02.00 Fri-Sat
book on weekends
credit cards accepted
£££
A light and spacious bar/casual restaurant, with an open deck upstairs looking out over Cardiff Bay and the busy streets of Mermaid Quay. Inside are booths and comfy leather chairs, with a swirling staircase giving the impression of travelling on an ocean liner. The food is simple and inexpensive using Welsh ingredients, Y-Fenni cheese in the risotto and Penderyn Welsh whiskey ribs.

### Zushi
The Aspect, 140 Queen Street
029 2066 9911
www.zuchicardiff.com
12.00-22.00 Mon-Sat, 12.00-17.00 Sun
book on match days
credit cards accepted
££
Just north of Queen Street station is this sushi bar, recently chosen by Wales international Gavin Henson as his favourite restaurant in Britain's *Observer Food Monthly Magazine*. Henson appreciates its laid-back style as well as its healthy range of sushi dishes, which you can take from the conveyor. They include incredibly tasty dishes such as peppered salmon sashimi and crab meat gunkan, but there are bigger options too, like stir-fried chilli beef, as well as daily specials.

### Norwegian Church Coffee Shop
Harbour Drive, Cardiff CF10 4PA
029 2045 4899
09.00-17.00 daily, last orders 16.30
bookings not taken
no credit cards
£
The cosy wood-panelled coffee shop at the Norwegian Church is always busy, which isn't surprising as they serve tasty home-made food at reasonable prices. Try the Norwegian open sandwich, with smoked salmon and sweet-cured herring, or a spinach and feta filo pie. The huge array of cakes and desserts will make your mouth water.

SALT

## Further afield

### La Cucina
Vale Hotel, Hensol Park, Hensol
Vale of Glamorgan, CF72 8JY
01443 667 877
12.30-14.00, 18.00-22.00 Mon-Sat
closed Sun
booking advised
credit cards accepted
£££
Smart but casual Mediterranean-style restaurant at the Vale Hotel, part of the golf club building but open to anyone. It is worth the journey as the atmosphere is relaxed with plenty of space around the tables, large picture windows and an open kitchen containing one of the few wood-burning stoves in Britain. They make very light pizzas, and the menu also includes a perfect asparagus, mushroom and mascarpone risotto, roast rump of lamb and fillet steak.

### Red Lion
Pendoylan, Vale of Glamorgan CF71 7UJ
01446 760 332
12.00-15.00 Tues-Sun, 17.00-23.00 Tues-Sat
closed all day Mon and Sun evenings
££
Iranian chef and new owner Comi Soroush has transformed this village pub into a destination for food lovers. It looks like a good pub should, with thick stone walls and wooden beams, and the wooden tables are simply set with black slate placemats and a single fresh flower. Soroush's signature dish of Persian chicken is sublime, but currently only available on the Early Bird menu from 6-7pm. The full menu includes such delights as roasted Cajun sea bass with mango and avocado salsa flavoured with coriander and lime juice.

# Shopping

Shops are generally open 9.30am-5.30pm Monday-Saturday. Thursday is late night, when shops stay open a little later than usual, most until about 8pm. On Sundays many shops, especially in the centre, are open 11am-5pm.

For a city to be a shopper's paradise it needs more than the ubiquitous chains – good shopping requires unique shops not found elsewhere. Cardiff's Victorian and Edwardian arcades contain the types of business that have been priced out of city-centres elsewhere: wig-makers, violin-makers and old-fashioned delis.

St David's Centre is a new shopping mall which occupies a large chunk of the middle of the city, with further shopping developments being planned.

**Eden Park** 
34 St Mary Street CF10 1AB
029 2038 8407;
www.eden-park.com/cardiff
09.30-17.30 Mon-Sat, 11.00-16.00 Sun
Established in 1987 by French rugby players Franck Mesnel and Eric Blanc who added a pink bow tie to their club kit for the French Championship final match. The chain is known for its quality wearable fashions with a strong rugby theme.

**Shop Rugby**
8 Duke Street, Cardiff CF10 1AY
029 2039 5522
www.shoprugby.co.uk
09.30-17.30 Mon-Sat, 11.00-16.00 Sun
Opposite Cardiff Castle and a short walk from the stadium, this is a stop for any rugby fan. They stock a wide range of jerseys and boots as well as t-shirts, gloves, track suits, shorts and rugby souvenirs, not just for Welsh clubs but for clubs worldwide.

**Craft in the Bay**
029 2048 4611
10.30-17.00 daily; free
Almost opposite the entrance to the Millennium Centre is another striking structure, an old maritime warehouse with a modern extension, now housing Craft in the Bay. This craft shops displays the best of Welsh arts and crafts, with some stunning creations in jewellery, fabrics, rugs, paintings, ceramics, glass, ironworks and mixed media. There are some incredibly talented Celtic artists working today, and this shop and gallery showcases some of the best.

**VISA**

## The Arcades

Cardiff has six glass-roofed arcades: Royal Arcade, Duke St Arcade, Wyndam Arcade, Morgan Arcade, High St Arcade and Castle Arcade. Located east and west of St Mary Street, these were built so that people could carry on shopping despite the wet Welsh weather. Some arcades are straight, some L-shaped, and others Y-shaped. All are fascinating and great to wander through, wet or dry, for you never know what you're going to find. In the High Street Arcade there is a harp shop opposite a tattoo parlour, with a joke and novelty shop near the New York Deli.

Wally's Deli, in the Royal Arcade, is the best deli in the city. The food and drink comes from all over the world: Greek Mythos beer, Polish salted pretzels, Italian polenta, vanilla pods, oyster sauce. At the other end of the same arcade look for Cardiff Antiques and Collectibles, stocking everything from vintage clothing to Elvis's autograph and lots of sporting photos, cricket bats and other memorabilia.

The Castle Arcade is built on two levels. It contains the fabulous Madame Fromage, which locals claim is the best cheese shop in Wales. Madame also carries a range of over 800 gourmet products from speciality producers around the world. If walking has made you peckish, take a break at the little café opposite the shop. String musicians should pay a visit upstairs to Cardiff Violins.

**VISA**

CASTLE ARCADE

# Golf and other sports

Cardiff is about much more than rugby. As the home of the Wales national football team and Cardiff City FC, soccer is well represented. Golf is another popular sport with numerous courses near to the city enabling players to enjoy the Welsh countryside.

## Golf

**Vale Hotel**
Hensol Park, Hensol
nr Cardiff CF72 8JY
014 4366 7800
www.vale-hotel.com/golf.html
Two 18-hole championship standard golf courses, including the Wales National course, as well as an all-weather driving range, putting greens, pro shop, club and other facilities.

**Cottrell Park Golf Club**
St Nicholas
Cardiff CF5 6JY
014 467 81781
www.cottrell-park.co.uk
Boasting two 18-hole courses, one of which is of championship standard, Cottrell Park offers something to golfers of all levels. A large clubhouse with a relaxed atmosphere does a great Sunday lunch.

**Radyr Golf Club**
Drysgol Road, Radyr
Cardiff CF15 8BS
029 2084 2408
www.radyrgolf.co.uk
With its beautiful views over across Cardiff to the Bristol Channel beyond, Radyr is one of Glamorgan's most idyllic golf clubs. It's a testing course however - every hole presents a different challenge, and the greens can be unforgiving. A welcoming clubhouse with bar and restaurant completes the setting.

**Hensol Golf Academy**
Duffryn Bach, Clawddcoch
Cowbridge CF71 7UP
014 4322 6901
Has a driving range and golf lessons are available.

**Vale of Glamorgan**
www.valeofglamorgan.co.uk
This website has details on the many other recommended golf clubs in the area.

## Cycling

**The Taff Trail**
www.tafftrail.org.uk
If you want some enjoyable cycling you need to get away from the heavy traffic of the city and out into the countryside. The Taff Trail extends for 55 miles (88 kms) from the Cardiff Bay waterfront to the market town of Brecon in the beautiful Brecon Beacons. Although there is some urban riding, the route also takes you through some of the best scenery north-west of Cardiff.

## Tennis

**Tennis Wales**
029 2046 3335
www.tennis.wales.org
Contact them to locate a convenient court at one of the clubs in and around Cardiff.

**The Welsh National Tennis Centre**
Ocean Way, Ocean Park, near Cardiff Bay
029 2045 6000
Six indoor acrylic courts.

## Sailing and Watersports

**Cardiff Harbour Authority**
029 2087 7900
www.cardiffharbour.com
An excellent source of information on what there is to do, in and around Cardiff Bay and further afield, with links to other local sailing and watersports clubs.

**Cardiff Bay Water Activity Centre**
029 2037 8161
On the banks of the River Taff as it leads down into Cardiff Bay is this activity centre which organises canoeing, sailing, rowing, water-skiing and power-boating. They have all the equipment and also run courses both for beginners and more experienced people.

**Llanishen Sailing Centre**
029 2076 1360
On the northern edge of the city is the Llanishen Reservoir surrounded by 69 acres of countryside. It's a Royal Yachting Association Training Centre, providing a variety of courses from one day to a week and longer.

**The Gower Watersports Association**
01792 234 502
www.gogwa.com
Fifty miles (80 kms) west of Cardiff is the gorgeous Gower Peninsula, with some of the best beaches in Wales for surfing and other watersports activities, such as diving, snorkelling, kayaking and bodyboarding. There's also some great fishing in the area.

THE VALE

## Spa and Fitness

### St David's Spa
St David's Hotel, Cardiff Bay
(see entry in Hotels section)
The spa has a 15-metre exercise pool, an 8-person jacuzzi, a sauna, a very well-equipped gym, 14 treatment rooms, a walk-through marine hydropool and a relaxation room with perfect views out over the Bay. Visitors can purchase a spa day-pass to make use of the facilities.

### Cannons Health Club
Welsh National Tennis centre
Ocean Way, Ocean Park
029 2045 6000
Gym and fitness studio with sauna, steam room, and a pool.

### Body Matters
Units 1 & 2 Wesley Hall, Bridge Street
029 2066 8600
Located in the city centre, is it has a sauna and tanning beds as well as gym facilities.

## Spectator Sports

### Cardiff City FC
029 2022 1001
www.cardiffcityfc.co.uk.
The club has a place in the Champions League, where they finished mid-table in 2005/2006. The team haven't finished among the honours in recent years, but in the past they have won the FA Cup and made it to the semi-finals of the European Cup Winners Trophy. Their home ground is at Ninian Park, west of the city centre.

### Cardiff Devils, Ice Hockey
Wales National Ice Rink, Hayes Bridge Road
029 2039 7198
www.thecardiffdevils.com
The Cardiff Devils are the number one ice hockey team in Wales.

### Cardiff Rugby Club
Cardiff Arms Park
029 2030 2000
www.cardiffrfr.com
The ground dates back to 1876. To check if there's a match on while you're in Cardiff, visit the website or call.

# Near Cardiff is the lovely Vale of Glamorgan with sandy beaches and secluded coves. Inland are woodlands with walking trails and even a vineyard.

### St Fagans National History Museum

St Fagans, Cardiff CF5 6XB
(two minutes south of Junction 33 of the M4,
off the A4232)
029 2057 3500

Also known as the National Museum of Wales, St Fagans opened in 1948 and was one of the first open-air museums in the world. It is the biggest heritage attraction in Wales and depicts the lives of Welsh people over the past 500 years.

Lovingly restored Welsh homes, shops, farms and other exhibits (including a beehive pigsty and a cock-fighting pit) have been moved here from their original locations throughout Wales. Welsh craftsmen continue to work here using traditional methods, including a baker who makes delicious bread.

The museum's buildings are set in the 100 acre grounds of St Fagans Castle, a 16th-century manor house with its own colourful flower-filled gardens.

**Vale of Glamorgan**
• glorious Welsh countryside
**St Fagans National History Museum**
• National Museum of Wales
**Llanerch Vineyard**
• the biggest commercial vineyard in Wales

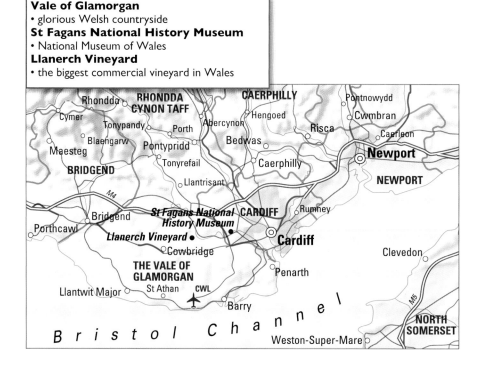

## Llanerch Vineyard

Hensol, Pendoylan, Vale of Glamorgan
CF72 8GG
01443 225 877
www.llanerch-vineyard.co.uk
10.00-17.00 daily, March-Christmas
£4

South Wales may not have the best climate for growing vines, but wine has been made here since Roman times. Today Peter and Diana Andrews continue the tradition. Seven of their 20 acres are given over to vines, growing six varieties of unusual grapes: Seyval Blanc; Triomphe; and the aptly-named Bacchus.

The Llanerch vineyard produces four white wines, a rosé and a sparkling rosé. It is now the largest commercial vineyard in Wales and the wines have won 20 awards at international competitions. The House of Commons sommelier regards these wines so highly he has placed Andrews' Cariad wines on their restaurant lists and serves them to visiting dignitaries.

A wine tasting is included in the admission charge, and all the wines are for sale at very reasonable prices.

The Llanerch Estate also offers accommodation, plus a vineyard trail and woodlands walking trails. The two small lakes are especially beautiful in spring and summer, when wild irises and orchids can be found. There is a café serving snacks, drinks and, of course, glasses of Cariad wine.

Cardiff is twinned with Nantes, and wine-maker Peter Andrews will be travelling to Nantes for the Wales matches. Peter will be representing his own and other Cardiff and Welsh wines. 'Some years ago I had the honour of being made a *Chevalier Bretvin,* a *confrère* which celebrates the muscadet of the *Pays de Nantes'* says Peter proudly, 'which involves a lot of dressing up and a lot of fun. It sounds very grand but the members are a real mix of people, from engineers to aristocrats, all of whom take their wine seriously. So I'm delighted to be able to go to the matches and promote Cardiff and Wales and our wine, all at the same time. The French are very nationalistic, of course, and so are the Welsh, but when wine-makers get together, the quality of the wine is all that matters.'

# EDINBURGH

# From the historic quarter around Edinburgh Castle to the elegant New Town, Scotland's capital city exudes an agreeable energy.

Edinburgh is a happy meeting ground of tradition and the avant garde, as evidenced by the Military Tattoo and the famous Fringe festival, both held in August. Called the 'Athens of the North', Edinburgh was the home of Scotland's kings and queens and is once again the seat of government. It is an arts capital with many fine galleries, museums, performing venues and a strong literary tradition.

The atmospheric Old Town recalls its medieval origins with tall tenements, steep staircases, and cobbled lanes leading to hidden courtyards. The genteel, neoclassical New Town is the handsome face of Edinburgh's prosperity. Together they've been designated a UNESCO World Heritage Site. With a constant influx of university students and tourists, Edinburgh has a lively nightlife and café scene.

CHARLOTTE SQUARE

## Getting around Edinburgh

The Lothian bus network runs Edinburgh's transport system (there is no tube/metro). Day passes cost £2.30 for unlimited travel, Ridacard costs £13 for one week or you can purchase a single ticket from the driver as you board the bus.
Lothian Buses: 0131 554 4494
www.lothianbuses.co.uk

**Tourist Office**
3 Princes Street, Edinburgh, EH2 2QP
0845 22 55 121; www.edinburgh.org
09.00-19.00 Mon-Sat, 10.00-19.00 Sun

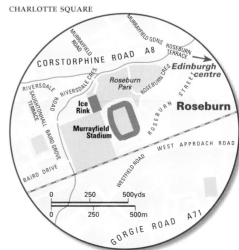

**Edinburgh Castle**
• the formidable fortress dominates the city from atop Castle Rock
**The Royal Mile**
• famous road lined with shops, restaurants, pubs and attractions
**Palace of Holyroodhouse**
• a tragic chapter in the life of Mary, Queen of Scots took place here
**National Museum of Scotland**
• Scotland's history is displayed in a fascinating array of artefacts and exhibits
**National Gallery of Scotland**
• a fine collection of Old Masters, Impressionists and Scottish artists

# MURRAYFIELD STADIUM

## Getting to the stadium

Located two miles west of the city centre, the stadium is easily reached by bus or even on foot. Walking to the stadium, with a few refreshment stops on the way, is very popular with local fans.

**Nearest airport**
Edinburgh Airport
0131 333 1000;
Located six miles west of Murrayfield. Take the A8 towards the city centre, which passes very close to the stadium.

**Car**
The main A8 road into the city centre from the west passes very close to Murrayfield. If travelling by car, use public carparks around the city and take a bus or walk to the stadium.

**Bus**
Prince's Street is lined with bus stops, stand on the south side and look for bus numbers 12, 22, 26 or 31, marked for the West End. Get off at the Murrayfield stop. The city's bus service is excellent, with route maps on all the stops and information displays showing how long to wait for the next bus.

**Train**
Edinburgh Waverley Station, where InterCity services arrive, is in the city centre and about two miles from Murrayfield, easily reached by taxi. Some local services also call at Edinburgh Haymarket station, which is about a mile from Murrayfield.

| Murrayfield capacity 68,000 | | |
|---|---|---|
| **Matches** | **Date** | **Pool** |
| Scotland v Romania | 18 September, Tues | C |
| Scotland v New Zealand | 23 September, Sun | C |

## The stadium and around

Murrayfield, Edinburgh EH12 5PJ
0131 346 5000

One of the world's great rugby venues, Murrayfield was built in 1925 on land belonging to the Edinburgh Polo Club. The Scottish Football Union, as it was then called, had bought the 19 acres out in the Costorphine suburb of Edinburgh in 1922. The new ground held 70,000 people, and Scotland celebrated their new home by winning the Grand Slam for the first time in their history (not that the phrase 'Grand Slam' had been invented at the time). They would have to wait 59 years before winning their next one. Murrayfield once rang to the sound of 104,000 people, its record crowd for a match when Scotland beat Wales 12-10 in March 1975. It was a world record attendance at the time, but hundreds who had tickets for the game were unable to get in, and the decision was taken to make all future internationals all-ticket matches, and with a much reduced capacity of 70,000. That Murrayfield record is not likely to be beaten, as the ground capacity now is down to 68,000 in line with recent trends towards having smaller stadiums.

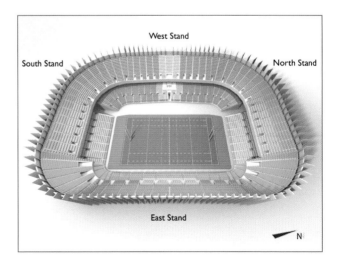

West Stand

South Stand

North Stand

East Stand

N

# Rugby bars

## Bars near the stadium

Around the stadium there are plenty of fast food places, and no shortage of bars that cater to sports fans. The best include:

### The Murrayfield Bar
57-59 Roseburn Terrace
0131 337 1574
11.00-24.00/01.00 daily
www.murrayfieldbar.com
Not to be confused with the bar at the Murrayfield Hotel, the Murrayfield has seven TV screens and two pull-down big sports screens. It's a nice wood-panelled bar and does food with a basic menu of such things as fish and chips, bangers and mash (both £5.95), and wine by the bottle from £9.95.

### Murrayfield Hotel
18 Corstorphine Road
0131 337 1844
9.00-01.00 daily, food served 9.00-21.00
The Murrayfield has a large modern bar, quite different from the other sports bars in the area. There are two big sports screens right behind the bar itself, so you don't miss any of the action while ordering.

### The Roseburn
1 Roseburn Terrace
0131 337 1067
Also known as The Fly-Half, the Roseburn has six screens and a small lounge bar whose walls are covered in sports photos, autographs and jerseys (including one from Gavin Hastings). There's a bigger bar on the corner, with wood panelling and red leather seats, and yet another bar off that – and they are all full on match days.

## Bars in the centre

### The Three Sisters
139 Cowgate
0131 622 6801; www.the3sisters.co.uk
One of Edinburgh's most popular pubs with the sporting crowd, the Three Sisters is noisy, usually full, and has a great atmosphere on match days.

### Kay's Bar
39 Jamaica Street West
0131 225 1858
A hidden gem with strong rugby connections, this cosy pub attracts visiting internationals for a drink. And the fans love it too. Well-kept beers and wines.

### The World Bar
55 Thistle Street
0131 225 3275
Small local pub showing rugby matches; the All Blacks memorabilia on the walls shows the landlord's allegiance.

### Sportsters Sports Bar & Diner
1a Market Street
0131 226 9560
Opposite Waverley Station, this bar has a good atmosphere, big screens, big portions and great prices.

### The Oxford Bar
8 Young Street
0131 539 7119; www.oxfordbar.com
With slices from ancient rugby posts framed on its walls and a famous Pie Machine at one end of the bar, this is a grubby and lovable pub which attracts an eccentric and interesting clientele. And not a big screen in sight.

### The Cambridge Bar
20 Young Street
0131 226 2120; www.thecambridgebar.co.uk
Just along from the Oxford, and also popular with rugby fans – probably because it serves good beer, good food (homemade burgers) and shows live rugby on a big screen.

0131 225 9846
www.historic
scotland.gov.uk
9.30-18.00 daily
last admission 45 minutes
before closing
£10.30

## Edinburgh Castle

Towering over the city centre from atop a volcanic crag nearly 122 metres (400 ft) high, Edinburgh Castle is an impressive monument. It is home to the city's oldest building (tiny St Margaret's Chapel built in the 12th century), Scotland's crown jewels and the Stone of Destiny. A fortified site since the 7th century, parts of the castle are still used by the British army. Today it's Scotland's biggest tourist attraction, with over a million visitors each year.

Surrounded on three sides by formidably steep cliffs, the castle's only entrance is through the Esplanade, a cobbled forecourt on the east side. Edinburgh's famous Military Tattoo with pipes, drums and brass bands takes place here every August. Inside, pick up an audiotape tour (included in the admission fee) to hear the fascinating history of the castle and its royal inhabitants. Mary, Queen of Scots gave birth to her son, the future King James VI of Scotland, in the Royal Apartments.

**Writers' Museum**
Lady Stair's Close
Lawnmarket, Royal Mile
0131 529 4901
www.cac.org.uk
10:00-17:00 Mon-Sat
free admission

**Palace of
Holyroodhouse and
the Queen's Gallery**
Canongate, Royal Mile
0131 556 5100
www.royal.gov.uk
£8 (£12.50 including
Queen's Gallery)
09.30-18.00 daily
last admission one hour
before closing

There are fantastic views over the city from the batteries, which are lined with cannons, including the 15th-century siege cannon Mons Meg. A one o'clock gun salute is fired every day from Mills Mount Battery. You can visit the Scottish National War Memorial and several museums, of which the highlight is the Honours of Scotland exhibit displaying the oldest crown jewels in Britain. Alongside is the Stone of Destiny, upon which the monarchs of Scotland have been crowned since the 9th century.

# The Royal Mile

The Royal Mile runs downhill through the Old Town from Edinburgh Castle to the gates of Holyroodhouse. It is actually a succession of four streets – Castlehill, Lawnmarket, High Street and Canongate – lined with shops, restaurants, pubs and visitor attractions. There's a fascinating mix of architecture, from medieval to modern, including the tall stone tenements called 'lands'. Narrow side passages called 'wynds' lead into atmospheric corners. To walk briskly from end to end takes a half an hour or more depending on your interest in the various attractions.

Near the castle are the **Scottish Whisky Heritage Centre**, **Tartan Weaving Mill** and **Camera Obscura**, with a birds-eye view of the city through its Victorian camera. Along Lawnmarket is **Gladstone's Land**, a 17th century merchant's house, and the **Writers' Museum**, which pays tribute to Sir Walter Scott, Robert Burns and Robert Louis Stevenson. The lofty crown spire of **St Giles High Kirk**, is a city landmark. Further along is the medieval **John Knox House**, alleged home of the religious reformer.

## Palace of Holyroodhouse and the Queen's Gallery

At the road's lower end is the Queen's official residence in Scotland, built on the grounds of the Abbey of Holy Rood during James V's reign in the 16th century. When the royals are not in residence, tours are available of the State Apartments and the Royal Apartments in the northwest tower, including the bedchamber of Mary, Queen of Scots, and the room where her secretary was murdered. In front of the palace, the Queen's Gallery displays changing exhibitions from the Royal Collection.

THE ROYAL MILE: JOHN KNOX HOUSE

## Museums and galleries

### Scottish Parliament Building

Horse Wynd
0131 348 5000
www.scottish.parliament.uk
09.00-19.00 Tues-Thurs when Parliament in
session, otherwise 10.00-18.00 Mon-Fri
10:00-16:00 Sat-Sun
building free, guided tours £5

Edinburgh's newest landmark stands
opposite the Palace of Holyroodhouse,
a striking contrast in both style and
substance. It was built to house the
independent Scottish Assembly, which
reconvened in 1999 for the first time
in nearly 300 years. (Since the Act
of Union in 1707, Scotland had been
directly governed from Westminster by
the Parliament of the United Kingdom.)
Designed by the late Catalan architect
Enric Miralles, the controversial
modernist building incorporates the
materials and motifs that represent
the Scottish landscape and heritage.
The building was completed in 2004.
Guided tours will take you beyond
the lobby to see the richly designed
chambers.

### Royal Museum of Scotland

Chambers Street
0131 247 4422; www.nms.ac.uk
10.00-17.00 Mon-Sat (Thurs till 20.00)
12.00-17.00 Sun; free admission

A magnificent atrium brings plenty of
space and light to this grand Victorian
museum. The eclectic collections
– everything from bicycles to butterflies
– cover three general themes: the
Natural World, Decorative Arts,
and Science and Industry. There are
antiquities and scientific instruments,
clocks and costumes, Egyptian
mummies, stuffed animals and an
enormous skeleton of a blue whale.
The breadth of the collection is as
impressive as the objects themselves.

NATIONAL MUSEUM OF SCOTLAND

### National Museum of Scotland

Chambers Street
0131 247 4422; www.nms.ac.uk
10.00-17.00 Mon-Sat (Thu till 20.00)
12.00-17.00 Sun; free admission

The contemporary sandstone building
with its round entrance tower is the first

clue that this fascinating museum aims to cover Scottish history in a refreshing way. Plan to spend a bit of time here.

Exhibits are organised chronologically over seven levels, depicting Scottish history and artefacts from the earliest days through to modern times. On Level 0, striking sculptures by Eduardo Paolozzi hold priceless objects made by early peoples. Environmental artworks by Andy Goldsworthy form backdrops for other artefacts. Level 1 displays Celtic treasures such as rare highland harps and the Monymusk Reliquary. The exhibits from the medieval to industrial ages include a gruesome beheading machine. There are free guided tours and audio sets to help you appreciate the collections. You can walk through to the Royal Museum on several levels. Be sure to visit the roof terrace for spectacular views over Edinburgh.

Opposite the National Museum in Candlemaker Row, notice the statue of the little Skye terrier called Greyfriars' Bobby. After his master's death in 1858, the loyal dog guarded his grave in nearby Greyfriars' churchyard for 14 years. The locals remembered him fondly with this memorial fountain.

### National Gallery of Scotland and Royal Scottish Academy

The Mound
0131 624 6200; www.natgalscot.ac.uk
10.00-17.00 Fri-Wed, 10.00-19.00 Thu; free

Inside and out, the gallery is an elegant home for Scotland's superb collection of European art from the Renaissance to the late 19th century. The neo-classical building was designed by William Playfair in the 1850s. The octagonal rooms and claret-coloured walls lend an intimate feel to the paintings. The collection is not too extensive and

can be viewed at a leisurely pace. Among the highlights are Rembrandt's *Self-Portrait at Age 51* and works by Vermeer, Titian and Raphael, as well as Canova's sculpture of *The Three Graces*. There are also some fine Impressionist works and a basement wing displaying works by leading Scottish painters.

Next door, the Royal Scottish Academy was also designed by Playfair. Major temporary exhibitions are shown here, including the annual RSA exhibition showcasing the works of Scotland's best living artists. The two galleries are linked below ground level, where there is a restaurant and large plaza.

### Arthur's Seat

If you're feeling energetic, you can climb 237 metres (823 feet) to the top of Arthur's Seat, an extinct volcano and the city's highest hill. The walk up is easier if you take the path up the back of the hill (facing away from the castle). From the top are excellent views over Edinburgh and across the Firth of Forth to Saint Andrews.

## Princes Street

Princes Street is the main thoroughfare in the city centre, and it's always busy. At its east end, Waverley Station is a hub of activity, with trains, taxis and buses coming and going. The Tourist Office is conveniently located above. To the east of the Tourist Office is the landmark clock tower of the Balmoral Hotel. To the west across Waverley Bridge is the soaring spire of the Scott Monument. This Gothic memorial by George Meikle Kemp is 200 feet high, making it the world's largest memorial to an author. It was erected in 1844 in honour of Sir Walter Scott, one of Scotland's great literary figures. His statue sits beneath the arch, while 64 characters from his novels are depicted in the ornamental sculpture. You can climb the 287 steps to the top of the spire for some giddy but fabulous views.

The north side of Princes Street is lined with chain stores which, apart from the Victorian facade of Jenners department store, are fairly bland. Luckily on the south side, the Scott Monument marks the start of Princes Street Gardens, running the length of the street and giving wonderful views of the castle and Old Town skyline. Amazingly, these sunken gardens at the base of Castle Rock were once a loch that was drained to create this great green space in the heart of the city. It is divided into the East and West gardens by The Mound, which runs uphill to the Royal Mile. On the west side is the Floral Clock, planted with more than 20,000 plants each year.

## New Town

North of Princes Street are the spacious, symmetrical streets of the New Town. In 1766 a young, unknown architect named James Craig won a competition to design a new residential area for the burgeoning city. The result was one of the most graceful examples of urban planning in Europe. Laid out in a grid pattern, the streets are linked by public squares, with Queen Street and Princes Street facing north and south respectively on to public gardens. Running through the centre is

PRINCES STREET

George Street, half a mile long and wide enough for a coach and six-horse team to turn full circle, with statues rising above the intersections.

The New Town was built as a residential area, but today it's the city's prime area for business and pleasure. Many banks and professional offices are located here, as well as upmarket shops and fashion chains. George Street is lined with popular restaurants and bars, the fashionable place for an evening on the town.

A stroll around the New Town reveals many fine architectural features on the buildings, such as fanlights, lamps, cast-iron work and other decorative details. At the west end of George Street, Charlotte Square, designed by Robert Adam in 1791, is one of the most prestigious addresses in the city. Handsome Georgian houses surround the green, with its equestrian statue of Prince Albert. You can visit the restored Georgian House at No. 7 for a glimpse of the late 18th-century lifestyle here. At the eastern end is St Andrew Square,

where the former Dundas House now houses the Bank of Scotland with a gorgeous domed ceiling in the banking hall.

## Old Town

The Grassmarket is a wide cobbled street that runs below the Royal Mile on the south side. Up until the early 20th century, it was the city's cattle market and was also notorious for the public hangings, riots and other insalubrious activities that took place here. Cowgate, one of the city's oldest streets, leads into it from the east, while the western end affords a stunning view up to Edinburgh castle. Today the Grassmarket is one of the city's liveliest nightlife areas, with lots of pubs and bars, many with live music.

West Bow leads into Victoria Street, one of the most picturesque in the city. For a charming view of it from above, follow Upper Bow Street off Lawnmarket on the Royal Mile. Steps lead down to it from the overlook.

# Restaurants

See page 288 for price guide.

### Restaurant Martin Wishart
54 The Shore, Leith, Edinburgh EH6 6RA
0131 553 3557
12.00-14.00 Tues-Fri, 19.00-21.30/22.00 Tues-Sat
bookings essential
credit cards
££££
You'll need to travel out to Edinburgh's port at Leith to find this, one of the city's top restaurants, but it's well worth the journey. It currently has one Michelin star and is aiming for a second, giving some indication of the food quality. The dining room is formal but unpretentious, and the food presentation first class. Cuisine combines top Scottish produce with French flair in dishes like roast woodcock in Armagnac *'en cocotte'*.

### The Witchery by the Castle
Castlehill, Royal Mile, Edinburgh EH1 2NF
0131 225 5613
12.00-16.00 and 17.30-23.30 daily
bookings essential
credit cards
££££
Just down from the entrance to Edinburgh Castle, the Witchery is one of the city's top choices for atmosphere, based in a 16th-century merchant's house. It's also a top choice for food, as years of success have given them supreme confidence in what they're cooking. Seasonal Scottish game and seafood are specialities, with Scottish lobster and Angus beef fillet being established favourites.

### The Dome Grill Room
14 George Street, Edinburgh EH2 2PF
0131 624 8624
12.00-23.00/24.00 daily
bookings not usually necessary
credit cards
£££
The New Town's George Street is one place to head if you've no set plans, as it's lined, east to west, with good eating options. The Dome was once a hospital, and the magnificent glass dome that gives it its name and character once provided light for the operating theatre. Now it's a bar, brasserie and Grill Room, always lively and a popular meeting place. The food's not fancy but is superb – Angus beef steaks, duck breast, and sea bass with fennel.

### Stac Polly
29-33 Dublin Street, Edinburgh EH3 6NL
0131 556 2231;
12.00-14.30 Mon-Fri, 18.00-23.00 daily
bookings suggested
credit cards
£££
Just up from the National Portrait Gallery in the New Town, with another branch on Grindlay Street in the West End, Stac Polly is where you can get traditional Scottish food with a modern twist, in a smart but very relaxed setting. Haggis puff pastry parcels are an essential starter. The restaurant name comes from a mountain in the Highlands, by the way, and it means 'the peak of the peat moss'.

### Whighams Wine Cellars
13 Hope Street, Edinburgh EH3 9JR
0131 225 8674
12.00-22.00 Mon-Sat, 12.30-22.00 Sun
bookings not usually necessary
credit cards
£££
You'll find the wonderful Whighams between Charlotte Square and the western end of Princes Street. On a busy night you'll have to squeeze your way through the crowds at the bar and grab a table in one of the booths or the dining room. The

THE DOME GRILL ROOM

stripped-down look adds to the noise and the relaxed atmosphere, but the food is way above standard wine bar fare. Succulent scallops, perfect risottos, a great wine list and cheerful service make for a perfect night out.

**Duck's at Le Marché Noir**
2-4 Eyre Place, Edinburgh EH3 5EP
0131 558 1608
12.00-14.00 Tues-Fri, 18.30-22.00 daily
bookings essential
credit cards
££
You'll find Duck's in the north of the New Town, by King George V Park. Just about every Scottish international has eaten here at one time or another, and many visiting players know about it too. You'll need to book ahead, as you'd expect with a place that combines excellent food with reasonable prices, with an eclectic menu that ranges from haggis samosas to roast fig tart and, of course, an excellent breast of duck.

**The Lot**
4 Grassmarket, Edinburgh EH1 2JU
0131 225 9924;
11.00-late (last orders 21.30) Mon-Sat,
12.00-18.00 Sun; bookings not usually necessary
credit cards
££
The Lot, at the end of Grassmarket, has wonderful views up to Edinburgh Castle, and if you drink or dine at a pavement table you'll see constant visitors taking the photograph. Inside is a light and airy dining room, with light blue walls adorned by the work of Edinburgh artists. All profits from here go to a charity but you don't need that as an excuse to sample the fabulous food. Try chicken breast stuffed with haggis in a whisky sauce.

**Le Monde**
16 George Street, Edinburgh EH2 2PF
0131 270 3900
09.00-22.00 daily, bookings not usually necessary
credit cards
££
Stylish and fun, this new place on George Street combines a hotel with a brasserie-style restaurant on several floors. You can eat anything anywhere – at the big upstairs bar, at the pavement tables or in the Moulin Rouge-style restaurant. The menu is kept simple (pan-fried Scottish salmon, Scottish steaks, chicken breast) but everything's perfectly done, and there's a very relaxed atmosphere everywhere.

THE LOT

**Henderson's Salad Table**
94 Hanover Street, Edinburgh EH2 1DR
0131 225 2131
08.00-22.45 Mon-Sat; bookings not accepted
credit cards
£
Just north of George Street in the New Town, Henderson's is the kind of vegetarian restaurant which attracts non-vegetarians too, for the standard of its cooking. There's a bistro round the corner, or the salad bar where you can pop in for a quick meal, or linger in the adjoining cellar-like wine bar, with live music a few nights a week. Check the daily specials on the blackboard, with dishes like vegetarian goulash both tasty and filling.

## Shopping

As befits a capital city, Edinburgh has no end of shopping experiences. You can find the latest fashions in the designer stores and boutiques of the New Town, imaginative gifts in the offbeat shops of the Old Town, and quality Scottish woollens and textiles almost everywhere. This is also a good place to source a broader range of whiskies than you'll find at home. Good foodie gifts include Scottish cheeses, smoked salmon, oat cakes, shortbread and the rich, super-sweet fudge called tablet.

Shops are generally open 9.30am-5.30pm Monday-Saturday. Thursday is late night, when shops stay open a little later than usual, most until about 8pm. On Sundays many shops, especially in the centre, are open 11am-5pm. You cannot buy alcohol before 12.30pm on a Sunday.

### Princes Street and the New Town

The famous Princes Street can be disappointing, as it's mainly lined with all the high street chain stores you find anywhere in Britain. You'll find even more in the Princes Mall and the St James Centre at the east end of the street. But head into the nearby streets of the New Town and you'll find plenty of upmarket shops selling designer fashions, jewellery, perfumes and other goods.

**Jenners**
48 Princes Street; 0131 225 2442
Often called the 'Harrods of the North', this *grande dame* of Edinburgh department stores has been trading here since 1838. It's got everything from high quality clothing to homewares and a fabulous food hall.

**Harvey Nichols**
30-34 St Andrew Square; 0131 524 8388
Edinburgh knew it was seriously cool when the famous London department store opened this New Town branch in 2002. It has five stories of high fashion designer labels, a food hall, restaurant and bar, with fantastic views over the city.

**Eden Park**
101 Hanover Street
0131 226 6440
www.eden-park.com/edinburgh
Established in 1987 by French rugby players Franck Mesnel and Eric Blanc who added a pink bow tie to their club kit for the French Championship final match. The chain is known for its quality wearable fashions with a strong rugby theme.

**VISA**

## The Royal Mile

The Royal Mile has many uniquely Scottish shops selling high quality textiles, jewellery and foodstuffs.

### Geoffrey (Tailor) Kiltmakers
57-59 High Street; 0131 557 0256
This is one of the best places in town to get a traditional, custom-made kilt and other items of Highland dress. The family-run business also specialises in '21st Century Kilts', fashionably made in modern styles and materials, even leather if you like.

### The Tappit Hen
89 High Street; 0131 557 1852
Behind the nondescript storefront, this small, pleasant jewellers sells a quality range of Scottish jewellery with unusual Celtic designs not often found elsewhere. It specialises in Celtic wedding rings and has a variety of gift items such as flasks and pewter tankards.

### Ragamuffin
278 Canongate; 0131 557 6007
If you're tired of tartan, check out the stylish selection of designer knitwear from Scotland, Ireland and beyond, made with natural fibres in a variety of colours and textures. There's also a collection of jackets and fleeces made with the 'angels don't trudge' label.

### Royal Mile Whiskies
379 High Street; 0131 225 3383
Hundreds of single malt whiskies are stocked in this specialist shop. The knowledgeable staff partake of regular blind tastings and recommend their favourite discoveries to customers.

## Grassmarket and Victoria Street

A handful of delightfully offbeat and one-of-a-kind shops can be found around Grassmarket and Victoria Street. Several sell foodstuffs such as cheeses, oils and vinegars, teas and whisky.

### Anta
93 West Bow (Victoria Street)
0131 225 4616
Tartans and tweeds are given a whole new look with the contemporary designs of this family-run Highland company. Beautiful textiles and hand-painted stoneware are inspired by the Scottish landscape. They also sell stylish luggage and a quirky range of accessories such as handbags, mini-kilts and ties.

### Iain Mellis Cheesemonger
30a Victoria Street;
0131 226 6215
Rounds of traditional British farmhouse cheeses are piled high in this delectable shop, along with cheeses from Ireland and the Continent. They also sell specially roasted coffees, teas from around the world and chocolate.

### Mr Wood's Fossils
5 Cowgate, Grassmarket
0131 220 1344
This unique shop in the Grassmarket is known round the world for its quality fossils and minerals from Scotland and abroad. Among Mr Wood's discoveries of rare plant and animal fossils is 'Lizzie', the oldest reptile ever found.

**SHOPPING**

VISA

# Golf and other sports

## Golf

Scotland is called the home of golf with some justification. Mary Queen of Scots is said to have been a keen golfer and reputedly played rounds on Musselburgh Links in 1567. Some of the most beautiful courses in the world are among the 500 or so spread throughout the land. Many of them are within easy reach of Edinburgh, and there are several options within the city.

### Historic courses

**The Old Golf Course
Musselburgh Links**
Balcarres Road, Musselburgh EH21 7SD
0131 665 5438
www.musselburgholdlinks.co.uk
Just six miles east of Edinburgh on the coast is this 'oldest course in the world' where golf has been continuously played since 1672. It was then a 7-hole course and is now a par-34 9-hole course. For a feeling of the history of the game, it can't be beaten. A round costs £9 weekdays and £9.50 weekends.

**The Old Golf Course
St Andrews Links**
St Andrews, Fife KY16 9SF
01334 477036
www.standrews.org.uk
Vying with Musselburgh in its claims to be the oldest course in the world, The Old Golf Course here is just one of several courses at St Andrews. Prices range from £10 for two rounds on the 9-hole Balgove Golf Course to £115 to play a round on the par-72 Old Golf Course itself. You could also play on the par-71 New Golf Course, which was opened in 1895, for £55.

Make plans well in advance if you want to play here because courses, and accommodation, book up quickly. Many people naturally want to stay at the Old Course Hotel (www.oldcoursehotel.com) but there is a range of accommodation from 5-star luxury down to comfortable and inexpensive guesthouses. The city of St Andrews is 55 miles northeast of Edinburgh, on the beautiful Fife coast.

### The game's origins

No-one knows with absolute certainty the true origins of golf, with several countries claiming credit for its invention. It was certainly played in Europe in a vaguely recognisable form as long ago as the 13th century, and there are Dutch paintings from the 18th century showing a similar game being played on ice and land. However it seems that the Scots invented the hole – and developed it into the game that we know today. The Honorable Company of Edinburgh Golfers laid down the rules of the game at St Andrews in 1754. The name golf is thought to originate from an old Scots verb 'to gowff' meaning to 'strike hard'.
At **St Andrews** there is a **British Golf Museum** with audio-visual displays to take you through the history of the game.
www.britishgolfmuseum.co.uk

## Edinburgh City courses

**Braid Hills**
Braid Hills Approach, Edinburgh EH10 6JY
0131 447 6666
www.edinburghleisure.co.uk
Braid Hills is only three miles south of the city centre, and has two public 18-hole courses, one a par-64 the other a par-70. A round costs from £15 depending on the time of your visit.

**Silverknowes Golf Club**
Silverknowes Parkway, Edinburgh EH4 5LB
Tel: 0131 336 3843
golf@edinburghleisure.co.uk
www.edinburghleisure.co.uk
Only three miles northwest of the centre and with beautiful views over the Firth of Forth, the public course here is an 18-hole par-71, with prices starting at £13.

## Freedom of the Fairways

The Scottish Borders, with 21 golf courses, is less than an hour's drive from Edinburgh. The Freedom of the Fairways golf passport offers excellent value, giving you access to 10 of these courses for 3 or 5 consecutive days. Information is available at tourist offices, on tel: 0870 608 0404 or online at www.visitscottishborders.com

BORDERS LANDSCAPE

## Adventure Sports

**Ratho Adventure Centre**
South Platt Hill, Ratho, Edinburgh EH28 8AA
0131 333 6333
www.adventurescotland.com
10:30-22:30 Mon-Fri; 09:30-20:00 Sat-Sun
free admission, charges for activities vary

The world's largest indoor climbing arena was spectacular enough when it opened in 2003, having cost over £24 million, but following a major refurbishment, it promises now to be even better. Incorporated into the Centre, which is in a former quarry that has been enclosed, are scuba diving facilities, mountain biking and several other activity sports.

## Football

Glasgow may have the historical edge on Edinburgh when it comes to soccer, with their two teams, Rangers and Celtic, but Edinburgh is the home of Hibernian and Heart of Midlothian. Both play in the Scottish Premier League, and with home matches alternating on weekends during the season (August-May approximately), there's a good chance to catch a home match.

### Heart of Midlothian
Tynecastle Stadium, McLeod Street
0870 787 1874
www.heartsfc.co.uk
The stadium for Hearts is the Tynecastle, two miles southwest of the city centre.

### Hibernian Football Club
Easter Road Stadium, 12 Albion Place
0131 661 2159
www.hibernianfc.co.uk
Hibs play at the Easter Road Stadium, about a mile east of the city centre on the way to Leith.

## Hiking in the Highlands

**Walkabout Scotland**
2F2, 70 Strathearn Road, Edinburgh EH9 2AF
0845 686 1344
www.walkaboutscotland.com
There are dozens of walking tours of Edinburgh, but if you want to do some real hiking then the Southern highlands are within striking distance for a day visit. This enterprising company has three organised day tours to take you walking in some of Scotland's spectacular scenery, on Mondays, Wednesdays and Fridays. You can start the day in Edinburgh and a few hours later be up Ben Lawers, Scotland's 10th-highest mountain, and still be back in time for supper. Other tours take in Ben Lomond, overlooking Loch Lomond, and Ben A'an, the easiest option by Loch Katrine at 1,450ft.

# Some of Scotland's loveliest scenery is right on Edinburgh's doorstep. The Scottish Borders region stretches east to the coast and south to the border with England.

The Borders has an idyllic, rolling landscape perfect for walking, cycling, fishing and other outdoor sports. Old picturesque mill towns lie along the banks of the River Tweed, a legacy of the traditional weaving trade. Peaceful though it is today, during medieval times it was often the scene of cross-border warfare between the English and the Scots. When they weren't fighting the English, locals had to defend their land against the reivers, or cattle thieves.

**Smailholm Tower,** which stands on a lonely outcrop near Kelso, is a 15th-century defensive tower that was used to keep watch for invaders. Many towns still hold annual pageants called the Common Ridings, gathering to

**Kelso**
• pretty town along the river
**Peebles**
• attractive base for exploring
**Jedburgh**
• visit the abbey and the Mary Queen of Scots house
**Melrose Abbey**
• the best preserved of the region's great medieval abbeys

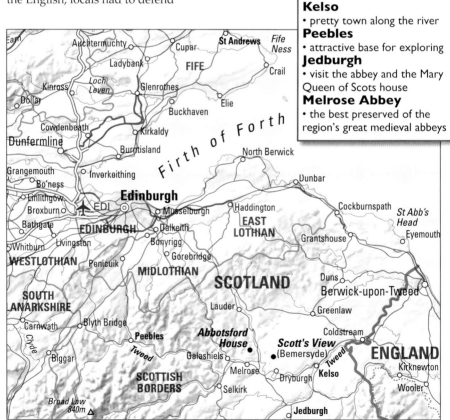

KELSO

patrol their lands on horseback as their ancestors did.

Set along the River Tweed, **Peebles** makes an attractive base for exploring the Borders. It's the starting point for several good walks which follow the river past Neidpath Castle, a medieval tower house, across old railway bridges and through woodlands and farmland.

The ruins of four great medieval abbeys can be visited on a scenic drive. **Melrose Abbey** is the best preserved, with much carved detail remaining in its pinkish facade. The heart of the Scottish hero Robert the Bruce was buried here. **Jedburgh Abbey**, the largest, is an impressive sight. In town you can also visit the Mary Queen of Scots House, a fortified house where she took refuge in 1566. Little is left of **Kelso Abbey**, once the largest and richest of them all, set in the pretty town centre. **Dryburgh Abbey** stands in lovely grounds on the banks of the Tweed, and is the burial place of Scotland's great writer, Sir Walter Scott.

You can visit several stately homes in the Borders, but perhaps none is more interesting than the home of the great man himself, **Abbotsford House**. Scott's descendants still live in one wing, but you can see his impressive library and the wood-panelled study where he wrote. These and other rooms are filled with mementoes of historical figures.

One of the best places to admire the beautiful landscape of the Borders is from the hilltop known as **Scott's View**. Sir Walter often came here to take in the panorama looking across the River Tweed to the Eildon Hills. According to local lore, during his funeral procession to Dryburgh Abbey, his horses stopped here of their own accord.

### Tourist Offices

Information on these and other attractions is available from the Tourist Offices in Peebles High Street and other Borders towns. Or contact the Scottish Borders office 0870 608 0404 www.visitscottishborders.com

# TRAVEL BASICS

# France

## Climate

France is a large country, temperate in the north and sub-tropical in the south. Host cities are spread across the nation, so be prepared for all kinds of weather. In the south, Marseille and Montpellier have warm climates buffered by the Mediterranean, while Toulouse is affected by its proximity to the mountains of the Pyrenees. Nantes and Bordeaux are influenced by the Atlantic, Lyon by the Alps. September temperatures should be in the low 20's C, warm and sunny, with some autumn rain on the south coast. Temperatures cool as October advances, and as you go north. Lens could be chilly (13-15 C) in September, and rain is always possible in Paris in October.

## Documents and Health

If you're an EU national or from the US, Canada, Australia or New Zealand and are planning to stay for less than three months, you don't need a visa. All other foreign nationals will be required to show a short-stay visa on entry.

EU travellers should carry a European Health Insurance card, which entitles them to free medical and dental treatment and local rates for prescriptions.

No special immunizations or medications are necessary for travel to France, but all travellers, especially children, should be up to date with routine vaccinations such as tetanus.

Rabies is endemic in France, but human cases are extremely rare and vaccination is not necessary (although EU pet owners bringing an animal into France must show a rabies vaccination certificate along with a European Pet Passport).

### Pharmacies

Pharmacies in France are usually easily recognizable by an illuminated green cross sign, and are extremely helpful. For minor ailments you can use them almost like a doctor: they will give diagnoses and prescribe pharmaceuticals. In the south of the country there are occasional cases of scorpion or hornet stings. These are usually only of minor discomfort and local pharmacies are equipped to deal with them. In addition, pharmacists can often identify edible species of mushrooms for you.

## Arriving

### By Air
www.aeroport.fr
Travellers arriving from other EU countries will most likely fly direct to the match cities. Refer to the stadium pages of each city for the nearest airport. If you are arriving from outside the EU, chances are you will be landing at Paris Charles de Gaulle airport and then taking a connecting flight or train. Shorthaul flights from budget airlines are already expensive for Rugby World Cup 2007, so a train pass could be a good option. At the time of writing airport security is high, and will probably continue to be so throughout Rugby World Cup 2007. Expect armed police with sniffer dogs at all entry points.

### Eurostar
www.eurostar.com
Eurostar operates up to 17 services daily between London and Paris. Journey time is approximately 2½ hours, and the majority of these trains stop at Lille. The fastest time from London to Lille is about 1 hr 40. Eurostar in London departs from Waterloo station and arrives in Paris at Gare du Nord.

### Cross Channel Ferries
Those travelling by car between the UK and France can choose from a number of cross-channel car ferries:
• Brittany Ferries
www.brittany-ferries.co.uk  0870 907 6103
08.00-19.30 Mon-Fri, 09.00-17.00 Sat, 09..00-16.30 Sun
Portsmouth to St Malo, Caen and Cherbourg; Poole to Cherbourg; Plymouth to Roscoff
• Condor Ferries
www.condorferries.co.uk  0870 243 5140
Poole to St Malo, Weymouth to St Malo, Portsmouth to Cherbourg
• LD Lines
www.ldline.co.uk  0870 420 1267
Newhaven to Dieppe and Le Havre
Portsmouth to Le Havre
• Norfolkline
www.norfolkline-ferries.com  0870 870 1020 daily
08.00-20.00
Dover to Dunkerque (formerly Hoverspeed)
• P & O Ferries
www.poferries.com  0870 598 0333
Dover to Calais, up to 25 crossings daily
• Seafrance
www.seafrance.com
Dover to Calais, 15 crossings daily
• Speedferries
www.speedferries.com  0870 220 0570
Dover to Boulogne

### Eurotunnel (Le Shuttle)

Alternatively you can travel by Le Shuttle, the train service operating through the Channel Tunnel:

• www.eurotunnel.com

## Getting around

Transportation in France is easy and well-organised with modern facilities and equipment. Roads are usually well-signed and trains generally run on schedule.

Special buses and parking facilities will be available during Rugby World Cup 2007, keep your eye out for Park-and-Ride (*parking-relais*) signs on major routes near the stadiums. There will also be special shuttle buses from train stations and airports. These be well-signed in English and French.

### Trains

Train connections are excellent throughout France and the country boasts some of the fastest trains in Europe (TGVs). It may be worth flying into Paris and continuing to the host cities by train rather than by a connecting flight.

Charles de Gaulle has its own TGV station in Terminal 2, where you can board direct high-speed trains to Nantes, Bordeaux, Lyon, Toulouse, Montpellier and Marseille. Or there are RER trains every fifteen minutes to the Gare to Nord, from where it's easy to get to anywhere else in Paris including all mainline stations. From Gare du Nord you can also take Eurostar trains to London and travel on to Cardiff and Edinburgh. The main-line stations in Paris for the French host cities are as follows:

Gare du Nord - Lens, St Denis
Gare Montparnasse - Nantes, Bordeaux, Toulouse
Gare de Lyon - Montpellier, Marseille, St Etienne, Lyon

### Buses

Long-distance buses generally only operate where rail services are poor. However there are good shuttle services from many airports and train stations. For instance, there's an hourly bus from Charles de Gaulle right across Paris to Gare Montparnasse. Special services are planned for Rugby World Cup 2007. At the time of writing there are no concrete details, but look for signs upon arrival.

### Driving

France has a dense network of roads and motorways, making road access to all the host cities relatively easy. But be warned: the French love their cars and at busy times the *bouchon* or traffic jam is common, even on toll roads. If you're bringing your own car, make sure you have a green card from your insurer, as well as a warning triangle, spare bulbs and headlamp deflectors if it's right-hand drive.

Car hire in France is easy to arrange and is best done in conjunction with an air ticket – the best deals are on the internet. It's often possible to arrange a dropoff at another city if you're using one of the major companies. Parking in French cities can be a problem as there are often more cars than spaces. This will be even more the case during Rugby World Cup 2007 and you are advised not to even attempt parking near the stadiums: parking will be reserved for press and corporate use and restricted for security reasons. Park-and-Ride (*parking-relais*) schemes are being organised to handle match traffic on all major routes.

Driving in France can be unnerving at first because the French can be aggressive and they like to drive fast. However the roads are kept in good repair and the signage is good, especially on toll roads. The French drive on the right-hand side of the road, so be careful if you're used to driving on the left – overtaking can be tricky without a passenger to help you. If you take your car across the Channel to Cardiff and Edinburgh matches, remember that you'll be changing over to the left side. There are signalling differences too: in France a headlamp flash means that you're claiming right of way; in the UK it means you're giving it.

Remember there's a loose adherence to *priorité à droite* (priority from the right) and you may be surprised when cars unexpectedly enter your lane from the right. This is less of a problem than it was, but it still happens. On a roundabout, cars already in circulation always have priority.

Signage in France can also be slightly confusing as road signs may appear to be pointing sideways when they're directing you straight ahead. Signs do not indicate what direction you are travelling, ie. north or south, so it is useful to know the names of larger cities further along your route as smaller towns may not appear on road signs until you are quite close to the destination.

When you approach a town, you will often be given two choices: *centre-ville* or *autres directions*. To carry on through and avoid the centre choose *autres directions*, to travel into the centre choose *centre-ville*.

### Taxi

All taxi drivers must be registered and cars are metered. It is a requirement for a Parisian taxi driver to speak a second foreign language and most choose English. Therefore, chances are, whether he admits it or not, your driver does speak English. If you are catching a taxi at Gare du Nord, it is helpful to briefly check your map for your destination to avoid being given the scenic tour of Paris, even better if you can give your instructions in French.

## Holidays

There are no national holidays in France or the UK in September or October, but it's worth knowing that in France a lot of attractions, shops and even restaurants are closed on Mondays. In the southern part of France too, there's a loose siesta time in the middle of the day when some things are shut. It may be as long as from noon until 4pm, or just from one until two, or it can be anywhere in between.

## Tourist information

Before you travel, read this book. There are web links to tourist offices for host cities in their individual sections, but see also:
• www.france2007.fr
Official website for the tournament
• www.rth07.org
Official hospitality and tour operator site
• www.franceguide.com
French tourist board
• www.sncf.com & www.eurostar.com
Railway information
• www.bonjourlafrance.net
Airfares, transport and much more general advice

## Disabled travellers

France can be tricky for disabled travellers: there are seldom kerb ramps, streets can be steep and are often cobbled, and older hotels sometimes lack lifts (elevators). However, improvements in accessibility are being made all the time and each of the participating stadiums is fully wheelchair-accessible (see individual city sections for more information).

SNCF Accessibilité (0 800 154 753) has information (French only) for travellers with physical, sight and hearing disabilities. At railway stations and airports, porters wearing red jackets are free of charge. On TGVs you can book a place in the first class carriage at no extra charge (and on Eurostar trains there are two wheelchair spaces per first class carriage; you don't need to book). The **Guide du Voyageur à Mobilité Réduite** is available

free at main train stations, and gives details of all facilities. Rental cars with hand controls are available at Paris, Lyon and Marseille airports. *Access in Paris* by Gordon Couch and Ben Roberts, published in Britain by Quiller Press and available from RADAR (£6.95), is an excellent guide to accommodation, monuments, museums, restaurants and travel to and in the city.

## Emergencies

Numbers to call:
• **15** Ambulance
• **17** Police and Gendarmerie
• **18** Fire (Sapeurs Pompiers, who also offer a first aid and ambulance service and often arrive before an ambulance, especially in rural areas)

## Thefts and losses

In the event of a theft, a police report will be required if you are going to make an insurance claim. Report to the local police station. If a passport was lost or stolen, contact your embassy. If only credit cards were stolen, and these have been cancelled, it may not be necessary to make a police report – credit card companies are often satisfied with a telephone report.

## Embassies in Paris

• Argentina
6 rue Cimarosa
01 45 53 14 69
• Great Britain and Northern Ireland
35 rue du Faubourg-St-Honore
01 42 66 91 42
• Ireland
4 rue Rude
01 45 00 20 87
• New Zealand
7ter rue Léonard-de-Vinci
01 45 00 24 11
• Australia
4 rue Jean-Rey
01 40 59 33 00
• South Africa
59 quai d'Orsay
01 45 55 92 37
• Italy
51 rue de Varenne
01 45 44 38 90
• Canada
35 ave Montaigne
01 44 43 29 00

• Japan
7 ave Hoche
01 47 66 02 22
• Namibia
80 avenue Foch
01 44 17 32 65
• Romania
5 rue de l'Exposition
01 40 62 22 03
• Georgia
104 avenue Raymond Poincaré
01 45 02 16 16
• USA
2 ave Gabriel
01 43 12 22 22
• Uruguay
15 rue Le Sueur
01 45 00 81 37
• Morocco
5 rue Le Tasse
01 45 20 69 36
• Portugal
3 rue de Noisiel
01 47 27 35 29

## Communication

### Postage
Stamps are for sale in tabacs and post offices (identifiable by their blue on yellow signage); sometimes stamps are sold along with postcards.

### Telephone
If possible avoid making calls from your hotel – sometimes you can be charged double or triple the standard rate. All French telephone numbers have ten digits, the first two of which are the area code and can be dropped if you're calling from the same city. To make international calls dial 00, wait for the tone and then dial the country code, area code (minus the initial zero) followed by the number.

### Internet
France lags a few years behind the US on internet availability but is catching up fast. The internet is now available in many hotels and internet cafés. French modem sockets are not compatible with UK or US ones; it's inexpensive however to buy a French lead for your laptop, or use wifi if available.

## Money

### Banking hours
In northern France standard banking hours are 09.00-16.30 or 17.15 Mon – Fri. In the south things are a bit different: a lot of banks are closed on Mondays and are open instead Tue-Sat with a lunchtime siesta, 08.00-12.00 and 13.30-16.30.

### Cashpoints
ATMs which you can use with a credit card are getting more common and debit cards (Maestro, Cirrus) can be used almost anywhere. In restaurants a handheld machine which reads your card at your table is pretty standard, so remember to bring all your pin numbers.

### Shopping
You will be required to show ID (driving license or passport) when purchasing items with a foreign registered debit or credit card.

## Practical

### Language
English is the second language of the country and there is often someone who can speak it, if you don't speak French. Surprisingly, although you'd think English should be most commonly spoken in Paris, this is not always the case. Parisians often seem to feel that foreigners should address them

## Restaurant Listings

### pricing
Restaurants are listed according to price range, signified by the € symbol. Prices are average per person for 2-3 courses including a glass of house wine.

| €€€€ | €60 and over |
| €€€ | €30-€60 |
| €€ | €15-€30 |
| € | €15 and under |

### booking
It is advisable to book ahead during the tournament, as all listed places are bound to be busy.

in French, so it's best to know at least the basic phrases. The French set great store by basic politeness, so in a shop or café always say *bonjour* before you begin on any other queries. Likewise, *merci* and *au revoir* should be used whenever relevant, and handshaking is more often employed during an informal greeting than in the UK or USA.

### Smoking
At the time of writing, smoking is set to be banned from places such as offices, universities and railway stations from February 2007. Cafés, bars, restaurants and nightclubs could be given up to a year to prepare to enforce the new anti-smoking laws.

### Toilets
French public toilets can be anywhere from spotless to horrific on a cleanliness spectrum and there are still open-air *pissoirs* for men and 'Turkish' squat toilets in chic cafés. It may be safest to use the facilities in your hotel, a museum or restaurant. Automatic pay toilets you find in the street are self-cleaning, though this is no guarantee. Be careful as children have become locked inside. It is not advised to use public toilets located along the motorway or at the toll stations as these are often disgusting. Bring your own toilet paper.

Although this is gradually changing, it is still common for French owners to allow their dogs to relieve themselves on the pavement and poop-scoopers are still too rarely used, so watch your step.

## Tipping
A service charge of 12.5 or 15% is added to the bill in a restaurant (it should say *service*

*compris*, service included on your bill), but most people leave a few euros cash on the table on top of this, or round up the bill. Some bars have taken to cheekily adding a spurious 'tip not included' message next to the legally required service compris line on the till receipt, in the hope of getting some extra – always read the bill carefully.Elsewhere cloakroom attendants usually receive 30-50c, and taxi drivers expect 10% of the fare.

## Time

France is in the Central European Time Zone which observes daylight saving time and so during the tournament will be two hours ahead of Greenwich Mean Time (GMT).

# United Kingdom

## Climate

Weather in the UK is less predictable than you will find in France. In September and October temperatures will be similar to those in northern France or a degree or two lower. Rain is a strong possibility; sadly in Edinburgh it is almost inevitable.

## Arriving

### By Air

You can fly to Edinburgh from Paris Charles de Gaulle (and also direct from Toulouse, Marseille, Bordeaux and Lyon). Cardiff isn't directly accessible by air from France, but if you're in London you can fly from Heathrow, although it is only a couple of hours away by road or rail.

**Eurostar** See page 284

**Eurotunnel** See page 284

**Cross Channel Ferries** See page 284

## Getting around

### Train

To continue your journey to Cardiff, you'll need to head for Paddington: take the Bakerloo tube line from Waterloo. For Edinburgh, go to Euston on the Northern line (7 stops) or to King's Cross station via the Northern and Victoria lines (8 stops, change at Euston).Train times are approximately 2 hours to Cardiff and 4½ hours to Edinburgh.

### Driving

In the UK, remember that you'll now be driving on the left. The change takes many drivers time to adjust.

## Visas

For onward travel from France to the UK, Fiji and Georgia foreign nationals are required to hold a UK visa. Please make sure you have one before travelling.

## Smoking

Please remember that smoking in enclosed public spaces is banned in the UK, and you may be liable to an on-the-spot fine of £50 if you light up in the wrong place.

## Tipping

Good news for those making the transition from France to the UK: restaurant service is often a mere 10% (unless specified) which is left at your discretion, and bars and pubs expect no tipping at all. Taxi drivers are usually happy with just 10%.

## Time

The UK is one hour behind France and during the tournament will be observing British Summer Time (GMT +1).

## Disabled travellers

The UK is one of the world's most advanced countries in terms of ease and access for disabled visitors. Various government schemes mean that most venues and destinations cater fully for disabled travellers, and staff usually go out of their way to help.

## Emergencies

For all emergency services dial **999** or **112**. An operator will forward you to the service you require.

## Tourist Information

Some useful websites:
- www.visitbritain.com
- www.visitwales.com
- www.visitscotland.com

---

### Restaurant Listings

**Pricing**

Restaurants are listed according to price range, signified by the £ symbol. Prices are average per person for 2-3 courses including a glass of house wine.

| | |
|---|---|
| ££££ | £60 and over |
| £££ | £30-£60 |
| ££ | £15-£30 |
| £ | £15 and under |

THERE IS NO LOVE WITHOUT COMMITMENT. THERE IS NO LOVE FOR ONE ANOTHER WITHOUT RESPECT. THERE IS NO LOVE OF THE GAME WITHOUT TEAM SPIRIT. THERE IS NO LOVE FOR THE OVAL BALL WITHOUT FRIENDSHIP. AND IT'S BECAUSE IT HAS ALWAYS INSPIRED ALL THOSE WHO KNOW IT THAT THERE IS NO RUGBY WITHOUT LOVE. SOCIÉTÉ GÉNÉRALE HAS BEEN THE RUGBY PARTNER AT EVERY LEVEL FOR 20 YEARS.

1987-2007 BECAUSE WE LOVE rugby.

SOCIETE GENERALE

www.paramourdurugby.com

# Essential French

## Courtesy

| | | |
|---|---|---|
| Please | S'il vous plaît | *seel voo play* |
| Thank you | Merci | *mair-see* |
| You're welcome | Je vous en prie | *zher voo zon-pree* |
| Sorry (excuse me) | Pardon | *par-don* |
| Excuse me (may I pass?) | Excusez-moi | *ek-skew-zay mwa* |
| Yes | Oui | *wee* |
| No | Non | *non* |

## Greetings

| | | |
|---|---|---|
| Good morning/afternoon | Bonjour | *bon-zhoor* |
| Good evening | Bonsoir | *bon-swar* |
| Good night (to sleep) | Bonne nuit | *bonna nwee* |
| Hello (informal) | Salut | *sa-lew* |
| Good-bye | Au revoir | *o rer-vwar* |
| My name is . . . | Je m'appelle | *zher ma-pel* |
| How are you? (formal) | Comment allez-vous? | *ko-mont allay-voo* |
| See you later | À bientôt | *A byun-to* |

## For Help

| | | |
|---|---|---|
| Excuse me . . . | Excusez-moi . . . | *ek-skew-zay mwa* |
| Sir | monsieur | *mer-soo-er* |
| Madam | madame | *ma-dam* |
| Miss/Ms | mademoiselle | *mad-mwa-zel* |
| Do you speak English? | Parlez-vous anglais ? | *par-lay vooz on-glay?* |
| I'm sorry . . . | Pardon . . . | *par-don* |
| I don't speak French | Je ne parle pas français | *zher ner parl pa fron-say* |
| I don't understand | Je ne comprends pas | *zher ner kom-pron pa* |
| I would like . . . | Je voudrais . . . | *zher voo-dray* |
| Do you have . . .? | Avez vous . . .? | *avvay-voo* |
| Help! (in an emergency) | Au secours ! | *o skoor!* |

## Directions

| | | |
|---|---|---|
| Where? | Où ? | *oo* |
| Where is the toilet? | Où est la toilette? | *oo ay la twa-let* |
| How do I get to . . .? | Pour aller à . . .? | *por allay a* |
| Is there a bus to . . .? | Est-ce qu'il y a un car à . . .? | *ess-keel ya un car a* |
| Where do I buy tickets? | Où est-ce que je peu acheter des billets ? | *oo ess-kuh zhe per ash-tay day bee-yay* |
| Left/Right | À gauche/À droite | *a gosh / a drwat* |
| Straight on | Tout droit | *too drwa* |

## Requesting a Table/Making Reservations

| | | |
|---|---|---|
| Have you got a table for . . . ? | Avez-vous une table pour . . . ? | *avvay vooz oon tar-bler poor . . .* |
| two, three, four | deux, trois, quatre | *der, trwa, katrer* |
| breakfast | petit déjeuner | *per-tee day-zher-nay* |
| lunch | déjeuner | *day-zher-nay* |
| dinner | dîner | *dee-nay* |

| I'd like to reserve a table . . . | Je voudrais réserver une table . . . | *zher voo-dray ray-zair-vay oon tar-bler* |
| for tonight | pour ce soir | *poor ser swar* |
| tomorrow night | demain soir | *der-mun swar* |
| at eight o'clock | à huit heures | *a wee terz* |
| Do you have a reservation? | Avez-vous un réservation? | *Avvay voo zun ray-zay-va-syon ?* |
| I have a reservation. | J'ai une réservation | *zhay un ray-zay-va-syon* |

## Ordering/Asking for Things

| The menu (please ) | la carte s'il vous plaît | *la kart seel voo play* |
| Fixed price menu | menu à prix fixe | *mu-new pree fiks* |
| Wine list | la carte des vins | *la cart day vuns* |
| What is the house speciality? | Quelle est la spécialité de la maison ? | *kess-kuh say la spe-syal-ittay der la may-zon* |
| What would you recommend? | Qu'est-ce que vous conseillez? | *kess-kuh voo con-say-yay* |
| I'll have this | Je prends ceci | *zhe pron ser-see* |
| I'd like a . . . | Je voudrais | *zhe voo-dray* |
| beer | une bière | *oon bee-air* |
| glass of wine | un verre de vin | *un vair der vun* |
| bottle of wine | une bouteille de vin | *oon boo-tay der vun* |
| glass of water | un verre d'eau | *un vair doh* |
| knife/fork | un couteau/une fourchette | *un koo-toh/oon foor-shet* |
| spoon | une cuillière | *oon kwee-yair* |

## Paying the Bill

| The bill, please | L'addition, s'il vous plaît | *la dee-syon, seel voo play* |
| Is service included? | Le service est compris? | *ler sair-vees ay kom-pree* |

## Essential Shopping French

| Open | Ouvert(e) | *oo-vair(t)* |
| Closed | Fermé | *fair-may* |
| How much is this? | Ça fait combien? | *sa fay kom-byun?* |
| Can you write down the price? | Pouvez-vous écrire le prix? | *poo-vay-voo ay-kreer ler pree* |
| Do you take credit cards? | Prenez-vous les cartes de crédit ? | *prunnay-voo lay kart der kray-dee?* |
| I'd like to buy . . . | Je voudrais . . . | *zher voo-dray . . .* |
| Do you have anything . . .? | Avez-vous quelque chose . . .? | *avvay voo kelka shoze* |
| larger | plus grand | *ploo gron* |
| smaller | plus petit | *ploo per-tee* |
| Do you have any others? | Avez-vous quelque chose d'autre? | *Avvay voo kelka shoze do-trer?* |
| I'm just looking. | Je regarde | *zhe rer-gard* |

## Words to watch out for

*Journée* means day, not journey (which is *voyage*).
*Car* means coach or bus, not car (which is *voiture*).
*Vacances* means holidays, not vacancies (which are *postes vacantes*).
*Menu* means a fixed-price menu, not a paper menu (which is *carte*).
*Librairie* means bookshop, not library (which is *bibliothèque*).
*Information* means news, not information (which is *renseignement*).
*Avertissement* means a warning, not an advertisement (which is *une réclame*)
*Monnaie* means cash, coinage or change, not money (which is *argent*).

## Menu reader

**A**
**abats** offal
**abricot** apricot
**à emporter** to take away
**agneau** lamb
**aiguillette de boeuf** slices of rump steak
**ail** garlic
**amande** almond
**ananas** pineapple
**anchois** anchovies
**andouillette** spicy sausage
**anguille** eel
**à point** medium (cooked)
**artichaut** artichoke
**asperge** asparagus
**assiette anglaise** selection of cold meats
**au gratin** baked in a milk, cream and cheese sauce
**au vin blanc** in white wine
**avocat** avocado

**B**
**banane** banana
**bavaroise** light mousse
**béarnaise** with béarnaise sauce (made with eggs & butter)
**béchamel** white sauce
**beignet** fritter, doughnut
**beurre** butter
**bière** beer
**bifteck** steak
**bifteck de cheval** horsemeat steak
**bisque** thick soup
**blanc de blancs** white wine from white grapes
**blanquette de veau** veal stew
**bleu** rare (meat)
**boeuf** beef
**boeuf bourguignon** beef in red wine
**boeuf braisé** braised beef
**boeuf en daube** beef casserole
**boudin noir** black pudding
**bouillabaisse** fish soup from the Midi
**bouillon** broth
**bouillon de poule** chicken stock
**bouquet rose** prawns
**braisé** braised
**brioche** round roll
**brochette** kebab
**brut** very dry (wine)

**C**
**cabillaud** cod
**café** coffee (black)
**café au lait** white coffee
**café complet** continental breakfast
**café crème** white coffee
**café glacé** iced coffee
**calamar/calmar** squid
**calvados** apple brandy
**canard** duck
**canard à l'orange** duck in orange sauce
**carbonnade** beef cooked in beer
**cari** curry
**carotte** carrot
**carré d'agneau** rack of lamb
**carte** menu
**carte des vins** wine list
**casse-croûte** snacks
**cassis** blackcurrant
**cassoulet** bean, pork & duck casserole
**céleri** celeriac
**céleri en branches** celery
**cerise** cherry
**cervelle** brains
**champignon** mushroom
**chantilly** whipped cream
**charcuterie** sausages, ham and paté: pork products
**cheval** horse
**chèvre** goat's cheese
**chevreuil** venison
**chicorée** endive
**chocolat chaud** hot chocolate
**chocolat glacé** iced chocolate
**chou** cabbage
**chou-fleur** cauliflower
**chou rouge** red cabbage
**choux de Bruxelles** Brussels sprouts
**cidre** cider
**citron** lemon
**concombre** cucumber
**confit de canard** duck preserved in fat
**confiture** jam
**coq au vin** chicken in red wine
**coquille Saint-Jacques** scallops in cream sauce
**côtelette** chop
**crabe** crab
**crème** cream, creamy sauce or dessert; white coffee
**crêpe** pancake
**crêpes Suzette** pancakes flambéed with orange sauce
**crevette grise** shrimp
**crevette rose** prawn
**croque-madame** grilled cheese & ham sandwich with a fried egg
**croque-monsieur** grilled cheese & ham sandwich
**crustacés** shellfish
**cuisses de grenouille** frogs' legs

**D**
**déjeuner** lunch
**digestif** liqueur
**dinde** turkey
**dîner** dinner
**doux** sweet

**E**
**eau minérale** mineral water
**endive** chicory
**en papillote** baked in foil or paper
**entrecote** rib steak
**entrée** starter
**épinards** spinach
**escalope** veal
**escargot** snail
**estouffade de boeuf** beef casserole

**F**
**flageolets** kidney beans
**flambé** served flaming
**flan** custard tart
**foie gras** goose or duck liver preserve
**fonds d'artichaut** artichoke hearts
**fraise** strawberry
**framboise** raspberry
**frisée** curly lettuce
**frites** chips
**fromage** cheese
**fruits de mer** seafood

**G**
**garni** with potatoes & vegetables
**gâteau** cake
**gelée** jelly
**génoise** sponge cake
**glace** ice cream
**gratin** baked cheese dish
**gratinée** grilled cheese layer
**grillé** grilled

**groseille blanche** whitecurrant
**groseille rouge** redcurrant

**H**
**haricots** beans
**haricots verts** green beans
**homard** lobster
**hors-d'oeuvre** starter
**huître** oyster

**I**
**infusion** herb tea

**J**
**jambon** ham
**julienne** soup with chopped vegetables
**jus de pomme** apple juice
**jus d'orange** orange juice

**K**
**kir** white wine with blackcurrant liqueur

**L**
**lait** milk
**langoustine** scampi
**lapin** rabbit
**lard** bacon
**léger** light, not rich
**légume** vegetable
**lentilles** lentils
**lièvre** hare
**limande** lemon sole
**limonade** lemonade

**M**
**mangue** mango
**maquereau** mackerel
**marron** chestnut
**massepain** marzipan
**menthe** peppermint
**menu du jour** today's menu
**millefeuille** custard slice
**morille** morel (mushroom)
**morue** cod
**moules marinière** mussels in cream and wine sauce
**mousse au chocolat** chocolate mousse
**mousseux** sparkling
**moutarde** mustard
**mouton** mutton
**mulet** mullet

**N**
**navet** turnip
**noisette** hazelnut
**noisette d'agneau** small round lamb steak
**noix** walnut
**nouilles** noodles

**O**
**oeuf** egg
**oignon** onion

**P**
**pain** bread
**pain au chocolat** chocolate filled croissant
**palette de porc** shoulder of pork
**pamplemousse** grapefruit
**parfait glace** layered ice cream
**pâté de canard** duck paté
**paupiettes de veau** stuffed veal slices
**pêche** peach
**petit déjeuner** breakfast
**petit pain** roll
**petit pois** peas
**petits fours** small pastries
**pistache** pistachio
**plat du jour** dish of the day
**poire** pear
**poireau** leek
**poisson** fish
**poivre** pepper
**pomme** apple
**pomme de terre** potato
**pommes frites** French fries
**porc** pork
**porto** port
**potage** soup
**pot-au-feu** beef & vegetable stew
**provençale** with tomatoes, garlic & herbs
**prune** plum
**pruneau** prune
**purée** mashed potatoes

**Q**
**quenelle** meat or fish dumpling
**quiche lorraine** egg tart

**R**
**râble de chevreuil** saddle of venison
**raclette** Swiss dish of melted cheese
**radis** radish
**raisin** grape
**ratatouille** dish of stewed peppers, courgettes, aubergines & tomatoes
**rémoulade** mayonnaise flavoured with herbs & mustard
**riz** rice

**S**
**sablé** shortbread
**saint-honoré** cream puff
**salade russe** salad of diced vegetables in mayonnaise
**salade verte** green salad
**sanglier** wild boar
**saucisson** salami-type sausage
**saumon** salmon
**saumon fumé** smoked salmon
**sec** dry
**sel** salt
**service (non) compris** service (not) included
**service inclus** service charge included
**sole meunière** floured sole fried in butter
**soufflé au chocolat** chocolate soufflé
**soupe à l'oignon** French onion soup
**soupe aux poireaux et pommes de terre** leek & onion soup
**steak au poivre** peppered steak
**steak frites** steak & chips
**steak tartare** raw minced beef with onions, herbs and raw egg
**sucre** sugar
**supreme de volaille** chicken in cream sauce

**T**
**tarte** tart, pie
**terrine** pâté
**thé** tea
**thé à la menthe** mint tea
**thon** tuna
**tomate** tomato
**tournedos** round beef steak
**tripes** tripe
**truite meunière** floured trout fried in butter

**V**
**veau** veal
**vermicelle** vermicelli
**viande** meat
**vin** wine
**vin blanc** white wine
**vin rouge** red wine
**volaille** poultry
**VSOP** mature brandy

**Y**
**yaourt** yoghurt

# HOTELS

HOTEL LE BRISTOL, PARIS

**HOTELS**

## France

### Pricing

Price ratings are for a standard room per night. In France, rates are usually given for the room (not per person). Breakfast is almost always extra.

€€€€€ €400 and up
€€€€ €300-400
€€€ €200-300
€€ €100-200
€ under €100

## Paris

### Hotel Le Bristol Paris
112 rue Fauberg Saint-Honoré
metro: Miromesnil
01 53 43 43 00
www.hotel-bristol.com
€€€€€
Located on a very fashionable street, and with every amenity one would expect from a classic 5-star, the Bristol is an obvious choice for those seeking a luxurious hotel. With two Michelin stars, the restaurant is located just off the lobby in winter; it moves to a gorgeous courtyard in summer. Just near the courtyard there is a comfortable and elegant bar. Service is excellent, and the rooms are large and well-appointed. Paris views are to be had from the small rooftop pool, with Sacre Coeur on one side and the top of the Eiffel Tower on the other.

### Four Seasons George V
31 avenue George V; metro: George V
01 49 52 70 00
www.fourseasons.com/paris/
€€€€€
Definitely the place to stay for a special treat, the George V knocks you out with its style, from the enormous and elaborate flower displays that adorn the hotel, like floral works of art, through to the upper rooms with their views of the Eiffel Tower. It also has one of the city's best restaurants in *Le Cinq*, and is well-located halfway between the river and the Champs-Élysées.

### Les Jardin du Marais
74 rue Amelot; metro: St-Sébastien Froissart
01 40 21 22 23
resabastille@homeplazza.com
www.homeplazza.com
€€€
A large hotel (265 rooms) very well located

between the Marais and Bastille with many lively restaurants and bars within walking distance. It's also only a short taxi ride from Gare du Nord. The hotel is made up of several buildings facing an interior courtyard which is a good arrangement for people travelling in groups. Rooms are decorated in a contemporary version of Art Deco. Suites come with a functional kitchen complete with plates and cookware. An ideal base.

### Montalembert
3 rue de Montalembert; metro: rue du Bac
01 45 49 68 68
www.montalembert.com
€€€
The Montalembert is as achingly stylish as only a Paris hotel can be, yet at the same time it manages to be friendly and relaxing. Each room is decorated differently but every room has a marble bathrooms and plenty of space.

### Hôtel de Latour-Maubourg
150 rue de Grenelle; metro: Latour-Maubourg
01 47 05 16 16
info@latourmaubourg.com
www.latourmaubourg.com
€€
Conveniently located right in front of the metro stop. A small but charming boutique hotel with a Turkish bath and a small fitness room in the basement. It faces a busy square but double glazing means rooms are quiet.

### Hôtel de la Bretonnerie
22 rue Sainte Croix de la Bretonnerie
metro: St Paul, Hôtel de Ville
01 48 87 77 63
www.bretonnerie.com
€€
Set in a 17th-century building between place des Vosges and Hôtel de Ville, you won't find a better located hotel for rugby bars and fun restaurants. Some rooms are decorated with tapestries and four-poster beds while others have sloping ceilings and wooden beams under the eaves.

### Hôtel Saint-Merry
78 rue de la Verrerie; metro: Hôtel de Ville
01 42 78 14 15
www.hotelmarais.com
€€
A small (12 rooms) hotel set in a converted presbytery with exposed stone walls, tiled floors and carved wood panelling and doors. There is no lift or air-conditioning. Breakfast is served in the room or you may prefer to skip the charge and go to the café downstairs where they have excellent croissants.

### Hôtel Mansart
5 rue des Capucines; metro: Opera
01 42 61 50 28
www.esprit-de-france.com
€€
A Paris hotel for traditionalists in a central location just north of place Vendôme. It's styled in the manner of Louis XIV's architect, Mansart, and is old-fashioned and plush without being overpriced.

### Saint Thomas d'Aquin
3 rue du Pré-aux-Clercs; metro: rue du Bac
01 42 61 01 22
www.aquin-paris-hotel.com
€€
Chic doesn't get cheaper than this. Right in the heart of Saint-Germain, just across the river from the Louvre, is this delightful and stylish hotel which you feel ought to be costing twice as much. The rooms have tastefully expensive furniture and subtle colour schemes, yet it's all very modern too, with free wi-fi access.

### Hôtel des Marroniers
21 rue Jacob; metro: Saint Germain des Près
01 43 25 30 60
www.hotel-marronniers.com
€€
The name means chestnut trees, and they are to be found in the quiet retreat of the hotel's back garden, along with statuary and tables for afternoon tea. The rooms are plush with rich colours, but the price is cheaper than you might expect for this surprising spot in the heart of Saint Germain.

### Hôtel Bel Ami
7-11 rue St Benoit; metro: St Germain des Près
www.designhotels.com
€€
Part of the Design Hotels group, this is a comfortable hotel decorated in chocolate and cream. It's well-located and attracts a younger clientele.

### Hôtel du Danube
58 rue Jacob; metro: Saint Germain des Près
01 42 60 34 70
€
An older hotel decorated with wooden furniture and floral upholstery that is a bargain at €70 for a double room. It's clean, quiet and very well located.

### Hôtel de Nevers
83 rue du Bac; metro: Saint Germain des Près
01 45 44 61 30
hoteldenevers75@aol.com
€

### Mondiresa
01 56 82 66 14
www.mondiresa.com
Mondiresa are the Official Accommodation Bureau for Rugby World Cup 2007. They manage accommodation for the teams, VIPs, sponsors, businesses, official agents, tour operators and the media. If you fit in any of these categories and you are seeking accommodation, contact Mondiresa on the Paris number above, or visit their website for more information.

### Interhome
www.interhome.co.uk
If you are planning on making any of the Host Cities a base from which to operate, you might consider renting an apartment for a longer stay. Interhome offer a wide choice of apartments in all price ranges. A typical reservation is for 7 days.

### Alcove and Agapes
8 bis rue Coysevox; metro: Guy-Môquet
01 44 85 06 05
www.bedandbreakfastinparis.com
Another option is to stay in a Parisian home. Lots of people rent rooms out, and you may choose a host to suit your interests – whether artistic, gourmet, according to age or the languages they speak. Their excellent website allows you to find just the right place and person to suit your needs, ideal for those who want something more personal than a hotel.

A small but friendly family-run hotel with cozy rooms that have shutters and window boxes.

### Hôtel des Grandes Écoles
75 rue du Cardinal Lemoine
metro: Cardinal Lemoine
01 43 25 28 15 CHECK 01 43 26 79 23
www.hotel-grandes-ecoles.com
€
Located where rue Mouffetard meets Saint Germain is a charming country-style hotel. The château-like building surrounds a green courtyard in the middle of the Latin quarter. The rooms are on the floral side, but there's a warm welcome and a very rural feel to it all. Delightful and popular – bookings are only accepted 4 months in advance.

### Hôtel Plessis
25 rue du Grand Prieuré; metro: République
01 47 00 13 38
€
Don't let the fact that this is just a 2-star hotel

put you off – it's a lovely little place and a great bargain. It's a few minutes from both place de la République and the Marais, in the untouristy and lively Oberkampf area. Rooms are small and basic but bright and clean with TV, modem, phone, hair dryer and other facilities.

### Hôtel Roma Sacré-Coeur
101 rue Caulaincourt;
metro: Lamarck Caulaincourt
01 42 62 02 02
www.hotelroma.fr
€
If you want a true feel for Montmartre choose this quirky hotel where artists including George Braque have stayed. The rooms are decorated in very bold colours, so don't expect a restful look to them, but it's on the north side of the Butte, away from the more overly touristy parts of the area, and a place of terrific character.

## Lens, Arras & Lille
see page 296 for price guide

### Lens

#### Espace Bollaert
13 route de Bethune; 03 21 78 30 30
€€
This is the only 3-star in Lens and many of its rooms have a view of the stadium. The hotel isn't new, but beds are comfortable and there is a dining room on the ground floor.

#### Hôtel de France
2 place de Général de Gaulle; 03 21 28 18 10
€
A small 2-star hotel located across from the train station.

### Arras

#### Hôtel d'Angleterre
7 place du Maréchal Foch; 03 21 51 51 16
hd.arras@free.fr
€€€
Considered to be the best hotel in Arras, it is a 4-star, located right on the square near the train station.

#### Hôtel de l'Univers
3/5 place Croix-Rouge; 03 21 71 34 01
www.hotel-univers-arras.com
€€
A large comfortable hotel arranged around a quiet courtyard. This is a Best Western hotel and part of the Najeti hotels-and-golf group so there are special offers that combine hotel stays and green fees. The staff is friendly and

there are plenty of opportunities for golf and other excursions.

#### Holiday Inn Express
3 rue du Docteur Brassart; 03 21 60 88 88
reservations@hiexpress-arras.com
€
Sometimes its good to know exactly what to expect and this Holiday Inn maintains the chain's standard. It is located opposite the train station and beside a large underground carpark.

#### La Maison d'Hôtes La Corne d'Or
1 place Guy Mollet; 03 21 58 85 94
franck@lamaisondhotes.com
€
A small guest house lovingly restored by its owners, Franck and Isabelle Smal, who have an apartment at the rear of the house.

### Lille

#### Central Reservation Service
Tourist Office, 1 place Rihour
03 59 57 94 00
resa@lilletourism.com
Lille Tourist Office offers a free hotel booking service. They have a database of over 44 hotels and tourism residences and are open seven days a week.

#### L'Hermitage Gantois
224 rue de Paris; 03 20 85 30 30
www.hotelhermitagegatois.com
€€€€
Lille's most prestigious hotel is beautifully set in a converted hermitage and is decorated with taste and style. There is a piano bar and a Turkish bath and stunning rooms.

#### Alliance Hotel Couvent des Minimes
17 quai du Wault; 03 20 30 62 62
www.alliance-lille.com
€€€€
This contemporary hotel is in an old convent and its traditional brick and stone architecture is complemented by modern furnishings. It is well-located in the centre near place Rihour and has a peaceful interior courtyard that was once a cloister.

#### Crowne Plaza
335 boulevard de Leeds; 03 20 42 46 46
www.lille-crowneplaza.com
€€€
A modern 4-star hotel that is across the street from the Eurostar. It has all the conveniences you'd expect from this reliable hotel chain and it is a short 15-minute walk to the centre.

## Grand Hôtel Bellevue
5 rue Jean Roisin; 03 20 57 45 64
www.grandhotelbellevue.com
€€
This is a 19th century hotel with very large rooms, some facing onto the Grand'Place. The entrance is tucked away down a side street and there is a busy nightclub on the ground floor.

## Hôtel Mercure de l'Opera
2 boulevard Carnot; 03 20 14 71 47
www.accorhotels.com
€€
This traditional hotel is very well located in the centre of Lille next to Grand'Place. The rooms are rather faded but the location is excellent.

## Hôtel de la Treille
7/9 place Louise de Bettignies; 03 20 55 45 46
www.hoteldelatreille.fr.st
€
A nicely decorated 3-star in the heart of Lille's shopping district that is good value for money.

## Le Brueghel
5 parvis Saint Maurice; 03 20 06 06 69
www.hotel-brueghel.com
€
A 19th century style hotel near Flanker rugby bar and Gare Lille Flandres. Room prices hover around €100 per night and they have triples and family suites.

# Nantes
see page 296 for price guide

## Grand Hotel Mercure
4 rue du Couedic; 02 51 82 10 00
H1985@accor.com; www.accorhotels.com
€€€
A modern 4-star hotel located in the old town near the castle. Service is friendly and efficient, the environment is elegant and air-conditioned with a restaurant and bar on the ground floor. The rooms are large, clean and comfortable and each has a TV, hairdryer and minibar.

## Le Jules Verne
3 rue du Couedic; 02 40 35 74 50
hoteljulesverne@wanadoo.fr
€€
This centrally located 3-star is part of the Arcantis chain. It is decorated in a contemporary Art Deco style using rich colours and they have a variety of rooms. There are plenty of bars in the surrounding streets and it is an easy walk to catch a tram to the stadium.

## Brit Hotel Nantes La Beaujoire L'Amandine
45 boulevard des Batignolles; 02 40 50 07 07
amandine@brithotel.fr; www.brithotel.fr
€€
The better of the two hotels that are situated near La Beaujoire stadium. Decoration is contemporary without being overly generic. There is a pleasant restaurant where they have a large screen showing the tournament.

## Ibis Nantes La Beaujoire
5 rue du Moulin de la Haveque
02 40 93 22 22
www.accorhotels.com
€
The Beaujoire stadium is only 800 metres away, so this is a good location for attending the match. It's less expensive and more generic than L'Amandine but with 81 rooms, including 3 for disabled persons, a restaurant with bar, and covered parking, it is good value for money.

## Hôtel Pommeraye
2 rue Boileau; 02 40 48 78 79
info@hotel-pommeraye.com
www.hotel-pommeraye.com
€
An old world hotel beside the 19th century Pommeraye shopping arcarde. The rooms are a bit faded but comfortable and located in a good part of town for rugby bars and screens.

## Abat Jour
17 rue Geoffroy Drouet; 02 40 74 35 95
abat.jour@wanadoo.fr; www.hotelabatjour.com
€
A small but comfortable hotel located near passage Pommeraye and place du Commerce.

# La Baule

## Hôtel Le Brittany
7 avenue des Impairs; 02 40 60 30 25
www.hotelbrittany.com
€€
A very modern hotel, virtually right on the beach with king size beds and a balneotherapy spa. The place to come for relaxation.

## Hôtel St Pierre
124 avenue de Lattre de Tassigny; 02 40 24 05 41
www.hotel-saint-pierre.com
€
Just a 5-minute walk from the beach is this

charming *villa bauloise,* built in the 19th century in the local architectural style. It has been updated and newly decorated with polished hardwood floors and large wrought iron beds. The staff is very welcoming and they serve wonderful coffee and croissants for breakfast.

### Hôtel Les Pléiades
28 boulevard René Dubois; 02 51 75 06 06
www.les-pleiades.com
€
An old residence from the beginning of the last century that has been entirely renovated and is available only on a 7-day minimum rental. Close to the beach and all amenities.

# Lyon
see page 296 for price guide

### Villa Florentine
25 montée Saint Barthélemy; 04 72 56 56 56
florentine@relaischateaux.com
www.villaflorentine.com
€€€€€
A luxury 4-star villa set in a former convent high in the Fourvière district with fabulous views over Vieux Lyon. The Renaissance style of the original building has been preserved, but inside, the 28 rooms are decorated with contemporary chic. There is a pool and an excellent restaurant. Price range €150-800.

### Cour des Loges
2-8 rue du Boeuf; 04 72 77 44 44
www.courdesloges.com
€€€
The loveliest hotel in Lyon, stylishly built in and around the old courtyard of one of Vieux Lyon's 17th century houses. It was originally a college and has 62 rooms, suites and apartments, all individually designed. Some have fireplaces, others have beamed ceilings or gardens, all chicly modern. There are also rooftop terraced gardens and an indoor pool.

### Hôtel Globe et Cécil
21 rue Gasparin; 04 78 42 58 95
www.globeetcecilhotel.com
€€
This charming 3-star hotel is on an old street, about 50 metres from place Bellecour. Its 60 rooms are each individually – and stylishly – decorated, some with balconies, antique furniture, tapestries and marble fireplaces. Breakfast is included and the service is faultless.

### Phénix Hôtel
7 quai de Bondy; 04 78 28 24 24
www.hotel-le-phenix.fr
€€
This has been a hotel since the 16th century and is a good choice for Vieux Lyon, as it's on the edge of the old town and also steeped in its history. The rooms are immaculate but there's also a bohemian feel about it, with occasional jazz concerts and a reputation for being the haunt of actors and artists.

### Grand Hôtel Château-Perrache
12 cours Verdun-Rambaud, Esplanade de la Gare
04 72 77 15 00
www.accorhotels.com
€€
Right by the Gare Perrache and very convenient if you have an early departure, this Mercure hotel is comfortably modern but has Art Nouveau styling in public areas. It's only a short metro stop to the stadium and has a small business centre, a restaurant for lunch and dinner, and a bar open from 8am till late.

### Novotel Lyon Gerland
70 avenue Leclerc; 04 72 71 11 11
www.accorhotels.com
€€
If you want to be near the stadium then the Sofitel could hardly be closer. It's about five minutes from the Stade, and from the Gare Perrache on the other side of the Rhône. It has 187 rooms, with its own bar, restaurant and an outdoor unheated swimming pool. There is also private secure parking. The rooms are what you would expect from a modern hotel, designed for comfort rather than character, but with all the modern conveniences.

### Hôtel Élysées
92 rue P. Eduoard Herriot; 04 78 42 03 15
elysee-hotel@wanadoo.fr; www.elysee-hotel.com
€
Although only officially a 2-star hotel, the Élysées is well-located in the heart of the Presqu'île. It's friendly and efficient, clean and charming, with 29 ensuite rooms. They all have a hair-dryer, phone and satellite TV, though some are a little on the small side. However, if you want inexpensive accommodation in the city centre, it's perfect.

### Hôtel Saint-Vincent
9 rue Pareille; 04 78 27 22 56
www.hotel-saintvincent.com
€
Lovely location just behind the Quai Saint-

Vincent, with easy access to Vieux Lyon, the Croix Rousse and the Presqu'île areas. All 32 rooms have direct-dial phones and satellite TVs, and are spread around four separate buildings which have recently been refurbished. Its 2-star rating belies the attractive décor, the comfort and the friendliness of the staff.

## Saint-Étienne

see page 296 for price guide

Saint-Étienne is not a big tourist or business destination and so lacks the top-of-the-range hotels you might expect elsewhere. However, there are plenty of good mid-range options.

### Mercure
rue de Wuppertal; 04 77 42 81 81
H1252@accor.com; www.accorhotels.com
€€

Out in the Parc de l'Europe, about 2.5km southeast of the city centre, the Mercure has 120 air-conditioned rooms as well as its own bar and restaurant. The rooms are conventionally modern, comfortable, and all have mini-bar, cable TV and wifi high-speed internet access. It's only five minutes by taxi into the centre yet very close to the Mt Pilat Regional Park.

### Hôtel Furania
18 rue de la Résistance; 04 77 32 19 82
€

The Furania may only have two stars but it is a delightful place, perfect for all the city centre sights and activities. It has been wonderfully decorated by the new owners, who obviously have an artistic flair. Contemporary artworks adorn the breakfast room, while elsewhere there are Oriental rugs and travel photographs on the walls. The rooms are basic but clean, and the warmth of the welcome makes it a great place to stay.

### Hotel du Midi
19 boulevard Pasteur; 04 77 57 32 55
contact@hotelmidi.fr; www.hotelmidi.fr
€

Three kilometres due south of the city centre, the Midi has 33 simple but modern and perfectly comfortable rooms. They are all ensuite with satellite TVs and free wireless internet access. There's a bright lounge with comfortable armchairs, and also private parking if you're driving. The hotel is family-run and the owners are very obliging.

### Le Plateau de la Danse
Boulain, 42230 Saint-Victor-sur-Loire
04 77 90 36 90
leplateaudeladanse@yahoo.fr
€

Well-placed for exploring the Gorges de la Loire yet only 15km from Saint-Étienne's centre, this *chambre d'hôte* provides four ensuite rooms in a lovely 18th-century farmhouse. The owners, Martine and René Joseph, speak English, and the house is non-smoking and doesn't allow pets. The rooms are large and very homely, like staying in a friend's house, and outside is a colourful garden with a swimming pool.

### Hôtel Tenor
12 rue Blanqui; 04 77 33 79 88
contact@hoteltenor.com; www.hoteltenor.com
€

Only a block away from the central place de l'Hôtel de Ville, the 2-star Tenor has 64 ensuite rooms, all with satellite TV and desks. The décor is basic but the rooms are a good size and comfortable. The hotel also has its own basement car park, which is very useful if you're driving and want to be in the city centre.

### Hôtel Terminus du Forez
31 avenue Denfert Rochereau; 04 77 32 48 47
hotel.forez@wanadoo.fr
www.hotel-terminusforez.com
€

Close to the station is this slightly quirky 3-star hotel, where some rooms are decorated in colonial style and some in Egyptian, while in the public areas there's also a touch of art deco. It certainly makes for a characterful place to stay. All the rooms have satellite TV, phones and high-speed internet access, and the reasonable rates make it a good choice just a few minutes from the centre of town.

## Bordeaux

see page 296 for price guide

### Les Sources de Caudalie
Chemin de Smith Haut Lafitte
33650 Bordeaux-Martillac; 05 57 83 83 83
sources@sources-caudalie.com
www.sources-caudalie.com
€€€€€

This exclusive 4-star spa resort is part of the Smith Haut Lafitte vineyard and it's run by the same family. The Caudalie offers 49 luxury rooms and suites, with one suite set on its own island. Guests can also enjoy vinotherapy, an outdoor pool and jacuzzi, whirlpool bath, Turkish bath, gym, tennis, two restaurants and 16,000-bottle wine cellar. The resort has its own helicopter pad and a 3-hole golf course.

### Mercure Mondiale
18 parvis des Chartrons; 05 56 01 79 79
H2877@accor.com; www.accorhotels.com
€€€
Tucked away in the Cité Mondial, set back slightly from the riverfront, this Mercure is a good mid-range option between the city centre and the Chartrons district. It's modern and big, with 96 rooms, though the friendly little reception desk makes it feel much more homely. There's also a fabulous rooftop breakfast terrace with impressive city views.

### La Maison Bordeaux
113 rue Albert Barraud; 05 56 44 00 45
contact@lamaisonbord-eaux.com
www.lamaisonbord-eaux.com
€€
This boutique hotel is a short walk north of the city centre, a walk worth making as the rooms here are chic, with calming colours and a cool sophistication. They all look over the courtyard garden, and have free internet access. As well as being a designer, the owner belongs to a wine-making family and can arrange private visits to the chateau and cellars.

### Hôtel Notre-Dame
36-38 rue Notre-Dame; 05 56 52 88 24
hotelnotredamebx@free.fr
www.hotelnotredame.free.fr
€€
Well located in the historic Chartrons district of wine dealers and antique shops, the Notre-Dame is the kind of French hotel that belies its 2-star rating. The 21 rooms are simple, comfortable and clean, and all have cable TV, internet, phone and a hair dryer. The rooms may be generic but the hotel is in a beautifully-restored 19th-century mansion, with plenty of atmosphere.

### Hôtel Des Quatre Soeurs
6 cours du 30-Juillet; 05 57 81 19 20
4soeurs@mailcity.com; http://4soeurs.free.fr
€
In a perfect location close to place de la Comédie just a few doors down from the Tourist Information Office, the Quatre Soeurs has been here since the 18th century. A portrait of Richard Wagner hangs by the front door, as the composer was a guest here in 1850. Book a room at the front if you can, as they are bigger and brighter than the interior rooms that overlook an inner courtyard.

### Hôtel de Sèze
7 rue de Sèze; 05 56 81 72 42
hotel.seze.medoc@wanadoo.fr
www.hotel-deseze-royalmedoc.com
€
A very central 18th-century mansion, decorated with wood-panelling, mirrors and chandeliers. The de Sèze has simple but attractive modern rooms. There is a sister hotel next door, the Royal Médoc, with a similar standard and price.

### Hôtel de la Tour Intendance
14 rue de la Vieille Tour; 05 56 44 56 56
info@hotel-tour-intendance.com
www. hotel-tour-intendance.com
€
Charmingly individual hotel on a pedestrianised street near place Gambetta. Rooms in the main building are plain but comfortable, and those in an annex around the corner are more stylishly decorated but smaller, and there's no lift. A good affordable choice, with friendly and accommodating owners.

# Toulouse
see page 296 for price guide

### Crowne Plaza Hotel
7 place du Capitole; 05 61 61 19 19
hicptoulouse@alliance-hospitality.com
www.ichotelsgroup.com
€€€
The Crowne Plaza overlooks place du Capitole, Toulouse's main square. There couldn't be a better location for Rugby World Cup 2007 festivities. There are 163 rooms and 10 suites spread over six floors (completely refurbished in 2005) as well as two restaurants and a cocktail bar.

### Hôtel Garonne
22 descente de la Halle aux Poissons
05 34 31 94 80
contact@hotelgaronne.com
www.hotelgaronne.com
€€€
The 4-star Garonne is in the heart of the old part of town but in a quiet side street that leads down to the river, near Pont Neuf. There are only 14 rooms and each is sumptuously decorated with oak floors, velvet curtains, warm colours and with all the modern accoutrements: mini-bar, broadband, digital safe, satellite TV.

## Hôtel Mermoz
50 rue Matabiau; 05 61 63 04 04
information@hotel-mermoz.com
www.hotel-mermoz.com
€€€
Excellent little 3-star hotel in the city centre, named after the pilot Jean Mermoz in honour of the local aeronautic industry. It has great character with a very friendly atmosphere and while rooms are basic, they are comfortable. The hotel is set back from the road and entered through a courtyard. The 50 air-conditioned rooms all have free wifi access.

## Hôtel des Beaux Arts
1 place du Pont Neuf; 05 34 45 42 42
contact@hoteldesbeauxarts.com
www.hoteldesbeauxarts.com
€€
Down by the river, near Pont Neuf, the grand 18th-century façade of this 3-star hotel conceals a cosy place that mixes chic with tradition. There are just 18 rooms, plus one suite, some having lovely river views. The best is room 42 right at the top with its own private terrace.

## Hôtel Mercure Saint Georges
rue saint Jérome; 05 62 27 79 79
H0370@accor.com; www.mercure.com
€€
Mercure hotels don't always have a lot of character, but they do provide comfortable accommodation at a reasonable price. This one is well-located in the city centre with 120 rooms and 28 larger apartments, as well as a restaurant and bar. Place Saint Georges, busy with bars and restaurants, is just a short stroll away.

## Hôtel Les Bains Douches
4 rue du Pont Guilheméry; 05 62 72 52 52
accueil@hotel-bainsdouches.com
www.hotel-bainsdouches.com
€€
This brand new 3-star hotel has a 4-star feel, although it's a little out of centre, near place Dupuy, an area with its own lively atmosphere. The rooms and public areas are all eye-catchingly designed, using Starck-like simplicity made warmer by accents of bright colours. A very striking place to stay.

## Oliviers
avenue du Général Leclerc, 11000 Carcassonne
04 68 26 45 69
infos@hotel-lesoliviers.fr
www.hotel-lesoliviers.fr
€
Ideally situated if you're driving into Carcassonne, just off a main road and only a short walk into the walled city, this new 2-star hotel is very comfortable. It has 29 rooms and 31 larger apartments, fully-equipped for self-catering. There's also a pool and a dining room, and all rooms are air-conditioned and have free high-speed internet access.

# Montpellier
see page 296 for price guide

## Le Jardin des Sens
11 avenue Saint-Lazare; 04 99 58 38 38
www.jardindessens.com
€€€
Twelve ultra-stylish rooms in this 4-star place that's some way north of the city centre. It's chicer than chic, designed by Bruno Borrione, who worked for Philippe Starck – and it shows. It has its own pool (though one suite also has a private pool), and a restaurant that is acclaimed in its own right, focussing on the cuisine of Languedoc.

## Hôtel le Guilhem
18 rue Jean-Jacques Rousseau; 04 67 52 90 90
contact@leguilhem.com; www.leguilhem.com
€€€
Wonderfully positioned in a quiet traffic-free street in the heart of the medieval quarter, this member of the Chateaux et Hôtels de France has 36 incredibly comfortable air-conditioned rooms, all of them different, all of them plush. There's also a dining room and a garden for breakfast when it's fine. Some rooms have lovely views over this old part of the city.

## Holiday Inn
3 rue du Clos Rene; 04 67 12 32 32
www.holidayinn-montpellier.com
€€€
Very conveniently located midway between the train station and the main place de la Comédie, the 4-star Holiday Inn was originally built in 1898 and was once the home of Queen Elena of Italy. The public areas retain some of the grandeur, and the old winter garden and courtyard terrace are still there, while the 80 bedrooms are thoroughly modern.

## Sofitel
1 rue des Pertuisanes; 04 67 99 72 72
H1294@accor.com; www.sofitel-montpellier.com
€€€
Right in the futuristic Antigone district,

HOTELS

the Sofitel has 88 rooms and one suite, all recently renovated with a bold blue and red colour design that manages to combine the Mediterranean with a sober business feel. The Ciel d'Azur restaurant has terrific city views, and the whole place is a cut above the typical Sofitel hotel.

### Mercure
218 rue Bastion Ventadour; 04 67 99 89 89
H3043@accor.com; www.mercure.com
€€
Only a few minutes walk from place de la Comédie, at the edge of Antigone, the 3-star Mercure is a reliable and comfortable choice. There are 120 rooms, a bar, a restaurant and a pleasant breakfast patio. The hotel has a more stylish look to it than similar business hotels. Staff are very friendly, perhaps because they're happy to live in Montpellier.

### New Hotel du Midi
22 boulevard Victor Hugo; 04 67 92 69 61
montpelliermide@new-hotel.com
www.new-hotel.com
€€
Right on place de la Comédie in the heart of town, no hotel has a better location – though thankfully the 44 rooms are all soundproofed. It's in the grand hotel style, but with luxurious modern rooms with wifi, satellite TV, mini-bar and so on. Something as simple as a noon check-out and 2pm check-in also makes a difference.

### Hôtel du Parc
8 rue Achille-Bège; 04 67 41 16 49
www.hotelduparc-montpellier.com
€
This lovely old 2-star hotel is good if you're driving into Montpellier as it has its own car park and is north of the city centre, but it's easily walkable or there's a tram. It's an 18th-century Languedoc mansion that once belonged to the Earl Vivier de Châtelard, but the 20 rooms are modern, stylish and all have air-conditioning.

### Le Lodge
4 route de Palavas, 34970 Lattes
04 67 06 10 20
info@lelodge.fr; www.lelodge.fr
€
Only about four miles south of the city centre and also very convenient for the beaches and the airport, Le Lodge offers a collection of bungalows nestling in a lush Mediterranean garden. The owners describe the décor as 'zen-like', but there is every modern convenience including free wifi access, air-

conditioning, swimming pool, jacuzzi and two restaurants: one casual and one more formal. All in all, an excellent base.

## Marseille
see page 296 for price guide

### Le Petit Nice
Anse de Maldormé, Corniche J.F. Kennedy
04 91 59 25 92
passedat@relaischateaux.com
www.petitnicepassedat.com
€€€€
Le Petit Nice could lay claim to being the best hotel in Marseille, graced as it is with a Michelin-starred restaurant and sumptuous rooms. There are 13 rooms and 3 suites spread around two Greek-island-white coastal villas along the Corniche, with their own pool of heated sea water, a solarium and all rooms having sea views.

### Sofitel Palm Beach
200 Corniche J.F. Kennedy; 04 91 16 19 00
H3485@accor.com; www.sofitel.com
€€€
The Sofitel is a good choice if you want modern business-like standards but want to be right by the sea along the Corniche. It's easy to reach the stadium and the city centre from here, either by bus or taxi. There are good sports facilities including tennis and water sports, a pool and fitness centre. All 150 rooms (plus ten suites) offer sea views.

### Hôtel la Résidence du Vieux Port
18 quai du Port; 04 91 91 91 22
hotel.residence@wanadoo.fr
www.hotelmarseille.com
€€€
A 3-star hotel perfectly located on the north side of the Vieux Port. Each of the 40 rooms has wonderful views over the port activities and beyond, to Basilica Nôtre-Dame. There are several different types of room, but all are comfortable, air-conditioned and sound-proofed – essential in this quayside location.

### Tonic
43 quai des Belges; 04 91 55 67 46
tonic.marseille@wanadoo.fr
www.tonichotel.com
€€
This chic and slick member of the small Tonic Hotel chain only has a 3-star rating but it has a 4-star feel. Sixteen of its 60 air-conditioned rooms look right over the western end of the Vieux Port, and the morning fish market. Its a perfect place to be

based, modern yet still friendly.

**Hôtel Hermes**
2 Rue Bonneterie; 04 96 11 63 63
hotel.hermes@wanadoo.fr;
www.hotelmarseille.com
€€
Although the Hermes is only a 2-star hotel, it's a great little place right on the Vieux Port. Try to get the Nuptial or Terrace room, both of which have terrific views across the harbour to Notre-Dame. There's a roof terrace, and all 28 rooms have AC and soundproofing. The whole place was renovated in 2006 and belies its 2-star rating.

**Mercure**
11 avenue de Mazargues; 04 96 20 37 37
H3004@accor.com; www.mercure.com
€€
The 3-star Mercure Marseille Prado is one of the best options if you want to be near the stadium, as it's only a stroll away, as is the Congress Centre. It's also handy for the beach if that appeals more than hanging out in the heart of Marseille city. The 100 rooms are typically modern and comfortable – no surprises but a safe choice if you're not especially looking for a lot of character.

**Hôtel Alize**
35 quai des Belges; 04 91 33 66 97
info@alize-hotel.com; www.alize-hotel.com
€
The Alize is in an 18th-century building in a perfect spot overlooking the Vieux Port and quai des Belges, but you'll have to pay a little extra for a room with a port view. The rooms are simple but they are all ensuite, air-conditioned and soundproofed, and the management offers pleasing extras like newspapers and free wifi – not to mention a friendly welcome.

**Hôtel Béarn**
63 rue Sylvabelle; 04 91 37 75 83
hotelbearn@aol.com; www.hotel-bearn.com
€
Cheap and charming, the Béarn is a friendly family-run hotel, just a few minutes walk south of the Vieux Port but in a more residential district in the old back streets. Ask for one of the garden rooms for a better view and a quieter location. The owners are scuba enthusiasts and will organise dives for interested parties.

# United Kingdom
# Cardiff

Price ratings are for a standard room, per person per night

| | |
|---|---|
| £££££ | £300-400 |
| ££££ | £200-300 |
| £££ | £100-200 |
| ££ | £60-100 |
| £ | under £60 |

**The Vale Hotel**
Hensol Park, Hensol, Vale of Glamorgan, Cardiff CF72 8JY
www.vale-hotel.com
£££££
Home of the Wales rugby team, and top choice for other sports teams playing at the Millennium Stadium. Check the fixture list before booking and you might find yourself having breakfast next to some top international players from all kinds of sports. There are also two championship golf courses, the biggest spa in Wales with 19 treatment rooms and a state-of-the-art health club and gym. The bar is always busy, and there are two restaurants, with La Cucina being highly recommended.

**St David's Hotel and Spa**
Havannah Street, Cardiff Bay; 0292 045 4045
www.rfhotels.com
£££££
Cardiff's first 5-star hotel is unmissable on a promontory jutting out into Cardiff Bay, but the angled exterior belies the comfort inside. Every room has a balcony with glorious views of Cardiff Bay, and the spa and restaurant facilities are equally indulgent.

**Hilton**
Kingsway, Cardiff CF10 3HH; 0292 064 6300
www.hilton.com
££££
With views over Cardiff Castle, and its high local reputation for its restaurant and atmosphere, this is much more than your average city Hilton. The Health Club is excellent, and you might find yourself working out next to one of the visiting celebrities who favour Hilton's 5-star chic.

**Jolyon's Hotel**
5 Bute Crescent, Cardiff Bay; 0292 048 8775
www.jolyons.co.uk
£££
Directly opposite the impressive front of the Millennium Centre, you'd be home five

minutes after the end of any production there. New boutique hotel in an old Bay building which was once a seamen's lodge, the hotel has just six luxury bedrooms, all with wireless access and one with a whirlpool bath.

**Park Plaza**
Greyfriars Road, Cardiff CF10 3AL
0292 011 1111
www.parkplazacardiff.com
£££
This stylish new four-star hotel is right in the heart of Cardiff's modern shopping area, just a few minutes from most of the attractions. Even the standard rooms have a sophisticated look to them, and a highlight is original Welsh art in every room. There is also free wireless access and both US and European power sockets, as well as UK ones, in all rooms.

**Paramount Angel Hotel**
Castle Street, Cardiff CF10 1SZ
0292 064 9200; www.paramount-hotels.co.uk
££
Thanks to its Victorian origins the Angel got a location to die for, on the halfway line between Cardiff Castle and the Millennium Stadium. It has retained its classic Victorian feel as a slightly more formal hotel, but with all mod cons of course. Some good bargains if you book ahead.

**The Big Sleep**
Bute Terrace, Cardiff CF10 2FE
0292 063 6363
www.thebigsleephotel.com
£
Unusual boutique hotel based in an old 1960s office block near the Cardiff International Arena – unusual in that it doesn't have hiked-up boutique prices but its 81 rooms are both chic and affordable. It's co-owned by actor John Malkovich, who is an active partner in the hotel, and you should book well ahead for busy periods.

**Llanerch Vineyard B&B**
Hensol, Pendoylan, Vale of Glamorgan CF72 8GG
0144 322 5877
www.llanerch-vineyard.co.uk
££
Staying on a vineyard must be a temptation, and the rooms here are simple but superb, as evidenced by the many celebrities who have stayed here. Self-catering cottages and studios are also available in this peaceful setting, but only about 15 minutes drive into the city centre.

# Edinburgh

see page 305 for price guide

**The Balmoral**
1 Princes Street, Edinburgh EH2 2EQ
0131 556 2414
thebalmoral@roccofortehotels.com
www.thebalmoralhotel.com
£££££
One of the longest-established best hotels in the city, where members of the Scotland team sometimes stay, the Balmoral offers 5-star luxury and is a distinguished landmark itself, on Princes Street. It recently had a £7 million refurbishment, is right by the tourist information centre, and can boast a Michelin-starred restaurant. With its first class spa facilities too, little wonder that scarcely a month goes by without the hotel winning one award or another.

**Sheraton Grand Hotel and Spa**
1 Festival Square, Edinburgh EH3 9SR
0131 229 9131
grandedinburgh.sheraton@sheraton.com
www.starwoodhotels.com
£££££
Used by the Scotland rugby team, who come here to make use of the superb spa facilities, the Sheraton is within sight of Edinburgh Castle and a short stroll from the western end of Princes Street. There are plenty of good eating places around, although with three restaurants, two bars and an Executive Lounge, you may not need to venture outside. The rooms are as comfortable as you would expect from a 5-star hotel, and the hotel is a happy mix of luxury and tradition.

**Radisson SAS Hotel**
80 High Street, The Royal Mile EH1 1TH
0131 557 9797
sales.edinburgh@radissonsas.com
www.edinburgh.radissonsas.com
££££
Right on the Royal Mile and only five minutes from Waverley Station is the visually stunning Radisson. Although it's a modern hotel it looks like a medieval building, and inside is equally striking. All 238 rooms are distinguished by having black-and-white art photos of the city and surrounds by a local photographer, and (rare for a large chain hotel) free high-speed internet access.

**Le Monde Hotel**
16 George Street, Edinburgh EH2 2PF
0131 270 3900

hotel@lemondehotel.co.uk;
www.lemondehotel.co.uk
££££
This striking new boutique hotel is right
on buzzing George Street, and has its own
nightclub, bar, brasserie and restaurant next
door. Winner of the Scottish Hotel Design
Award in 2006, it offers 18 luxury suites,
each individually designed and inspired by
a world city, from Cairo and Marrakech to
Tokyo and LA. All have plasma TVs, wifi
access, Egyptian cotton sheets and a mini-bar
stuffed with luxury goodies. A unique place.

### Point Hotel
34 Bread Street, Edinburgh EH3 9AF
0131 221 5555
reservations@point-hotel.co.uk
www.point-hotel.co.uk
££
Conveniently located just south of
Edinburgh Castle and a short walk to
Princes Street, the Point has 140 rooms
which manage to be both minimalist and
comfortable at the same time. It's won
awards for its stylish design, but unlike
many boutique hotels the Point also
manages to keep its prices minimalist too. Its
restaurant and the Monboddo Bar also rate
highly on the local scene.

### Allison House Hotel
17 Mayfield Gardens, Edinburgh EH9 2AX
0800 328 9003
enquiry@allisonhousehotel.com
www.allisonhousehotel.com
££
This really delightful family-run hotel offers
visitors 11 large, comfortable rooms with
complimentary sherry and whisky decanters
when you arrive, and free wifi internet
access. It's on the south side of the city with
regular buses or a 30-minute walk into the
centre and owner David Hinnrichs is a
passionate rugby fan who's happy to share
his knowledge about the local rugby scene.

### Murrayfield Hotel
18 Corstorphine Road, Edinburgh EH12 6HN
0131 337 1844
murrayfield@festival-inns.co.uk
ww.festival-inns.co.uk
££
Ideal base if you want to be near the stadium
as you can't get much closer, and the
rugby bars are all around – including the
Murrayfield's own. There are thirty rooms
split between the main building and the
adjacent lodge, and they're simple but have
all mod cons. The private car park is a bonus
in Edinburgh, and it's only a 15-minute walk
into the centre.

### Tontine Hotel
High Street, Peebles EH45 8AJ
0172 172 0892
stay@tontinehotel.com; www.tontinehotel.com
£
This delightful hotel dates back to 1806 and
still has its 19th-century cobbled courtyard,
setting it back slightly from the High Street.
Its bar and excellent restaurant are very
popular with locals, and its 36 ensuite
rooms include some overlooking the High
Street and others looking back over the
valley of the River Tweed. The Adam Room
Restaurant has a working Adam fireplace
and a minstrel's gallery, as well as inventive
Scottish cuisine.

CROWNE PLAZA, LILLE

# Index

Edinburgh

Cardiff

Lens

Saint-Denis

Paris

Nantes

Lyon

Saint-Étienne

Bordeaux

Marseille

Montpellier

Toulouse

iRB RUGBY WORLD CUP 2007 | SNCF

WORLDWIDE PARTNER

SPEEDING UP MEETINGS

## SNCF, taking you to meet your finest matches.

sncf.com

*boosting rail with new ideas* SNCF

EIFFEL TOWER

# Rugby World Cup 2007: Official Travel Guide

## Credits

**Senior Editor:** Robin Bell
**Editor:** Hope Caton
**Authors:** Mike Gerrard, Donna Dailey, Hope Caton
**Design:** Sharon Platt
**Additional research:** Nigel Britton
**Sub-editor:** Helen Sterne
**Rugby history quotes and source material:** David Ray, Rugby School

### Photography

William Webb Ellis Cup, Syd Millar, courtesy IRB; rugby match courtesy Stuart Hill, Rugby School; Bernard Lapasset courtesy RWC 2007 Organising Committee.

**Paris, Saint-Denis:** Hope Caton except pg 20, 22, 23 courtesy of Saint-Denis Office de Tourisme; pg 25 courtesy of Le Stade; pg 33 iStock international; pg 56 Moulin Rouge; pg 57 Lido; pg 64 Le Golf National; pg 67 Versailles; pg 68 Giverny; pg 69 Parc Astérix.

**Lens & Lille:** Hope Caton except pg 76 Kipling's grave, courtesy Loos-en-Gohelle Memorial; pg 77 Vimy Memorial courtesy CDT Pas-de-Calais/Pascale Morès; pg 79, Christophe Bailleul; pg 82 by permission Musee des Beaux-Arts d'Arras; pg 89 Sharon Platt.

**Nantes:** Hope Caton except pg 95 courtesy Ludovic Mocard; pg 96 A Delaporte; pg 98 Katia Forêt; pg 102 Hotel du Golf International de La Baule; pg 103 courtesy Angers Loire Tourisme.

**Lyon:** Donna Dailey except pg 129 courtesy Peter Deilmann.

**Saint-Étienne:** Donna Dailey except pg 142 Jean-Jacques Maleysson.

**Bordeaux:** Donna Dailey except pg 160 Golf du Médoc; pg 161 Les Sources de Caudalie.

**Toulouse:** Donna Dailey except pg 173 Trevor Brennan, De Danù Irish Bar; pg 186 Golf de Teoula.

**Montpellier:** Donna Dailey except pg 207 Bruce Gordon-Smith.

**Marseilles:** Donna Dailey except pg 231(top) Diamond Diving; (bottom) Diver Group

**Cardiff:** Donna Dailey except pg 248 Alamy Images; pg 250 Amgueddfa Cymru-National Museum Wales; pg 261 Llanerch Vineyard.

**Edinburgh:** Donna Dailey.

**Travel Basics:** Donna Dailey.

**Hotels:** pg 294-295 Hotel Le Bristol, Paris; pg 307 Lille Crowne Plaza.

**pg 316-317:** Bruce Gordon-Smith.

### Maps

**City and regional maps:** David Burles and Jane Voss of Anderson Geographics Ltd, Bracknell, Berkshire, UK; © 2007 The Purple Guide Ltd.

**Stadium maps:** Rugby World Cup 2007 Organising Committee, used by permission.

This product contains mapping redrawn from Ordnance Survey data. © Crown copyright 2006. All rights reserved. Ordnance Survey Licence No.100046085

City maps for Bordeaux, Lens, Lyon, Montpellier, Paris/Saint-Denis, Nantes, Saint-Étienne and Toulouse were re-drawn from source maps provided by Blay Foldex. © Blay Foldex No 23065.

**Cartes - Plans - Guides**
40 - 48, rue des Meuniers
93108 MONTREUIL CEDEX (FRANCE)
Tél.: 33 (0)1 49 88 92 10 - Fax : 33 (0)1 49 88 92 09
www.blayfoldex.com

## Acknowledgements

Mike Gerrard, Donna Dailey and Hope Caton would like to thank the following for their generous help in the research of the book:
**General:** Peter Mills and Amanda Monroe at Rail Europe; Jonathan Smith at Rugby School, Warwickshire.
**Paris, Saint-Denis:** Marie Périvier (you are a star) at Saint-Denis Office de Tourisme; Charlotte Danchin, Alexia Gabille, Gilles Smadja (Mayor), Ville Saint-Denis; Veronique Potelet at the Paris Tourist Office; Hôtel Les Jardins du Marais, Paris; Claire Barrett at Mason Rose PR; Hôtel Le Bristol, Paris; Renaud Huck (thanks for the restaurant tips).
**Lens & Lille:** Bruno Capelle, Office du Tourisme Lille; Crowne Plaza Lille; Marlene Varey and Lens Office de Tourisme; Angela Convers and Jean-Marie Prestaux, Office de Tourisme d'Arras; Holiday Inn Express, Arras; Espace Bollaert, Lens; Grand Hôtel Bellevue, Lille.
**Nantes;** Virginie Proux at Pays de Loire Office de Tourisme; Elise Barbier C'ap d'Atlantique Office de Tourisme; Katia Forêt, Nantes Office de Tourisme; Olivier Bouchereau, Angers Loire Tourisme; Hôtel Abat Jour, Nantes; Helen Ramsamy, Anjou Tourisme; Bleu Marine Hotel in Angers; Hôtel St Pierre, La Baule; Sarah Manser at Red Lemon PR.
**Saint-Étienne:** Brigitte Arfi at the Office de Tourisme in Saint-Étienne.
**Bordeaux:** Gwenaëlle Towse and the Office de Tourisme de Bordeaux; Maggie Garratt, Eric Hertz and the Chateau de Mirambeau.
**Toulouse:** Mélissa Buttelli and Philippe Verger, Office de Tourisme in Toulouse; Charlotte Wilmots, Mango PR; Philippe Miro at the Office Municipal de Tourisme in Carcassonne.
**Montpellier:** Caroline Berland at the Office de Tourisme de Montpellier.
**Marseilles:** Silvie Allemande at the Office du Tourisme et du Congres in Marseille.
**Cardiff:** Glenda Davies and Lowri Jones at Visit Cardiff; Ian Everett at Destination PR; the Vale Hotel and Pat & Charles Aithie (thanks for the beers).
**Edinburgh:** Mark Linklater at Scotland's Personal Hotels; the Tontine Hotel in Peebles; the Allison House Hotel; Sheraton Grand Hotel, Edinburgh.

BÉZIERS, *NEXT PAGE*

**RUGBY WORLD CUP 2007.**

*France 2007*